AMERICAN ORIENTAL SERIES
VOLUME 59

THE CASE FOR FRICATIVE-LATERALS IN PROTO-SEMITIC

AMERICAN ORIENTAL SERIES
VOLUME 59

AMERICAN ORIENTAL SOCIETY
NEW HAVEN, CONNECTICUT
1977

THE CASE FOR FRICATIVE-LATERALS IN PROTO-SEMITIC

BY

RICHARD C. STEINER

AMERICAN ORIENTAL SOCIETY
NEW HAVEN, CONNECTICUT
1977

PHOTOGRAPHED BY CUSHING-MALLOY, INC.
ANN ARBOR, MICHIGAN, UNITED STATES OF AMERICA

TO MY DEAR SARA

לזכר נשמות

זקני היקר ר׳ יואל בר׳ יחיאל מיכל הלוי

זקנתי היקרה מרת שיינדעל עלקע בת ר׳ מרדכי יהודה הכהן

דודי הנעלה ר׳ יהודה בר׳ ישראל שרגא

תנצב"ה

This monograph is a revised and expanded version of my University of Pennsylvania doctoral dissertation (defended, 1973), the research for which was supported in part by a grant from the National Foundation for Jewish Culture. Professor Henry Hoenigswald -- whose brilliant lectures were my introduction both to the problem of the Proto-Semitic *ś* and to the methods needed for solving the problem -- was the supervisor. My sincerest thanks go to him for assuming this burden, in spite of the fact that I was not even a student in his department, and for all the other help he has given me over the years.

Thanks are also due to the other members of my committee -- Professors Roger Allen, Barry Eichler, and Svi Rin -- and also to the chairman of the Near Eastern section of the Oriental Studies department, Professor Erle Leichty. Every one of them was a great source of support and advice during those difficult years spent on the brink of poverty.

It was my great privilege to have served as a research assistant to Professor William Labov. The work I did for him opened my eyes to the fact that the root causes and mechanisms of sound change are universal and that the Semitic linguist cannot afford to ignore the rich body of typological data available outside of his discipline. For this, and for his many acts of kindness and generosity towards me, I will forever be grateful.

I am also greatly indebted to another member of Professor Labov's research team, Malcah Yaeger, for reading and criticizing my book at two different stages of its development. Several important insights of hers are acknowledged in the footnotes.

It is a particularly pleasant duty to acknowledge my indebtedness to my three Israeli teachers and advisors: Professors Haim Blanc, Joshua Blau, and Shlomo Morag. Professor Morag was my first teacher of Semitic linguistics, and Professor Blau, through his mimeographed lecture notes, was my second. Both of them were kind enough to read and comment upon an earlier version of this monograph. Professor Blanc spent so many hours reading and criticizing my dissertation and answering questions in connection with it that I hardly know how to thank him. His penetrating comments and vast bibliographical knowledge are reflected on page after page of this monograph.

I would like to take this opportunity to thank Professor Robert Hetzron for his friendship and encouragement at times when it was most needed. I also want to thank him and two other good friends, Professors Daniel Boyarin and Federico Corriente, for their valuable comments on individual chapters of this monograph.

I am deeply grateful to Professors Moshe Levison and David Segal for the hours they spent answering my questions on the statistics of incompatibility (Professor Segal is also the author of the pun in the title of this monograph) and to Rabbis Sigmund Handelman and Gedaliah Shaffer for doing the lengthy calculations required by the Fischer exact test on their respective computers.

Let me also take this opportunity to thank the University of Pennsylvania, the American Scandinavian Foundation, and the National Foundation for Jewish Culture for the fellowships and assistantships which supported me and my family for five years. I would also like to express my gratitude to the officers of the American Oriental Society -- Professors Ernest Bender, Stanley Insler, Johannes Renger, and Hugh Stimson -- who provided a great deal of help, financial and otherwise, in bringing this book to publication. Thanks also to my brave typist, Mrs. Frankie Shahar, for persevering through two months of grueling and mind-numbing work.

Last but definitely not least I would like to thank my wonderful family, who helped me in so many ways, both large and small. My cousin, Dr. Bruce Maliver, lent me the Selectric used to type the final copy of my dissertation. My brother, Professor Mark Steiner, took out books for me from the Columbia University Library. My parents provided me with a fine home and a good education, and continued to help out in innumerable ways after I left home. My wife, Sara, created the warm, stable environment which enabled me to work at top efficiency. From the beginning of our marriage, seven years ago, she has done her utmost to maximize my time for writing and research by relieving me of all household duties and shielding me from even the most minor disturbances and interruptions. For all this, I thank her and the rest of my family from the bottom of my heart.

תם ונשלם שבח לא-ל בורא עולם
שהחינו וקימנו והגיענו לזמן הזה

January, 1976

Richard Steiner
Yeshiva Univ.

Table of Contents

Abbreviations and Symbols

PS	Proto-Semitic
ESA	Epigraphic South Arabic
MSA	Modern South Arabic
OA	Old Aramaic
BA	Biblical Aramaic
OB	Old Babylonian
PC	Proto-Chadic
AHw	See *List of References*
BDB	See *List of References*
CAD	See *List of References*
KBHK	See *List of References*
l̥	Symbol for voiceless lateral approximant
ɬ	Symbol for voiceless fricative-lateral (alveolar or unspecified)
ʟ̝̊	Symbol for voiceless *velar* fricative-lateral
ɮ	Symbol for voiced fricative-lateral (alveolar of unspecified)
ʟ̝	Symbol for voiced *velar* fricative-lateral
ś, *ḍ*	Conventional symbols for the two PS phonemes which are the subject of this monograph; also used for the reflexes of these phonemes in some of the Semitic languages.
ṡ, *ŝh*, *ṫh*	Symbols for MSA ɬ in Thomas 1937.
ẑ, *ẑh*, *d̂h*	Symbols for MSA ɮ in Thomas 1937.
ش	*šīn*, Arabic reflex of PS *ś*.
ض	*ḍād*, Arabic reflex of PS *ḍ*.
שׂ	*śin*, Hebrew reflex of PS *ś*.
וּ ֻ	are transliterated *u*
וֹ ֹ	are transliterated *o*
ָ	is transliterated *å*
ַ	is transliterated *a*
ֶ	is transliterated ɛ
ֵי ֵ	are transliterated *e*
ִי ִ	are transliterated *i*
בגדכפת	are transliterated *b̲ g̲ d̲ k̲ p̲ t̲*

Ethiopic 1st order vowel is transliterated *ä*
Ethiopic 2nd order vowel is transliterated *u*
Ethiopic 3rd order vowel is transliterated *i*
Ethiopic 4th order vowel is transliterated *a*
Ethiopic 5th order vowel is transliterated *e*
Ethiopic 6th order vowel is transliterated ə
Ethiopic 7th order vowel is transliterated *o*
/ / is used in phonemic notation.
[ ] is used in phonetic notation.
‹ › is used in graphemic notation.

Introduction

MODERN SOUTH ARABIC AND THE LATERAL HYPOTHESIS

The Omani Dependency of Dhofar or Ẓufār in South Arabia is the Semitist's answer to Shangri-La. Wendell Phillips, explorer and personal friend of the now-deposed Sultan Said bin Taimur, describes the area in *Unknown Oman* (1966:168-70):

> In 1833 Andrew Crichton wrote, 'The whole of the southern waste is a wall of naked rocks, as dismal and barren as can well be conceived.' This statement was almost true except it overlooked the south-west monsoon ... from which Dhofar derives its unique climate, with its inflow of fog and drizzling summer rain yielding five inches on the coast and fifteen inches in the mountains .... As these air currents ... blow north-west along the Somaliland coast, they traverse no area of land (except the island of Socotra) and thus arrive saturated with moisture over Dhofar, causing a green carpet to arise from the earth. If ever this barrier of Somaliland were eliminated, all of south-west Arabia would climatically resemble Dhofar; and if Somaliland extended farther to the east the arid deserts would soon bury sweet-smelling Dhofar under the sands.
>
> Here smiling plenty is found in the very bosom of desolation, for the narrow half-moon shaped coastal plain of Dhofar is an abnormal feature in this otherwise arid South Arabian coast, as it is the only major fertile region between Muscat and Aden ...
>
> The Qara Mountains rise steeply to the north, limiting the coastal plain to a maximum width of ten miles. ... Within these mountains lovely secluded little lakes and gorges are rich with tropical ferns and running streams ...
>
> Within and adjacent to these Qara Mountains, a natural asylum for primitive aborigines has existed where there are still nine illiterate tribes speaking four different Semitic tongues -- Shahari, Mahri, Batahari, and Harsusi ...

Now, given that the Qara Mountains are the most inaccessible part of a remote country that until 1970 had no radios, newspapers, printing presses, paved roads or secondary schools to bring foreign ideas across its tightly closed borders, it is not particularly daring to claim -- as does Patai (1969:146,192) -- that the Qara tribes have preserved several ancient customs which their less isolated neighbors long ago abandoned in favor of the prevailing Islamic-Middle Eastern norms. But it is quite another matter to adopt a theory -- as did Cantineau ([1941] 1960:54, [1951-2] 1960: 283-7) followed by Leslau (1957:327), Diakonoff (1965:21-2, 1970:462), and Rabin (1971:1154) -- which, in effect, credits the Qara languages with having preserved the ancient phonetic values of two Semitic phonemes (*ḍ and *ś) more faithfully than many of the most archaic and/or ancient Semitic languages, including Old Arabic (8th century CE), Old Aramaic (10th century BCE), Ugaritic (14th century BCE), and Old Babylonian (20th century BCE)!

What are the phonetic values of ḍ and ś in the Qara languages, or Modern South Arabic (MSA) as they are commonly called? The former is a voiced fricative-lateral -- an *l* made with friction. The latter is a voiceless fricative-lateral, differing from the former only in the absence of voicing, and similar to Welsh *ll*. Substitute "glottalized" for "voiced" (and, concomitantly, "affricate" for "fricative") in the description of ḍ, and "Proto-Semitic" for "Modern South Arabic," and you have the lateral hypothesis as it finally emerged, after nearly a century of development, in Jean Cantineau's highly influential exposition of "Le consonantisme du sémitique" ([1951-2] 1960:283-7).

THE HISTORY OF THE LATERAL HYPOTHESIS

On the second of May, 1861, one of Europe's leading philologists delivered a lecture to the Royal Academy of Sciences in Berlin, entitled "Über die Arabischen Sprachlaute und deren Umschrift." In that lecture, Richard Lepsius advanced the hypothesis that, in early Islamic times, Arabic ḍ was an "emphatic assibilated *l*." This brilliant solution to one of the most perplexing problems of Arabic philology seems to have attracted little attention at the time. Lepsius' biographer, writing one year after the master's death, makes no mention of this lecture, beyond listing it in the bibliography (Ebers 1887). It was not until the famous Arabist Karl Vollers adopted the idea as his own (to the extent that he often forgot to give credit to the real discoverer) that it began to take hold in Arabist circles. By this time, investigators in South Arabia had uncovered a lateral ḍ in Ḥaḍramī Arabic (van den Berg 1886:

239) and in Mehri (von Maltzan 1873:259), the implications of which Vollers (1894:174) was quick to point out. Explorations in South Arabia continued, and fifteen years later Rudolph Ružička (1909:171) was able to tie in several new discoveries from that area with Lepsius' hypothesis. Ružička was also, it seems, the first scholar to recognize, however hazily, the significance of several Arabic loanwords in Spanish in which Arabic *ḍ* is rendered as *ld*.

The next contribution to the lateral theory was an article by N.V. Yushmanov (1926) which reviewed the evidence for lateral *ḍ* in Arabic and MSA and added a few new details (e.g. the rendering of *ḍ* with *l* in Arabic loanwords in Hausa). An important innovation of this article was the claim, implicit in the author's use of the term "z'ˡad *protosémitique*" (ibid., 43), that *ḍ* was already a fricative-lateral in PS. Two years later, Gotthelf Bergsträsser ([1928] 1963:135) made this claim explicit.

The next few decades brought several restatements of the case for lateral *ḍ* (Colin 1930a:92,101-2, Cantineau [1941] 1960:54-6, [1951-2] 1960:286-7) but no important new discoveries until 1956, when Jacques Ryckmans and Riekele Borger independently identified Ruldayu -- a deity of the Arabian city Adumatu mentioned in an Assyrian inscription -- with the pre-Islamic deity Ruḍā. A year later, Borger adduced this equation as evidence for a lateral realization of Arabic *ḍ* already in the seventh century BCE (1957:10).

During the same period, the lateral hypothesis acquired a new dimension thanks to Cantineau's suggestion ([1941] 1960:62-3) that Proto-Semitic, like MSA and (Pre-) Arabic (cf. Arabic *qišda* - *qilda*), had a lateralized *ś* as well as a lateralized *ḍ*. A year later, a similar but independent suggestion by Yeḥiel Gumpertz (1942:114) appeared in print, with evidence drawn from Akkadian (the famous merger of *š* with *l* before apical stops and spirants), Greek (the Semitic loanword *balsamon*), and, of course, MSA.

Gumpertz's work was quickly forgotten, but Cantineau's ideas were followed up in the mid-sixties by Kalevi Koskinen and Igor M. Diakonoff. Koskinen (1964:45-7) argued for a lateral realization of *ś* in Hebrew based on the alleged incompatibility of *ś* and *l* in that language. Diakonoff (1965: 22) used Cantineau's version of the lateral hypothesis to account for the Proto-Semitic doublets *ḍḥq* - *śḥq* (and the above-mentioned conditioned merger of *š* with *l* in Akkadian), and thus, indirectly, provided new evidence for lateral *ś*. We shall have more to say about these matters in the next section.

THE PROBLEM

The original lateral hypothesis was confined to Arabic and to ḍ. Lepsius believed that the lateral realization of ḍ was a post-Islamic innovation (1861:136):

> Dass diese Aussprache des z̲ schon bis *Xalil*, warschcinlich schon bis Mohammed zurückging, beweist übrigens noch nicht, dass sie nicht einer noch früheren gefolgt sei, und es scheint mir sehr natürlich dass z̲ ursprünglich nur die tönende Aussprache von s̲ darstellte.

The discovery that MSA also had a lateral ḍ forced a certain modification of this position, but not as drastic a one as might have been expected. Voller's position (1894: 174), like that of Brockelmann (1908:29), is quite compatible with Lepsius' ideas about the lateness of the lateral realization of ḍ:

> Eine nicht minder grosse geschichtliche Tragweite besitzt die Ueberlieferung, dass ض klassisch ein laterales *z* sei und durch diese Artikulation dem *l* nahe komme. Viele Umstände, das frühe Schwinden dieses Lautes aus der Ueberlieferung, das Fehlen desselben in der lebenden Sprache und -- wie es scheint -- die Zugehörigkeit zu der lexikographisch dünn gesäten Reihe Kanaanäisch צ, Aramäisch צ, Arabisch ض deuten darauf, dass diese auffällige Varietät des z̲ nur ein kurzes Leben und eine geringe Verbreitung gehabt hat. Nehmen wir die beiden Tatsachen zusammen, dass der entsprechende laterale Verschlusslaut im Mehri noch jetzt vorkommt und in der gelehrten Ueberlieferung der Malaien auftritt, die aus Ḥaḍramaut oder Umgegend ihren Islam erhalten haben, so liegt die Annahme nahe, dass der südarabische Stamm, dem dieser Laut eigen war, gerade zur Zeit der Kristallisation der phonetischen Ueberlieferung -- in Medina oder in Baṣra -- momentan eine gewisse Rolle spielte, um bald darauf in dem grossen Amalgamations-Prozess der islamischen Stämme zu verschwinden.

Vollers was able to avoid an early date by assuming that the lateral realization of ḍ spread across dialect-, or even language-, boundaries, from South Arabic to the neighboring dialects of North Arabic. But even if Vollers had stayed within a strict family-tree framework, he would not have been required to date the lateral realization of ḍ any earlier than the common ancestor of Arabic and MSA, a language which is much younger than Proto-Semitic. This brings us to the heart of the problem: How is it possible to reconstruct for

Proto-Semitic a feature which is attested in only a small group of languages, each of which is a close relative and a close neighbor of the others?

The problem is even more acute in the case of the lateral realization of *ś*, which is attested only in MSA. As Moscati (1954:38) put it:

> La realizzazione sudarabica moderna e molto remota da quelle ebraica e semitica antica, ne tra esse e agevole stabilire una connessione ...

Naturally, Cantineau was not blind to this problem either. Not untypically, his response was to compensate for the lack of hard evidence with a typological argument ([1951-2] 1960:286):

> Cette prononciation a bien des chances d'être ancienne, car on ne voit pas pourquoi ni comment un *s* ou un *š* anciens se seraient latéralisés, tandis qu'on voit au contraire très bien comment une sifflante ou une chuintante latéralisée, perdant cette latéralisation (difficile à réaliser, surtout pour les étrangers) a abouti à une sifflante ou à une chuintante ordinaires.

But this argument is only superficially attractive. Examination of the historical record reveals that the "lateralization" of ordinary sibilants is not as unthinkable as Cantineau believed. Changes of this type are attested in Iranian (Bouda 1947:52), Ostyak (ibid., 53), the Biu-Mandara branch of Chadic (Newman and Ma 1966:226, although cf. Kraft 1971), and a nineteenth century Italian dialect (Malagòli 1939 s.v. *lisca* and passim, Teloni 1889).

The same typological argument is applied by Moscati (1954:31) to the lateral realization of *ḍ*, but here again there are no grounds for brushing aside the possibility that the lateral *ḍ* of Arabic and MSA developed from an earlier (unlateralized) *ḏ̣* (Brockelmann 1908:129, Vilenčik 1930:97, Magee 1950:77). There is no shortage of parallels. According to Vilenčik (loc. cit.), *ḏ* has shifted to *l* in Afghan, and mergers of *d* with *l* are attested in Latin (Buck 1933:123), Feʔfeʔ-Bamileke (Hyman 1972:21-2), Papago (Hale 1965:299), and, closer to home, the Jewish Neo-Aramaic dialect of Azerbaijan (Garbell 1965 passim).

Cantineau ([1946] 1960:200, [1951-2] 1960:287), and later Kurylowicz (1972:28), adduced, in addition, the incompatibility of *ḍ* and *š* in Arabic as evidence that PS *ś* was, like *ḍ*, a lateral; but since *ḍ* (and no doubt also *š*) is incompatible with *all* of the other sibilants (Cantineau [1946] 1960:200, Greenberg 1950:173), the incompatibility of ḍ and š can be easily explained without recourse to the lateral hypothesis.

Koskinen's more recent attempt (1964:45-7) to adduce incompatibility between *ś* and *l* in Hebrew as evidence for lateral *ś* in that language is unconvincing for a different reason. It is true that the number of triliteral roots containing *ś* with *l* is low (5 out of 1179), but so is the number of triliteral roots containing *ś without l* (70 out of 1179). Had Koskinen employed standard statistical procedures, he would have discovered that, even if *ś* and *l* were totally lacking in aversion for each other, the expected number of roots containing both would be only 41x95/1179 (*śl*-) + 41x105/1179 (*ś-l*) + 18x105/1179 (-*śl*) + 30x18/1179 (*lś*-) + 30x16/1179 (*l-ś*) + 95x16/1179 (-*lś*) = 10.7, and that the difference between this number and the observed number (5) is not quite significant at the .05 level ($\chi^2 = 3.7$). Thus, the assumption of incompatibility between *ś* and *l*, while by no means excluded, is unnecessary.

The remarks of Gumpertz and Diakonoff go a long way towards broadening the base of the lateral theory, but they are too brief and too modestly presented (to a large extent in footnotes) to have had much impact. The fact that Diakonoff's note on Akkadian *š* › *l* is not mentioned at all in the lengthy review which Edzard (1967) wrote for *Revue d'Assyriologie* (!) tells the whole story. Nevertheless, the case for fricative-laterals in Proto-Semitic is not nearly as much in need of the attentions of the present writer as he imagined when he wrote the early paragraphs of this section. At that time, he was still blissfully unaware that the "new" ideas which had inspired him to write this book were really the forgotten ideas of his predecessors.

יש דבר שיאמר ראה זה חדש הוא
כבר היה לעלמים אשר היה מלפננו
אין זכרון לראשנים וגם לאחרנים שיהיו
לא יהיה להם זכרון עם שיהיו לאחרנה

STRATEGY

After reviewing the evidence for the existence of two fricative-laterals in MSA (chapter ii), we shall proceed to identify the etymological counterparts of these two phonemes in the various Semitic languages (chapter iii). The rest of the book will be devoted to an investigation of the phonetic values of these etymological counterparts in the hope that some of them may have preserved something of the original, Proto-Semitic, values.

Our investigation will not be merely a survey of the commonly accepted values of the phonemes in question, for, in some cases (e.g. Akkadian š), these are based on insufficient and/or anachronistic evidence (see chapter xix). In other cases (e.g. Arabic š, Phoenician š), the accepted values may not hold for all dialects of the language in question (see chapter xi and chapter xvi, fn. 25). And in still other cases (e.g. Arabic š, Aramaic *q* › ʕ), the language in its attested stage may have preserved tell-tale alternations, doublets, and/or incompatibilities which came into being at an earlier stage, before the original phonetic value was lost (see chapters x, xiii, xiv, xx).

In general, our strategy will be to look for *l*'s: incompatibility with *l*, alternations with *l*, doublets with *l*, loanwords with *l*, spelling-variants with *l*, and mergers with *l*. Naturally, these *l*'s must be connected with the reflexes of PS *ḍ* and PS *ś*, if they are to be of any value for our purposes. A second general strategy will be to find out as much as possible about the behavior of the fricative-laterals in modern languages like Zulu, Welsh, Icelandic, and MSA, in order to be able to recognize similar behavioral patterns in the ancient Semitic languages.

Finally, we will not be put off by the fact that, due to various mergers, some of the etymological counterparts of the MSA fricative-laterals continue more than one Proto-Semitic phoneme. We will continue to hope that the two phonetic values which are of interest to us survived *some* of these mergers, even though the typological odds are stacked against us.

I.
Laterals: Definitions, Symbols, and Typology

A lateral, simply put, is an *l*. Why use a special term for one simple consonant? Actually, there are many kinds of *l*, and some of them -- the so-called "fricative-laterals" -- sound more like sibilants than *l*'s to most Americans and Europeans. It would be somewhat misleading to call these fricative-laterals *l*'s.

The term "lateral" calls to mind the articulatory characteristic which is common to all of the *l*'s and which sets them apart from all other consonants: the passage of air out of the side of the mouth instead of straight out the front. Bertil Malmberg (1963:44) explains the mechanics of this lateral air-flow:

> The consonants called laterals have this in common with stops and nasals: that the articulatory organ, the tongue, makes firm contact with the point of articulation in question (usually the teeth or the palate). But contrary to what happens in [those] groups, this contact takes place only at the middle of the oral cavity, while the air escapes from both sides of the place of articulation. Sometimes the lateral passage of air occurs on only one side (*unilateral* consonant) without any perceptible difference resulting. The English [l] (in *light, long, call*) is a lateral type ....

The class of laterals can, as intimated above, be further subdivided in many ways. Of fundamental importance to this monograph is the distinction between the lateral *approximants* (also called *sonorants* or *liquids*) and the lateral fricatives (also called fricative-laterals). The latter are characterized by the presence of audible friction at the point of articulation; the former by its absence or relative absence. Corresponding to this acoustic difference there is an articulatory difference, for friction is created by bringing the articulators close enough to constrict, but not block, the air which passes through them ("close-approximation"). Conversely, friction is avoided by keeping the articulators relatively apart ("open-approximation").

The common, garden-variety *l* is a voiced lateral approximant. Fricative-laterals are less familiar, although they can hardly be called rare. The voiceless fricative-lateral (written ɬ)[1] is in fact quite common in American Indian languages, e.g., Apache (Hoijer 1946:58), Chipewyan (Li Fang-Kuei 1946:398), Nez Perce, Wishram, Nootka and twelve other Indian languages of western North America (Nichols 1971: 842-5). Voiceless fricative-laterals are also found on islands at the periphery of Europe: in Welsh (Jones 1913:19, Rositzke 1939) and in Icelandic (Sveinbjörnsson 1933:64, Kress 1937:121, Rositzke 1939). In Asia they are found in the Modern South Arabic languages, in some dialects of Ostyak (Bouda 1947:53), a Ugric language, and in many North Caucasian languages (Trubetzkoy 1922), namely, Kabardian (Kuipers 1960:20, Henderson 1970:94) and the other Circassian languages (Bouda 1947:49-50, Dumézil 1952:243) and Ubykh (Dumézil 1952: 243, Dumézil and Namitok 1954:163) in the western Caucasus; Bats (Sommerfelt 1947:145) in the central Caucasus; and the Avaro-Andian languages (including Akhvakh with six different voiceless laterals) (Gudava 1964:20) and Archi in the eastern Caucasus. In Africa, they are found in a large number of languages, e.g. Sandawe, a Hottentot dialect (Copland 1938:62), the Chadic languages, especially those of the Biu-Mandara branch like Bura and Margi (Hoffman 1963:10, Newman and Ma 1966:226, Ladefoged 1968:29) but also those of the Plateau-Sahel branch (Newman 1965:57, Kraft 1971), the languages of the Iraqw group in Northeast Africa (Tucker and Bryan 1966: 571), and Southern Bantu languages of the Nguni group (which includes Zulu), the Sotho group, the Tsonga group, and, less generally, the Shona group (Doke 1954:33).

It is interesting to note that all of these languages (leaving aside Ostyak for which Bouda does not give complete data) have /l/ in addition to /ɬ/ except Ubykh and the Circassian languages (which do, however, have a voiced *fricative*-lateral)[2] and Nootka (which has no voiced consonants at all except for nasals and semi-vowels). This observation may be put in the form of an implicational universal: In languages which have voiced obstruents (stops and spirants), the presence of a voiceless lateral implies the presence of a voiced lateral.

It is tempting to speculate (*à la* Ferguson 1963:59 and Greenberg 1969:153) that at the root of this synchronic universal there is a diachronic universal to the effect that, in languages which have voiced obstruents, phonemic voiceless fricative-laterals are always the product of a secondary split involving /l/ (i.e. /l/ acquired a voiceless allophone which became an autonomous phoneme when the conditioning factor[3] was lost). Since secondary split, by definition, always leaves the original phoneme unchanged in some of its environments, this diachronic hypothesis would seem to account for the synchronic facts. Unfortunately, the historical record does not support this hypothesis, at least in its present form. Even the unsystematic investigation conducted by the present writer revealed that there are other sources of /ɬ/ besides /l/.[4]

Voiced fricative-laterals (written ɮ)[5] also occur in the languages of the world, but they are much rarer than their voiceless counterparts, perhaps because the ubiquitous voiced lateral approximants tend to discourage the formation and/or retention of a phoneme which would so greatly diminish their margin of safety. Whatever the reason, voiced fricative-laterals seem to occur only in Modern South Arabic, Ubykh, the Circassian languages, and several African languages, e.g., Sandawe, Bura, Margi and the Southern Bantu language groups mentioned above except for the Sotho group. All of these languages, except for Ubykh and the Circassian languages[6] also have /ɬ/ and /l/, so it seems that /ɮ/, /ɬ/ and /l/ form an implicational series. Old Arabic, as we shall see, was an exception: it had /ɮ/ and /l/ but not /ɬ/. However, this typologically abnormal situation, created by the retention of /ɮ/ after the shift of /ɬ/ to /š/, seems to have been short-lived.

We might also mention one other generalization that emerges from our survey: in some languages[7] which have /l/ and /ɬ/ (but not /ɮ/), the latter serves as a voiceless counterpart of the former in spite of the considerable acoustic difference between the two created by the presence of friction in one and its absence in the other.[8] The explanation is probably connected with the fact that the real voiceless counterpart of [l] -- the voiceless approximant [l̥] -- is scarcely audible[9] (Dieth 1950:149, Doke 1926:97). In such languages, then, [ɬ] is phonologically /l̥/, with friction added to make it audible.

One last point needs to be made. It is possible to produce a fricative-lateral at any point on the side of the tongue. Throughout most of this monograph we will be using the symbols ɬ and ɮ without regard to point of articulation. On those rare occasions when it is necessary to distinguish velar or uvular fricative-laterals from alveolar ones, ɫ and ɮ̄ will be used for the former, and ɬ and ɮ for the latter.

[1]Other symbols include: *ł* or *ƚ* in works on American Indian languages (but Slavicists and others use this symbol to denote a velarized *l*), *l̥* in studies of Icelandic (but many phoneticians reserve this symbol for the voiceless lateral *approximant*), ƀ (Smalley 1962-4:217), *ś* in works on Modern South Arabic (but nineteenth-century Semitists used this Polish symbol to write [ç], as in Polish, and most Semitists today use it as a phonetically

noncommittal transcription of Hebrew-Aramaic שׂ and its Proto-Semitic ancestor, a practice we shall follow in this monograph), ś in the Modern South Arabic word-lists of Thomas (1937), ʃ̌ in studies of Modern South Arabic by Johnstone (1968, 1970a,b) before he switched to ś (1972), ŝ and s̹ in articles dealing with South Arabic phonology by Beeston (1951, 1962b), *hl* in Icelandic and Zulu orthography, and *ll* in Welsh orthography. Kabardian has had many standard orthographies and hence many symbols for ɬ (Kuipers 1960:116).

[2]Henderson (1970:93) states that Kabardian "ɮ may be classified as both a voiced lateral fricative and a sonorant," but Kuipers (1960:20) writes that "only Kabardians who have been strongly subjected to the influence of some other language (Russian, Arabic, Turkish) to the extent of being more conversant in it than in Kabardian, occasionally pronounced voiced *l* as a pure liquid, but this sound is foreign to the language." In fact, none of the Northwest Caucasian languages has a lateral approximant except Abkhaz (Kuipers 1955:198).

[3]In Welsh, the conditioning factor was a preceding *h* weakened from **s* (Jones 1930:135, cp. ibid., 134), in Icelandic it was (or still is, depending on one's phonemic analysis) a preceding *h* weakened from **q*, **k̂*, and **k* (Johannesson 1956:1297-8); cf. also the following two synchronic rules of Apache phonology: /hl/ → [ɬ] (Hoijer 1946:71) and /l/ → [ɬ] */voiceless sibilant* (ibid., 73). A non-phonemic voiceless fricative-lateral with strong palatalization exists in the Yiddish of Carpathian Ruthenia (personal observation); the conditioning factor is a preceding *k* (e.g. [kɬ^{y}ayn] "small," [kɬ^{y}apn] "knock," etc.). The presence of glottalized ejectives in many of the languages which have ɬ suggests that such consonants (which are, of necessity, always voiceless) may have served as conditioning factors in many cases.

[4]Southern Bantu ɬ comes from an older voiceless palatal stop (Guthrie 1971:63, cf. also Doke 1954:42), and the Proto-Chadic source of Biu-Mandara ɬ may be **s* (Newman and Ma 1966:226, but cf. also Kraft 1971). The voiceless fricative-laterals in Archi and the Avaro-Andian languages seem to come from Proto-North Caucasian voiceless velar fricatives (Trubetzkoy 1922:199). Cf. also the non-phonemic lateral pronunciation of *s* in 19th century Leghorn (Italy) known as *la lisca* (Malagòli 1939 s.v., Teloni 1889), which probably involved a voiceless fricative-lateral rather than a liquid , judging from the positions in which the allophone appears (e.g. initially before stops as in *lperanza = speranza, ltampà = stampare*, etc.).

[5]Other symbols include: ɧ in works on African languages, ł (Smalley 1962-4:217), d̮ in works on Modern South Arabic, ź in the Modern South Arabic word-lists of Thomas (1937), ǯ in studies of Modern South Arabic by Johnstone (1968, 1970a,b) before he switched to ź (1972), *dhl* in Zulu orthography. It is ironic but not particularly significant that in the Kabardian adaptation of the Arabic alphabet (in use until 1923), the symbol for ɮ is not ض but ل (Kuipers 1960:116). Presumably, the introduction of this Kabardian orthography came long after Arabic ض had ceased to be a fricative-lateral.

[6]See fn. 2 above.

[7]E.g. Welsh, where the soft mutation or lenited form of *ll* is *l*, just as the soft mutation of the other voiceless consonants is voiced (Jones 1913:162); Apache, where *l* coalesces with a preceding *h* to form ɬ just as γ, *y*, *z*, ž coalesce with a preceding h to form *x*, *s*, *s*, š respectively (Hoijer 1946:73); and Chipewyan where the alternation ɬ ~ *l* is paralleled by θ ~ ð, *s* ~ *z*, and *x* ~ γ (Li Fang-Kuei 1946:400).

[8]Cp. the relationship between ʕ and ḥ in Arabic and between *y* and ç in various other languages.

[9]Nevertheless, Ladefoged (1971:11) reports a voiceless lateral approximant /l̥/ contrasting with /l/ in Burmese.

II.
Fricative-Laterals in Modern South Arabic

MODERN SOUTH ARABIC

The term Modern South Arabic (MSA) designates a group of South Semitic languages spoken on or near the southern coast of the Arabian Peninsula. Shahari[1] is spoken in the Omani Dependency of Dhofar (Ẓufār) and, in a somewhat different form, in the Kuria Muria Islands.[2] Mehri is spoken in Ẓufār and in the Mahra country (*bilād Mahra*) which lies between Ẓufār (whose western border is at Raʔs Ḍarbat ʕAlī) and Ḥaḍramawt (bounded on the east by Wādī Masīlah). The island of Socotra, formerly ruled by the Mahrite Sultans of Qishin, also has speakers of Mehri, but the indigenous MSA language of this island is Socotri. Botahari and Harsusi, closely related to Mehri and often said to be dialects of it, are spoken in Ẓufār.

The MSA languages are generally thought to be descended from a (thus far unattested) dialect or dialects of Epigraphic South Arabic (ESA), the language of the ancient inscriptions found mainly in southwestern Arabia but also in Ẓufār. They are set off from Arabic by their failure to show certain phonological innovations which are shared by every known Arabic dialect, including the Arabic dialect of Ẓufār (which is a second language to most speakers of MSA): the unconditional merger of *ḍ* and *ẓ*, and the chain shift *ś* › *š* › *s* in which š merged unconditionally with *s*. Furthermore, the MSA emphatics are not velarized as in Arabic but rather glottalized as in Ethiopian Semitic (Fresnel 1838b:544-5 [3], Yushmanov 1930:383-4, Johnstone 1970a:296fn, 1973:98fn, 1975a, 1975b:6-7) -- a little-known[4] fact whose implications for Semitic linguistics are enormous.[5]

If it is easy to show how the MSA languages differ from Arabic, it is more difficult to name the innovations[6] that justify their being grouped together. Several phonological innovations, which, at first glance, appear to set off MSA as a distinct branch of South Semitic, prove, upon closer examination, to have affected only some of the MSA languages. The raising of *ā* to *ō* or *ū*, for example, characterizes Shahari, Mehri, Harsusi, and Botahari, but is unevidenced in Socotri. The conditioned merger of *š* with *h*[7], on the other hand, is attested, with slight variations, in Socotri, Mehri,

Harsusi, and Botahari, but, with the exception of a few lexical items, not in Shahari (Leslau 1938:32-4, 1947a:183,195, 200). The merger of *h* and *ḥ*, reliably reported for Socotri (Leslau 1938:21[8], Johnstone 1975b:5), does not seem to be reflected in the spellings of Carter's Mehri informant (Carter 1847 passim) in spite of several instances of *ḥ* for *h*[9], and we should, therefore, no doubt, discount the evidence for such a merger in Thomas' Shahari, Mehri, Harsusi, and Botahari transcriptions. One phonological innovation which *does* seem to have affected the whole group is the de-emphatization of *ḍ* (Fresnel 1838b:546, Yushmanov 1930:384, Johnstone 1970a:296n), but even here it must be noted that in Socotri *ḍ* has retained a glottalized allophone (Johnstone 1973:98fn).

REPORTS OF FRICATIVE-LATERALS IN MODERN SOUTH ARABIC

Most of the published descriptions of the MSA languages come from doctors, diplomats, or just plain adventurers with no professional training in phonetics and with no knowledge of the descriptions of their predecessors. It is, therefore, quite astonishing that so many of them correctly identified at least one of the fricative-laterals in these languages.

The earliest description of the MSA fricative-laterals just barely missed being the earliest description of MSA (Wellsted's worthless Socotri word-list was published three years earlier). It is part of Fulgence Fresnel's description (1838b) of the phonetics of Ehhkili, also called Shhari (1838a:534) i.e. Shahari. This description, based on the speech of an informant who happened to be in Jidda (the seaport of Mecca) and sent to Paris in a series of letters, remains indispensable even today. The following section (1838b:538-9), full of French *esprit*, was formerly quite popular in European orientalist circles:

> [Il y a] trois lettres dont la prononciation détruit la symmetrie du visage.
>
> Toutes les langues que j'ai étudiées en Europe ont cela de commun, qu'on peut et doit les parler sans contorsions. Ainsi, lorsqu'un homme s'exprime en anglais, en russe, en arabe ou en chinois, si l'on conçoit la figure de l'orateur coupée de haut en bas par le plan que déterminent ces trois points, le milieu des lèvres, le sommet de la tête et le milieu de la nuque, les mouvements de ses organes vocaux seront exactement les mêmes de chaque coté de ce plan a chaque instant de son discours. Il n'en est pas toujours ainsi dans la langue ehhkili ou hhimyarique. Elle a des articulations qui exigent que la langue et la lèvre inférieure se portent à droite, d'où résulte une grimace que Mouhhsin lui-même

> trouve fort ridicule, parce qu'il a voyagé. Assurément, quand la reine de Saba prononçait [ces lettres], sa beauté devait en souffrir. M. Antoine d'Abadie, à qui je faisais remarquer ce phénomène, eut, ainsi que moi, l'idée de demander a Mouhhsin s'il n'y avait point dans son pays des gens qui, pour prononcer ces trois lettres, tournassent la langue du côté gauche. Notre Bedouin lui assura, comme il me l'avait assuré à moi-même, qu'on n'avait jamais vu d'exemple d'une pareille *gaucherie* ...

The phones described here can only be laterals, since laterals are the only phones which may be asymmetrical (with respect to the median line of the palate). Often, it is only the air-stream, escaping from the mouth on only one side, which is asymmetrical, but the tongue may also be positioned left or right of center and, in the case of fricative-laterals at least, even the lips may be pulled to the side (Sievers 1901:131). There can be no other explanation for Mouhhsin's facial contortions.

Fresnel goes on to explain that one of these three phones is "a kind of *z* or Arabic *dhal*" (op. cit., 540), the second is closer to the English *th* than any other sound (ibid., 554), and the third is like *ts* (ibid., 546). Significantly, the first of these replaces *l* for euphony (ibid., 539) even though it is completely different from it acoustically.

Fresnel was puzzled by this alternation of two sounds which sounded so different to him, although his informant found it quite natural. The explanation is really quite simple. It is true that *acoustically* the contorted z is completely different from *l* since the former is a fricative, i.e. made with friction, while the latter is an approximant, made with minimal friction. But once we realize that from an articulatory point of view both are laterals, with almost identical tongue-positions, their interchange ceases to be mysterious. It is simply a case of a voiced lateral approximant [l] becoming a voiced lateral fricative [ɮ] through an increase in friction.

Carter's description (1847:343) of a Mehri fricative-lateral is short and simple but says everything one needs to know:

> ش has a very peculiar sound in the Mahra dialect; it is formed by placing the tip of the tongue against the anterior part of the palate, and allowing the air to pass out of the mouth on one side or the other of it, in the manner of a lisp, following it with the sound of the letter *l*, as in شلوط[10] "fire," pronounced *shleeote*.[11]

The reason that Carter heard an *l* will be discussed in chapter xvi, but, whatever the explanation, its presence here confirms Carter's description of the lateral passage of air.

Glaser's description (1895:87) of a Shahari (?) fricative-lateral is almost as explicit:

> Dieses *š́* [in the word *šeḥrât*] ist an der rechtsseitigen Zahnreihe auszusprechen, also zum rechten Mundwinkel hinaus und ist nicht von einen gleichfalls an derselben Stelle articulirten ث zu unterscheiden. Etymologisch jedoch ist es ش [i.e. it corresponds to Arabic *š* but sounds more like Arabic *ṯ*].

Next we come to Jahn's description (1905:5) of a Mehri fricative-lateral:

> *ś*, laterales ش, wird artikuliert, indem man den Luftstrom durch die Verengung des Raumes zwischen dem rechten Gaumen und der Zunge, welche man durch Annäherung des rechten Zungenrandes an die rechten oberen Backenzähne herbeigeführt hat, und zwischen den beiden rechtseitigen Zahnreihen hindurchpresst.

All this is, as Yushmanov (1926:42) remarked, "un peu compliqué!" but the essentials are clear: the air is pressed through a narrow space between the right side of the palate and the right edge of the tongue and escapes between the upper and lower teeth on the right side of the mouth.

Thomas' description is of great interest (1937:236) in spite of the fact that it gives no articulatory details:

> The visitor to the Hadara habitat, whose ear is attuned to dialects of Modern Arabic, is immediately struck by two phonetic peculiarities -- the sounds of (*a*) lateralized consonants or lisped sibilants, and (*b*) of *ll* in the Welsh pronunciation of such a word as *Llanelly*.[12] It occurs with great frequency and is accorded not only to the *ḍh* consonant whose lateralization appears to have been an old Semitic usage lost in Modern Arabic, but is the value of the consonants *s, ṣ, sh, dh, <u>dh</u>, th, z,* judging from the Hadara pronunciation of those of their words akin to Modern Arabic ...

We have already mentioned that Welsh *ll* is a fricative-lateral. Jones (1913:19), for example, describes it as:

> ... a voiceless *l* pronounced on one side. It is produced by placing the tongue in the *l* position,

> raising it so as to close the passage on one side, and blowing between it and the teeth on the other. The common imitation *thl* conveys the effect of the "hiss" (voiceless spirant) in the *th*, and gives the side effect in the *l*. But *ll* is of course a simple sound which may be described shortly as a "unilateral hiss."

The Welsh *ll* is then indeed similar to the MSA fricative-laterals and we shall more than once call upon the Welsh fricative-lateral *ll* for parallels in the course of this research.

Lastly we find Johnstone's explicit statement (1970a: 296) that the MSA languages have a voiced fricative-lateral and a voiceless fricative-lateral.

LANDBERG'S ض AND THE ض-ISOGLOSS

The Swedish Arabist Count Carlo von Landberg is the author of several descriptions of the Arabic spoken in Ḥaḍramawt. One of them (1898:167) contains a brief reference to Mehri:

> ʔAwaɬ,[13] Hafiɬ, abyaɬ,[14] aɬmah,[15] etc.; dans toute cette contrée de même qu'en Daṯîna le ض est prononcé comme le *l* slave ou le *l* des paysans de la Haute-Bavière et des Hollandais. Cette prononciation est particulière des tribus qui ont le nom collectif de Himyar. Les Mahrites à qui j'ai causé l'avaient aussi et Maltzan, ZDMG 27, p259 a déjà relevé ce fait.

It is unclear from this statement whether the Mahrites with whom Landberg spoke had an *l*-like ض in their Arabic speech only, or (as the reference to von Maltzan 1873 suggests) in their native language as well. In a later description (1901: 637) he is more explicit:

> ض est prononcé dans tout le pays de Daṯîna et par les tribus dites ḥimyarites (Arabica V, 230) comme le ɬ slave, hollandais et de la Haute-Bavière. Comme c'est la règle dans la langue mahra, il faut supposer que nous sommes en présence d'une prononciation particulière de l'ancienne langue du sud.

Now when Landberg speaks of ض in Mehri, he means the Mehri phoneme which corresponds to Arabic ض, a loose but common way of speaking justified by the close relationship between the two languages. But when we examine the word-lists of other writers, we find that the Mehri phoneme which corresponds to

ض is not a velarized *l*, as Landberg claims, but one of the fricative-laterals (the voiced one) which we have been discussing.

We are now faced with a problem. Did Landberg make a mistake? Did he hear a voiced fricative-lateral as an *l*? Bravmann (1934:153) stops just short of an affirmative answer:

> Nach Landberg Hadram. p. 637 hat ḍ die Aussprache als emphatisches *l* in ganz Daṯīna...und im Mehri...--Allerdings ist es mir fraglich, ob das ḍ im Mehri so durchgängig als emphatisches *l* gesprochen wird. Jahn S.4 erklärt es als laterales ḍ, und umschreibt es bekanntlich mit ḍ̮. Seine definition dieses ḍ scheint übrigens ziemlich den Angaben nahezukommen die die Grammatiker vom ḍ geben...sodass dieser Laut uns im Mehri erhalten wäre...

But even if Landberg could confuse ض with *l*-- in spite of Fresnel's testimony[16] that he could not hear any resemblance between the two even though he tried -- could a native speaker do the same? Landberg (1901:637) tells us that: "بيضامد... fut écrit par un Karrâni d'éś-Śugra بلامظ." This spelling mistake must reflect a real merger of ḍ and *l* in the Arabic dialect of the karrâni, which suggests that Landberg may have been right about Mehri ḍ as well.

Actually a simple explanation is at hand for the discrepancy between Landberg's description and all of the above descriptions. It is contained in the statement by von Maltzan (1873b:259) alluded to above by Landberg (1898):

> Die beiden Zungenlaute ل [=*l*] and ض zeigen auch in Mehri recht deutlich ihre nahe Verwandschaft. In West-Mahra geht ض geradezu in *l* über:
>
> Beispiele
>
> *hlaiq*, eng (arabisch ضيق)
>
> *yetulian*, er verrichtet die Abwaschung (vom arabischen توضّأ).

The important part of this statement, which has been hitherto been ignored, is the phrase "in West-Mahra." Von Maltzan, like Thomas (1937:233), divides up the widespread Mahra tribe into eastern and western branches:[17]

> Es handelt sich hier also nur um zwei Zweige des Mahra-Dialects, die ich west- und ost-Mehri nenne. Ersterer wird vom Wâdi Mesîle und Sayhut an bis östlich von Keschîn,[18] auch auf der Insel Soqotra gesprochen. Er ist jedoch weniger rein, noch mehr mit Arabismen

> gemischt, als der andere, nebenbei scheint mir auch die Aussprache sehr verderbt. Das östliche Mehri ist die Sprache von Râs Fartaq und scheint in der Umgegend von Ḥaçûêl[19] ...am reinsten gesprochen zu werden.

Given these geographical data, it seems likely that the Mahrites whom Landberg met were West-Mahrites. All of the other authors cited above had East-Mahrite informants from Ẓufār (or, in Carter's case, the village of Ahsoel) or Shahari informants from the same area. It appears, then, that there is a *ḍ*-isogloss separating West-Mehri from East-Mehri.

That West-Mehri is characterized by a liquid, rather than (or alongside of)[20] a fricative, *ḍ* can be shown from another source: Bent's Mehri and Socotri word-lists (1900: 440-8). In these lists we find that Bent has transcribed Mehri *ḍ* with *l* in three out of five[21] examples:

Erkella "kick" (p. 443) cf. Carter (1847:351) *markadthat* (Mehri) "kick"; Leslau (1938:400) *rékoḍ* (Socotri) "fouler le sol"; Thomas (1937:304) *rikuś*[22] (Mehri) "kick."

Gailar "lion" (p. 446) cf. Johnstone (1970a:306) *k'ayẓ̌ar* (Mehri) "panther"; Thomas (1937:312) *qaiźur* (Mehri) "panther"; Ewald (1846:311) *k'eter* (Mehri) "lion"; von Maltzan (1873:229) *qaiṯer*[23] (West-Mehri) "lion,"

Athail "bone" (p. 446) cf. Thomas (1937:288) *adhaiź* (Mehri) "bone"; Jahn (1902:254) *aḍáyḍ* (Mehri) "Knochen"; Carter (1847:347) *athēth* (Mehri) "bone,"

The other two examples have *d* for *ḍ*: *Hader* "ready" (p. 443) and *Kadi* "judge" (p. 441), but these words are obviously Arabic. In fact, they are the very words that Bent asked his informant to translate.[24]

Bent's use of *l* to transcribe Mehri *ḍ* is significant since he never uses it for Socotri *ḍ* (*ld*, *dl*, *tl*)[25] or Socotri *ś* (*thl*, *kl*, *tl*, *hl*, etc.)[26] or Mehri *ś* (*zhl*, *zh*, *lth*, *tl*, *thl*, etc.).[27] In other words, if the Mehri *ḍ* that Bent heard had been a fricative-lateral, he would have used an *l*-*cluster*. It seems, then, that Bent heard Mehri *ḍ* as an ordinary *l*.

Bent collected his Mehri word-list while on Socotra, an island which was politically[28] and linguistically[29] tied to the West-Mehri dialect area. Thus, Bent's word-lists provide additional evidence for the existence of a *ḍ*-isogloss.

Anyone who has followed us this far will not be surprised to learn that the *Arabic* dialects of South Arabia are also divided by a *ḍ*-isogloss -- although in this case we should properly speak of a ḍ - ẓ - isogloss (in view of the unconditional merger which these dialects share with all other Arabic dialects). On the one hand, we have the ḍ - ẓ of Daṯīna and Wahīdī (east of Daṯīna at the western end of Ḥaḍramawt)[30] described by Landberg[31] as a lateral approximant and actually written with a *lām*, in one instance, by a native speaker; and on the other hand we have the Ẓufārī ḍ - ẓ described by Rhodokanakis (1911) as a spirant (p. x) and as coming close to the emphatic *lām* (p. 82; "Je höher sie hinter die Zähne schlägt, desto mehr nähert sich ḍ dem لام مفخمة = ḷ [=Landberg's ɬ]") -- in sum, a fricative-lateral. An intriguing note by Thomas (1937:331) suggests that ḍ - ẓ may be a fricative-lateral in eastern peninsular dialects outside of South Arabia as well:

> A lateralized ظ is met with in the modern Arabic of the borderland tribes of the eastern Rub'al Khali, who speak of the Abu Dhabi as Abu Źabi.

Unfortunately, Thomas' note has never been confirmed by other fieldworkers,[32] and Rhodokanakis' reliance on one Shahari-speaking tribesman (rather than several monolingual Ẓufārī Arabs) for all of his Arabic data (op. cit., xvi-xvii) may vitiate entirely the value of his description -- for our purposes, at least.

Our discussion of the ḍ-isoglosses would be incomplete if we did not mention the fascinating and undoubtedly ancient tradition quoted (anonymously) by Wallin in 1858 (p. 634) but, inexplicably, ignored by Semitists from that time on:

> *Wa-kāna s-sayyidu (ʕUmar?) yaqūlu: ʔinnamā ḍ-ḍādu ḍādu l-maġāribati ʔammā ḍādu l-mašāriqati fa-lāmun mufaxxama. Wa-xālafahu š-šayxu ʕĪd wa-qāla: ʔinnamā ḍ-ḍādu ḍādu l-mašāriqati wa-huwa l-laḏī ʕalayhi l-ʔijmāʕ.*
>
> The Master (ʕUmar?) used to say: It is the *ḍād* of the westerners which is the true *ḍād* [i.e. the *ḍād* of the orthoepists described as *rixwa* "fricative" and *min ḥāffati l-lisān* "lateral"] -- the *ḍād* of the easterners is an emphatic *l*. Sheikh ʕĪd differed with him and said: It is the *ḍād* of the easterners which is the true *ḍād*. The consensus of the scholars favors this latter opinion.

In a later chapter we will consider the possibility of corroborating this statement with other evidence, specifically, the fact that numerous African languages used *l* to render ḍ in Arabic loanwords, while Persian used z (Rubinchik 1965: 588). Here it suffices to note that the two realizations of ḍ described in this passage seem to be basically the same as those attested in present-day South Arabia.

HOW MANY FRICATIVE-LATERALS?

It seems virtually certain that there are exactly two fricative-lateral phonemes in the MSA languages -- one voiced and the other voiceless. Johnstone's system of transcription, which seems to be phonemic although he never says so explicitly, distinguishes two: ʃ̌ (= ɬ) and ǯ (= ɮ) (1970a:296). His discussion of the Socotri fricative-laterals (1968:517) is a little more explicit in this regard. Thomas' word lists (1937) show voiced ź (with free variants *d́h* and *źh*)[33] contrasting[34] with voiceless ś (with free variants *tĥ* and *sĥ*), in spite of a good deal of free variation between the two (perhaps partially due to mishearing).[35]

Thomas' *analysis* is another story. In it, Thomas gives a long list of consonants (some of them imported from Arabic!) which sometimes have lisped or lateralized "values" in MSA: *s, ṣ, sh, dh, ḍh, d̲h̲, th,* and *z*. Now this way of looking at the MSA fricative-laterals is quite misleading in view of the fact that *ś* and *s*, to pick one example, are totally unrelated in the MSA phonological system. But Thomas' statements are not sufficiently explicit to be called wrong -- they could after all be interpreted as a statement about the phonetic inventory. Murtonen (1966:139), however, obligingly adds the necessary precision by speaking of lateralized "variants" instead of "values." These variants, he adds, "seem to be only allophonic." This is demonstrably false. Despite Murtonen's claim to the contrary, there are a number of minimal pairs in Thomas' word-lists, e.g.

> Shahari *sōt* "strike" : *śōt* "fire"
> Shahari *sīn* "obey" : *śīn* "left"
> Shahari *sān* "they" : *śan* "we have"
> Mehri, Harsusi *zār* "stop" : *źār* "gazelle"
> Harsusi *zīd* "more" : *źaid* "fish" (ī and ai are free variants in Thomas' word-lists)

Murtonen makes much out of the considerable amount of free variation in Thomas' word-lists between lateralized and unlateralized sounds. But unless the free variation is between lateralized and unlateralized *correlates* (e.g. *d́h* and *dh*) it is difficult to see how that helps his case. All of the examples I have found of free variation between such correlates involve ź and *z*, which contrast in the above minimal pairs. Relatively rare symbols like *dĥ, zĥ* and *tĥ, sĥ* are always in free variation with z᷾ and s᷾[36] respectively -- never with their supposed unlateralized co-allophones.

It is curious that Thomas has, in addition to the analysis which misled Murtonen, a second analysis (op. cit., 239) which Murtonen ignored:

> The respective sound values of *s᷾*, *ṣ᷾*, *sh́*, *dh́*, *ḍh́*, *d̲h̲́*, *th́*, *ẓ᷾* are, to a European ear, practically indistinguishable. A lightly and a heavily lisped sibilant, as represented by *s᷾* and *z᷾*, seemed, to the writer's ear, the most that could be detected.

In this passage, Thomas presents his whole list of lateralized sibilants as variants of *s᷾* and *z᷾* rather than variants of the unlateralized sibilants.

A different problem arises in connection with Jahn's description of Mehri (1905:4-5). He also reports two lateral consonants, *ś* and *ḍ*, and these correspond fairly well to Thomas' *s᷾* and *z᷾* respectively; but *ḍ* is described as a stop. Now Jahn also says that *ḍ* is a lateral so that even if he did hear a stop, it must have had a lateral release, i.e. probably [dɮ]. But it seems more likely that he simply made a mistake of the kind recorded by Doke (1926:100): "many Europeans erroneously think that they hear a *d* in the fricative ɮ [of Zulu]." It is significant that no analogous mishearing is recorded for the Zulu *voiceless* fricative-lateral. It would be quite possible, then, for Jahn to make a mistake about *ḍ* without making the same mistake about *ś*.

A last problem arises from Fresnel's description. According to him, there are three distinct fricative-laterals in Shahari. From his examples it is clear that one of them is the reflex of PS *ś*, the second is the reflex of PS *ḍ*, and the third is the reflex of PS *l* in the vicinity of *i*. Thomas' Shahari word-list and Johnstone's Shahari texts show a split-and-merger in the same environment: *l* is merged with the reflex of PS *ḍ* before or after *i*. Now it is not impossible that this process was started but not completed by the mid-nineteenth century, in Fresnel's time. Thus we might suppose that there were three fricative-laterals in Shahari, one of which was an allophone of *l*. But Fresnel gives so few examples that it is hard to know whether we can rely on his data or not. It should also be pointed out that this possibility applies only to Shahari, because it is only in Shahari that this split-and-merger (*l* › ɮ / *i*) has taken place.

[1]The spelling of these names in English is far from standard. The spellings used here are Thomas', except for "Mehri" which follows the ear-

lier convention established by the Viennese Expedition.

[2]Until very recently, the only first-hand account of the Kuria Muria dialect was that of Hulton from 1840! Hulton found 23 speakers of Shahari on the island of Hallaniya and elicited a short list of words from them. It was not until 1975 that Semitists learned that a dialect of Shahari is still spoken in the area (Johnstone 1975b:3).

[3]Fresnel reports that the MSA emphatics

> "exigent un certain gonflement des amygdales, et sont, pour ainsi dire, *crachées* par une émission violente et subite de l'air comprimé dans le larynx. Le ص peut être représenté ... par *ss*, le ڝ [a palatalized allophone of ق] par *ttch* ou *tss*, le ط par *tt*, le ظ par *tth* et le ق par *ck*; mais à moins d'avoir ouï parler l'amharique (*amara*) ou éthiopien moderne on ne peut pas deviner ce que j'entends ici par *tt* ou *ck*."

[4]Johnstone himself is unaware that Fresnel reported the presence of glottalized ejectives in MSA nearly a century and a half ago. His recently published paper to the 1970 Hamito-Semitic Colloquium at the School of Oriental and African Studies in London begins as follows (1975:155):

> "Since ejectives occur in the languages of the Cushitic group (Bedawye, Agaw, Saho-ʕAfar, Sidamo, Galla, and Somali), but have not so far been recorded for the Semitic languages outside the Ethiopian area, it might reasonably be concluded that this was a N.E. African rather than a Semitic phenomenon."

Leslau's comment on the paper (ibid., 157) reveals that he is equally unaware of Fresnel's report, despite the fact that he devoted several lines to Fresnel's article and Yushmanov's analysis of it (Yushmanov 1930, cf. pp. 383-4 dealing with the glottalized emphatics) in his survey of South Arabic linguistics for *Current Trends in Linguistics* (1970:520):

> "I do not need to say that this is a minor revolution in so far as Semitic is concerned. We always thought glottalization was only a privilege of Ethiopic and some of the Cushitic languages. We have known Mehri, Šḥeri, Socotri for quite a while but we were never told that they had glottalized consonants."

[5]Since the presence of glottalized emphatics in MSA cannot possibly be attributed to a Cushitic substratum, as is frequently done with the Ethiopian ejectives, this evidence greatly strengthens the case for glottalized emphatics in PS (cf. Cantineau [1951-2] 1960:291-3 and the literature cited there).

[6]Retentions, of course, will not do, cf. Hoenigswald 1965:151. The fricative-laterals, which go back at least as far as Proto-South Semitic, clearly come under this heading.

[7]An interesting example of this merger is the MSA toponym *Hanun* (‹ESA *s*^{1}*ʔnn*), discussed in chapter iii, fn. 27.

[8]Leslau avoids the word "merger," which obviously applies here. The best proof is cited by Leslau himself: in addition to hypercorrections of *h* to š in Socotri (1938:34-5, cf. pp. 32-4 for the conditioned sound-change š › *h*), there are one or two hypercorrections of *ḥ* to š (ibid., 21).

[9]Cf. ظحر موتن "back" (Arabic *ẓahr*), واجح "face" (Arabic *wajh*), ناحر "river" (Arabic *nahr*), and probably also مظورح "tooth" (Arabic *ḍirs* ‹ **ḍirš*) since it is unlikely that š went directly to *ḥ* in this word (there are numerous examples of š › *h* but not of š › *ḥ*).

[10]This form was written by Carter's Mehri informant.

[11]I.e. [šliyot].

[12]Of course, the MSA voiceless fricative-lateral(s) resemble(s) Welsh *ll* more than the voiced fricative-lateral(s).

[13]ɫ = (Russian) velarized *l*. Not to be confused with our symbol ɬ = voiceless fricative-lateral.

[14]"White" = Classical ʔ*abyaḍ*.

[15]"Bone" = Classical ʕ*aẓm*; *ḍ* and *ẓ* are merged in this modern dialect as in all modern dialects (Colin 1930a:92).

[16]See above in this chapter.

[17]They define the boundaries of these branches differently, however;

von Maltzan seems not to have been aware of how far east the eastern branch went and Thomas may not have known how far west the western branch extended.

[18]Mehri Qâśän.

[19]Carter's Ahsoel (1847:342).

[20]Cf. fn. 23 below.

[21]A possible additional example is *Hat'hor* "yellow" (p. 445)(although Thomas (1937:328) has an ś in this word) since it may be identical with the word for "green" which has a *ḍ*.

[22]Thomas' ś instead of the expected ź is either the result of devoicing in word-final position or mis-hearing, for Carter's native informant writes ظ here (مركظات), a letter he uses consistently for the Mehri voiced fricative-lateral but never for its voiceless counterpart.

[23]The *ṯ* in this word is strange in view of von Maltzan's own testimony that *ḍ* › *l* in West Mehri. Jahn's informant from Qishin (Qâśän) also had *ḍ* in his inventory in spite of the fact that he should have been speaking West-Mehri, e.g. *ḍafḍât* (1902:174), *ḍarôb* (ibid., 175). Many solutions could be proposed but the problem clearly calls for further investigation.

[24]The Arabic words that Bent used are obviously the ones in the column labeled "dialect used in South Arabia..."; cf. p. 364 where Mrs. Bent descibes her husband's method of eliciting words.

[25]*Kaldi* "judge," *N'dlahak* "to laugh," *Entlahak* "laughter."

[26]*Thlef* "hair," *Thlaub* "leg," *Thlab* "stream," *Tadkleher* "one month" (Bent glosses "week" but the Arabic word he asked was *shahr* "month "), *Tlahas* "frankincense" (Bent glosses "myrrh gum" but the Arabic word he asked was *lobàn* "frankincense"), *Ihlop* "leg" (possibly for *Thlop,* cf. *Thlaub* "leg").

[27]*Arzhlìt* "tent," *Izhè* "evening meal," *Hamilthtòr* "buy," *Tlahas* "frankincense," *Thluf* "feather."

[28]As was pointed out above, the island of Socotra was ruled until recently by the Mahrite Sultans of Qishin. The town of Qishin or Keschîn is part of the West-Mehri dialect area, according to von Maltzan's statement quoted above.

[29]Cf. von Maltzan's statement, quoted above.

[30]This area is far to the west of Mahra-land, with practically the whole length of Ḥaḍramawt intervening. One wonders whether it is a completely isolated pocket or whether the lateral approximant *ḍ* - *ẓ* is found further east, in other parts of Ḥaḍramawt and in Mahra-land (where we know only about the Mehri *ḍ*).

[31]Cf. Landberg's descriptions, quoted above.

[32]After writing these lines, the present writer was informed by Professor F. Cadora that a student from Ḥāʔil whom he interviewed (and taped) in Beirut had a fricative-lateral *ḍ*-*ẓ*.

[33]The grapheme ‹ *źh* › occurs only in the Mehri word for "finger."

[34]Shahari *źaif* "feasts" (p.296) : *śaif* "asleep" (p. 284) and Mehri *aśiś* "get up" (p. 298) : *aźaiś* "bone" (p. 288). Note that *i* and *ai* are in free variation in Thomas' word-lists. Leslau's suggestion (1947a:182) that Thomas' ź is only an allophone of /ś/ is based not on any phonemic analysis of Thomas' data but rather on the alleged lack of any voiced counterpart to *ś* in the transcriptions of Thomas' predecessors (i.e. Jahn, Bittner, and the rest of the Viennese Expedition). Had Leslau examined the lexical distribution of ź, he would have seen that it corresponds to the Viennese Expedition's *d̮*, even though Jahn (1905:5) describes the latter as a stop. Moreover, Fresnel's ژ (1838b:540) is clearly a voiced fricative-lateral.

[35]Cf. Jahn 1905:5: "Bei der bildung dieses Lautes [i.e. *ḍ*], der von einem ungeübten Ohre leicht mit dem unten erwähnten Laute *ś* verwechselt werden kann..." Jahn's own glossary, compiled from transcribed texts (where free variation would naturally tend to show itself), does not show any free variation between *ḍ* and *ś*. Moreover, in places where Jahn and Thomas disagree in their transciption of a fricative-lateral, Carter's native infor-

mant seems always to agree with Jahn. On the other hand, it is possible that Jahn suppressed real phonetic variants -- he himself admits changing ʔ to ʕ in the texts of one speaker who differed from other Mehri informants in his ʕ-less speech.

[36]Cf. Rhodokanakis 1932:225 where Socotri *ś* = lateral *š* is said to have a free variant *s̊* = lateral *s*.

III.
Correspondence Sets Containing the MSA Laterals

The central problem of this monograph is to determine whether or not the two fricative-laterals of MSA are a survival from PS. In order to pursue this question, we must investigate the phonemes in other Semitic languages which correspond to the two MSA fricative-laterals in the hope of finding evidence which will bear on the phonetic nature of these phonemes. This investigation will begin in chapter iv. In this chapter, we will lay the groundwork by identifying the phonemes which will be the object of the investigation.

Ignoring special problems and special correspondences resulting from conditioned sound-changes (some of which will be taken up below), the correspondences are as follows:

	A	B
MSA	ɬ	ɮ
ESA	s^2	ḍ
Ethiopic	š > s	ḍ > ṣ
Arabic	š	ḍ
Aramaic	ś > s	q_2 > ʕ
Hebrew	ś > s	ṣ
Ugaritic	š	ṣ
Akkadian	š	ṣ
PS	*ś	*ḍ

Columns A and B are based on sets of cognates like those in the following charts:

Column-A Cognates

	"belly"	"lip"	"hair"	"sheep"	"ten"
Mehri (Jahn 1902)	*kirś*	--	--	*kébś*	*ðśer*
Mehri (Thomas 1937)	--	*s᷾ībith*	--	*kubs᷾*	*os᷾or* *os᷾ur*
Harsusi (Thomas 1937)	--	*s᷾ībith* *s᷾aibith*	--	--	*ōs᷾ir*
Botahari (Thomas 1937)	--	--	--	--	*as᷾īr*
Shahari (Thomas 1937)	--	--	--	***kubs᷾*** *kabus᷾*	*as᷾ūr* *as᷾ir*
Shahari (Bittner 1917)	--	--	--	*koś* *kób(e)ś*	*ʕáśer*
Socotri (Leslau 1938)	*šéreś*[1]	*śebeh*	*śáʕihor*	*kobś*	*ʕáśer*
ESA (Conti Rossini 1931, Jamme 1962)	--	--	--	--	*ʕs^2r*
Ethiopic (Dillman 1865)	*kärš*	*(šänfäf*[2]*)* Tigriña	*šəʕərt*	--	*ʕäšru*
Arabic (Wehr 1966)	*kirš* *kariš*	*šafa*	*šaʕr* *šaʕar*	*kabš*	*ʕašr*
Old Aramaic (Degen 1969)	--	*śptʔ*	--	--	*ʕśr*
Syriac (Payne Smith 1903)	*karsā*	*sp̱ā* *sep̱tā*	*saʕrā*	*kebšā* *(š!)*	*ʕsar*
Hebrew (BDB)	*kåreś*	*śåp̱å(h)*	*śeʕar*	***kɛḇɛś***	*ʕɛśɛr*
Ugaritic (Gordon 1965)	--	*špt*	*šʕrt*	--	*ʕšr*
Akkadian (CAD, AHw)	*karšu* *karašu*	*šaptu*	*šartu*	*kabsu* *(s!)*[3]	*ešir*

Column-A Cognates

	"winter"	"left, north"	"month, (new)moon"	"witness"
Mehri (Jahn 1902)	--	*ś̂īmel*	--	*ś̂ōhed*
Mehri (Thomas 1937)	*ŝaitū*	*ŝaimal*	*ŝaḥair*	--
Harsusi (Thomas 1937)	*ŝaitū*	*ŝimal*	--	--
Botahari (Thomas 1937)	*ŝeta*	--	--	--
Shahari (Thomas 1937)	*ŝetta*	*ŝīn* *ŝīl*	--	--
Shahari (Bittner 1917)	*ś́éte* *ś́éta*	*ś́iñ* *ś́i(y)n*	*ś́éher*	*ś́úhud*
Socotri (Leslau 1938)	*ś́éte* "(vent du) Nord"	*ś́ímhil* *ś́ém(h)el*	*ś́éher*	*ś́éhed* "regarder"
ESA (Conti Rossini 1931, Jamme 1962)	--	--	s^2hr	bs^2hd "in the presence of"
Ethiopic (Dillman 1865)	--	--	*šahr*	--
Arabic (Wehr 1966)	*šitāʔ*	*šamāl* *šimāl*	*šahr*	*šāhid*
Old Aramaic (Degen 1969)	*śtwʔ*	*śmʔl*	--	*śhd*
Syriac (Payne Smith 1903)	*saṯwā*	*semālā*	*sahrā*	*sahdā*
Hebrew (BDB)	*sĕṯåw*	*śĕmo(ʔ)l*	*śahăron* "moon ornament"	(*śåheḏ*) loanword?
Ugaritic (Gordon 1965)	--	*šmal*	--	--
Akkadian (CAD, AHw)	--	*šumēlu*	--	--

Column-A Cognates

	"sell"	"hate"	"burn, kindle"	"(good) tidings"
Mehri (Jahn 1902)	*śêm*	*mśénaʔ* "hässlich"	--	*beśêr*
Mehri (Thomas 1937)	*śōm*	--	--	--
Harsusi (Thomas 1937)	*śime* *śōm*	--	--	--
Botahari (Thomas 1937)	*śaim*	--	--	--
Shahari (Thomas 1937)	*śãm*	--	--	--
Shahari (Bittner 1917)	*śeʔm* *śem*	--	*śeróf*[10]	--
Socotri (Leslau 1938)	*śíom*	--	--	*bšr (š!)*[4] "apporter une nouvelle"
ESA (Conti Rossini 1931, Jamme 1962)	s^2*ʔm* "buy"	s^2*nʔ* "enemy"	--	*bs*^{2}*r*
Ethiopic (Dillman 1865)	*(sēma)* Harari[8]	--	--	*bəsrat*[5]
Arabic (Wehr 1966)	--	*šaniʔa*	--	*bišāra*
Old Aramaic (Degen 1969)	--	*śnʔ* "enemy"	*(śrp)* Egypt. Aram.	--
Syriac (Payne Smith 1903)	--	*snā*	--	*sḇartā*[6]
Hebrew (BDB)	--	*śåne(ʔ)*	*śårap̱*	*bĕśorå(h)*
Ugaritic (Gordon 1965)	--	*šnʔ*	*šrp*	*bšrt*
Akkadian (CAD, AHw)	*šāmu*[9] "buy"	--	*šarāpu*	*bus(s)urtu (s!)*[7]

Column-B Cognates

	"rib"	"(molar) tooth"	"frog"	"lizard"	"hyena"
Mehri (Jahn 1902)	*ḍálaʔ*	*mḍarâḥ*[12]	*ḍafaḍôt* *ḍafdât*	*ḍóbb*	--
Mehri (Carter 1847)	*dtheîlah*	*madthora*	*dthafzāt*	*dthob*	--
Mehri (Thomas 1937)	--	*muźerah*	*śofdāt* *(ś!)*[14]	*źōb* *źōp*	--
Harsusi (Thomas 1937)	--	--	*śofdaiyait* *źufīden*	*źōb*	--
Botahari (Thomas 1937)	--	--	--	--	--
Shahari (Thomas 1937)	--	--	--	*iźōb* *źōp*	--
Shahari (Bittner 1917)	*ḍélaʕ*	--	--	*ḍobb*	--
Socotri (Leslau 1938)	*ḍalḥ*[11]	*məźórəš*[13]	--	--	*ḍábʕah*
ESA (Conti Rossini 1931, Jamme 1962)	--	*ḍrs*^{1}	--	--	--
Ethiopic (Dillman 1865)	--	*ḍərs*	--	--	*ṣəʕb*[15]
Arabic (Wehr 1966)	*ḍilʕ* *ḍilaʕ*	*ḍirs*	*ḍifdaʕ*	*ḍabb*	*ḍabʕ* *ḍabuʕ*
Targumic Aramaic (Sperber 1959-62)	*ʕilʕā*	*(ʕaršā)* Syriac	*ʕurdʕānā*	*(ʕābā)* Syriac	*(ʔabʕā)*[16] Syriac
Hebrew (BDB)	*ṣelåʕ*	--	*ṣĕp̱ardeaʕ*	*ṣåb* "lizard"? "tortoise"?	*ṣåḇuaʕ*
Ugaritic (Gordon 1965)	*ṣlʕ*	--	--	--	--
Akkadian (CAD, AHw)	*ṣēlu*	--	*muṣaʔʔirānu*	--	--

Column-B Cognates

	"earth"	"egg"	"enemy"	"take, seize"
Mehri (Jahn 1902)	*árḍ*	*bīḍayt*	*ḍorr* "schaden"	*ḍáybat*
Mehri (Carter 1847)	--	--	--	*dthot*
Mehri (Thomas 1937)	--	--	--	*źōt*
Harsusi (Thomas 1937)	--	*bīź*	--	*źaibuṭ*
Botahari (Thomas 1937)	--	--	--	--
Shahari (Thomas 1937)	*airź*	--	--	*źubuṭ*
Shahari (Bittner 1917)	*erḍ*	--	*ḍerr* "schaden"	*ḍ(b)eṭ* *ḍoṭ*
Socotri (Leslau 1938)	--	--	*ḍer(r)* "battre"	*ḍéybet* "être saisi"
ESA (Conti Rossini 1931, Jamme 1962)	*ʔrḍ*	--	*ḍr*	--
Ethiopic (Dillman 1865)	--	--	*ḍärr*	*ḍäbäṭä*
Arabic (Wehr 1966)	*ʔarḍ*	*bayḍa*	*ḍarra* "second wife"	*ḍabaṭa*
Targumic Aramaic (Sperber 1959-62)	*ʔarʕā*	*beʕin* "eggs"	*ʕartā* "rival wife"	--
Hebrew (BDB)	*ʔɛrɛṣ*	*beṣå(h)*	*ṣar*	*ṣåbaṭ* "hold out"
Ugaritic (Gordon 1965)	*arṣ*	--	*ṣrt*	*mṣbtm* "tongs"
Akkadian (CAD, AHw)	*erṣetu*	*bēṣu*	*ṣerru*	*ṣabātu*

Column-B Cognates

	"laugh"	"ill"	"narrow"	"wash"
Mehri (Jahn 1902)	*ḍaḥâk*	*marîḍ*	*ḍayûq*	*reḥâḍ*
Mehri (Carter 1847)	*yadthahok*	--	--	*rahadtha* "clean"
Mehri (Thomas 1937)	*źiḥak* *ḍ́aḥak*	*maraź* "sickness"	--	*raḥaź*
Harsusi (Thomas 1937)	*źiḥak* *iźḥōq*	*mirīź*	--	*raḥaź*
Botahari (Thomas 1937)	*śahaq* *(ś!)*[18]	*mereź*	--	--
Shahari (Thomas 1937)	*źiḥak* *źaḥaq*	*marīź*	--	*raḥaź*
Shahari (Bittner 1917)	*ḍḥak*	*meríḍ*	*ḍiq*	*rḥaḍ*
Socotri (Leslau 1938)	*ḍáḥak*	*mrḍ* "caus. guérir"	--	*raḥaḍ*
ESA (Conti Rossini 1931, Jamme 1962)	--	*mrḍ*	--	--
Ethiopic (Dillman 1865)	*šaḥaqa* *(š̆!)*[19]	--	--	*rəḥədä* "sweat"[17]
Arabic (Wehr 1966)	*ḍaḥika*	*marīḍ*	*ḍayyiq*	*raḥaḍa*
Targumic Aramaic (Sperber 1959-62)	*ḥayyek̲*[20]	*mraʕ*	*ʕāq*	*(rḥʕ)* Egypt. Aram.
Hebrew (BDB)	*ṣåḥaq*	*nimråṣ?* "grievous"	*ṣuqå(h)* "pressure"	*råḥaṣ*
Ugaritic (Gordon 1965)	*ṣḥq*	*mrṣ*	*šṣq* "exert pressure"	*rḥṣ*
Akkadian (CAD, AHw)	*ṣâḫu?*[21]	*marṣu*	--	*raḫāṣu* "überschwemmen"

THE "MINOR" CORRESPONDENCES AND OTHER PROBLEMS

Shahari ź

Thomas' Shahari word-list (1937) has a number of instances of ź corresponding to *l* in other Semitic languages, and indeed in the other MSA languages:

> "dear (expensive)": *ghuźī, ghoyźī*, Mehri *gholī*, Harsusi *ghalī*, Botahari *ghālī*, Arabic *ġālī*.
> "egg": *gaiḥiźin, gaiḥiźun, guḥaiźil*, M *goḥalet*, Socotri *gehélihen*.
> "filled": *miźī*, M *mīla*, H *maila, milō*, Arabic *mali?*, Hebrew *måle(?)*, Akkadian *malū*, etc.
> "fish-hook": *kiźa, qiźa*, M *qailai*.
> "indigo": *nuź, nūiź*, M *nai?l*, H *nai?l, nīl*, B *anilit*, Arabic *nīl(a)*.
> "lungs": *kīźi*, M *killaiyitin*, Arabic *kulya* "kidney," Syriac *kulyā* "kidney," etc.
> "salt": *miź(a)ḥōt*, M *milḥāt*, H *milḥāt*, Socotri *milḥo*, Arabic *milḥ*, Syriac *melḥā*, Hebrew *mɛlaḥ*.
> "these": *iźenu*, M *iliyōma, ilih*, H *īlilma, īlīh*, B *ailan*, ESA (Sabaean) *?ln*, Arabic *(hā)?ulā?i*, Hebrew *?ellɛ(h)*, etc.
> "those": *iźukūna, iśekū*, M *laik*, H *īlik*, B *ailak, īlak*, Arabic *?ulā?ika*, etc.
> "Ali": *Aźi* < Arabic *ʕAlī*
> "God": *Ōź*, M *Abāl(i)*, B *Abaili*, H *Abāli*

In two of these cases, Shahari itself has allomorphs with *l* (*gōḥol* "eggs" and *aqalait* "fish-hook(s?)"; cf. also *kellēn, qalȁn* "infant" but *qiźūn* "infants").

These correspondences have not been included in our charts since they obviously result from a relatively recent conditioned sound-change in Shahari. Nevertheless, they are of interest for what they reveal about the nature of the Shahari voiced fricative-lateral.

The conditioning of the Shahari sound-change seems obvious. All of the above examples have *i* or *y* immediately before or after the new Shahari ź. Frictionless *l* remains (in *gōḥol, aqalait, kellēn, qalān*, and of course in many other words) where there is no high front vocalic segment in the immediate vicinity. However, there are numerous cases where *l* remains in spite of a contiguous *i* or *y* (e.g., *qaillas, qilzeṭe, qilaizuṭ* "button(s)," *daḥalīl* "hole," *khūli* "hollow," *khulif* "instead of," *qillīd, qailīd, aqilidit* "key(s)," *sailōt* "life," *dhakīl* "heavy," etc.). The above formulation will therefore have to be treated as only a first approximation.

It is interesting to note that other investigators, working independently and using different data, have noted this sound-change and isolated the same conditioning factor. The first discussion of the sound-change appears in the first published description of Shahari (Fresnel 1838b):

> Pour rendre le son du ژ, il faut chercher a prononcer un *z*, en portant l'extrémité de la langue sous les molaires supérieures du côté droit. Exemples: ژيش *zîsch*, de son pere; *ssouyzi*, il a prie. Ce qu'il y a de curieux, c'est que cette articulation barbare tient lieu de la plus douce consonne qui soit au monde, le ل *lâm* c'est à dire l'*l*, et ne la remplace que par euphonie (euphonie hhimyarique, bien entendu). En effet, ژيش est pour ليش *lisch*, mot qui en renferme trois, et correspond à l'arabe لأبيه, a son père, ou de son père. Le ژ lieutenant du ل, indique la possession ou le génitif, ou, plus généralement, la dépendance, (comme le ژ en éthiopien, et je crois dans les mêmes circonstances); le ى est ce qui reste du mot إيب *ip*, père, et le ش est le pronom affixe de la troisième personne masculine du singulier. Dans صيژى *ssouyzi*, qui a pour racine صلوت *ssolôt*, orient ou prière, le ى suivi du ژ, tient lieu d'un double ل *lâm*; c'est le mot صلّى, il a prié; avec d'autres voyelles que les voyelles arabes de ce mot: c'est صُلِّى *ssoulli* au lieu de صَلَّى *ssallâ*. Dans le ى qui remplace le premier ل *lâm*, on aperçoit une tendance aux *ll* mouillées. Cependant, après le son de la voyelle *ou* (ـُـ), je n'entends que celui du ى, consonne pure, comme l'*y* du mot *yeux*, et ensuite une espèce de *z* ou de ذ *dhâl* qui, pour mes oreilles, n'a aucun rapport avec l'*l*. Mouhhsin, qui est beaucoup plus pirate que grammairien, ne se doutait pas que cette lettre ژ pût tenir lieu d'un *lâm* (ل), et maintenant il en est parfaitement convaincu; mais comme le rapport acoustique qui doit exister entre ces deux articulations échappe complètement à nos sens, je n'ai pas voulu représenter la nouvelle articulation par un ل avec addition d'un point, de peur qu'on ne s'imaginât que le son de l'une a quelque ressemblance avec celui de l'autre.

Fresnel's remarkable insight that the sequence *yz* in *ssouyzi* had developed out of a palatalized *l*[22] was taken up by Yushmanov (1930:385) who pointed out the conditioning factor and showed -- using Fresnel's data -- that four other Shahari phonemes have palatalized allophones in the immediate vicinity of *i*.[23]

More recently, T.M. Johnstone (1970b:508fn) has described the same change in similar terms,[24] on the basis of his own fieldwork. His failure to cite Fresnel and Yushmanov would seem to indicate that he was unaware of their work on the subject.

It is also interesting to note that the same sound-change is known from the Bantu languages. Meinhof has reconstructed palatalized *l* as one of the two or three Ur Bantu ancestors of ɮ in the Bantu languages (Doke 1954:42).

The path which leads from a palatalized *l* to a fricative *l* is not difficult to find: when the blade of the tongue is raised for the palatalized *l*, the sides may also be raised to the extent that the passage of air between them and the palate is impeded. The result is a voiced fricative-lateral.

Mehri ɮ

In his *Grammatik der Mehri-Sprache in Südarabien* (1905: 9) Alfred Jahn notes that in Mehri "d̬ steht wie ḍ in ägypt.-arab. Dialekte öfters für ẓ" citing as examples *d̬ahâr* "er wurde sichtbar" (= Arabic *ẓahara*), *ḥad̬d̬* "Teil" (= Arabic *ḥaẓẓ*), and *mentad̬áyr* "auf etwas achtsam" (= Arabic *muntaẓir*). Sometimes a form with the expected ẓ is attested in Mehri alongside the form with d̬ (ibid., 6-7): *nôd̬ef* "abbürsten" alongside *nôẓef*, *hend̬áuf* "ausbreiten" alongside *henẓáuf*, *meḍállet* "Schirm" alongside *meẓallet*.

We have not included this correspondence in the charts because the Mehri lexical items on which it is based are almost certainly Arabisms from the local Ẓufārī dialect which the Mahra speak as a second language. In this dialect, as we have seen[25], ẓ has shifted to ḍ and merged with it; consequently, ḍ is the reflex of etymological ẓ.

It is interesting to note that Thomas' Mehri word-list (1937), which in general contains a much lower percentage of Arabisms than that of Jahn (1902),[26] seems to have no instances of ž for etymological ẓ with the exception of the place-name Žafūr (< Ẓafār, a variant of Ẓufār occurring in medieval texts).[27] This observation lends some support to our conviction that the ḍ = ẓ correspondence uncovered by Jahn is not what we would call a "genuine" correspondence.

ESA s^2

The voiceless, unemphatic sibilants of ESA have been the subject of a protracted, but rather sterile, debate. Fortunately, it is not necessary for us to enter deeply into this debate or review its long history, since all sides agree upon the point which concerns us most: that s^2 (⋟) corresponds to MSA ɬ, Arabic š, Hebrew ś, etc. (Cantineau [1932] 1935-45:314, Stehle 1941:520-1, 529, Leslau 1938a:32, Beeston 1951:14, LaSor 1957:168).

Similar unanimity once existed about the *phonetic value* of 𐩦 as well. In 1932, Cantineau wrote that "les trois systèmes de transcription [currently in use] s'accordent à le noter par ...š" (1935-45:315) and in 1943 Höfner could still claim that " 𐩦 ziemlich einheitlich ... mit š transkribiert wird" (1943:18).

This phonetic transcription of 𐩦 had already become standard in the nineteenth century, based as it was on two unassailable facts:

a) ESA 𐩦 was an adaptation of the Canaanite symbol W (= Hebrew ש) which stood for the phoneme š.
b) ESA s^2 corresponds etymologically to Arabic š.

Gradually, however, the realization began to dawn that, all other things being equal, more weight should be given to MSA than to Arabic in reconstructing the phonology of ESA. This realization, implicit in the work of Cantineau ([1932] 1935-45:316) was first made explicit by Leslau (1949:98):

> We think too much in terms of North Arabic when we discuss problems of Epigraphic South Arabic...

Beeston (1951:15fn) took up this theme and developed it:

> For [the nineteenth-century south-arabists], being as they were ignorant of the very existence of MSA, it was no doubt natural to assume a phonological identity between ESA s^2 and its etymological equivalent in Arabic, that being the nearest neighbor they knew to ESA. For us, who have to reckon with the evidence of MSA, the case is widely different.

In response to (a), it was pointed out that the verdict of comparative orthography was not unambiguous, since Canaanite W, in some areas at least[28], represented š and ś polyphonously (Cantineau [1932] 1935-45:315, Beeston 1962b:230). Other arguments for the standard transcription advanced by Stehle (1941:537,540) were convincingly refuted by Beeston (1951:15-6), who concluded that:

> The assumption that the ESA symbols s^1, s^2, and s^3 had the same phonetic value as their etymological cognates in MSA is one which is worth while considering at least as a working hypothesis.

Beeston later (1962b:225) retreated from this position, allowing that "doubt may subsist as to whether s^2 was realized, as in MSA, by [ɬ],[29] or, as in the Arabic of Sībawaihi's time, by [ç]." The present writer, however, continues to believe in the validity of Beeston's earlier arguments and conclusions, especially since the value [ç] is far from established even for Sībawaihi's Arabic.[30]

In any case, it is clear that the South Arabian inscriptions provide no *independent* evidence for or against the lateral hypothesis. Phonetic descriptions of ESA s^2 and, for that matter, of ESA *ḍ*, are based entirely on data from MSA, Arabic, or some other external source. It is for that reason that we have treated the controversy about s^2 in this chapter, instead of devoting a separate chapter to it.

Ethiopic *š* and *ḍ*

The chart indicates that *š* is merged with *s* in the traditional pronunciation of Geez. The same is true of *ḍ* (also transliterated *z'*) and *ṣ* (also transliterated *s'*). In fact, the mergers reflected in the traditional pronunciation seem to be very ancient. According to Ullendorff (1955:111):

> The present purely orthographical difference between *š* and *s* and between *s'* and *z'* can be shown to have reflected a real distinction in sound only in the earliest stages of Gəˤəz...

This conclusion follows from the fact that interchanges of *š* with *s* and *ḍ* with *ṣ* are already present in the Aksum inscriptions dated by Littman to the 7th-12th centuries and in the earliest Ethiopic manuscripts.

Accordingly, there is no direct evidence for the original pronunciation of Geez *ḍ* or *š*. Leander (1925:92) tried to show that the former was an emphatic [ẓ] in the earliest stages of the language, but his argument rests on the unlikely assumption that Proto-South Semitic *ḍ* was realized [ḏ̣].

Arabic *ḍ*

The phonetic value of Arabic *ḍ* will be discussed in great detail in the chapters that follow. The discussion will be based almost entirely on ancient sources since none of the modern dialects (Colin 1930a:92) and only some of the modern reading traditions show ض contrasting with ظ. Moreover, those reading traditions which do distinguish between ض and ظ, realizing the former as [ḍ] and the latter as [ḏ̣] or [ẓ], have certainly not preserved the original value of ض, which is known to have been a fricative.[31] How then did this realization arise?

It has long been recognized that the reading traditions in which ض is realized as [ḍ] are located in areas (usually urban) where colloquial ض - ظ is realized as [ḍ].[32] The "classical" pronunciation of ض as [ḍ] is nothing other than the colloquial pronunciation, as Fischer (1968:55) explains in the following passage:

> Im neuarab. Sprachgebiet hat das Phonem ض - ظ drei Realisationstypen: 1. ḏ̣ = stimmhafte, emphatische, interdentale Spirans, 2. ḍ = stimmhafte, emphatische, dentale Explosiva, 3. ḍ̌ = stimmhafte, emphatische, laterale Spirans. Die Realisation ḏ̣ findet sich in den sog. Beduinen-Dialekten des Nordens, die Realisation ḍ in den sog. Stadt-Dialekten, die Realisation ḍ̌ im Süden und zwar sowohl in den neuarab. als auch in den neusüdarab. Dialekten Südarabiens. Das ḍ der Stadtmundarten ist erst innerneuarabisch an die Stelle von ḏ̣ getreten: ḏ̣ > ḍ entspricht dem Ersatz der anderen Interdentalen ḏ und ṯ durch die entsprechenden Explosiva *d* und *t*. Der Ausspracheunterschied von städtisch ḍ und beduinisch ḏ̣ wurde von den Qoranlesern sekundär zur Differenzierung der Phoneme ض und ظ des Klass.-Arab. genutzt, indem sie für ض ḍ, für ظ ḏ̣ (ḍ̌) aussprechen. Diese Differenzierung zwischen ض und ظ ist zweifellos sekundär und enthält keine Reminiszenz an die alten Phoneme.

This theory, according to which the contrast ظ : ض was secondarily restored, becomes much more plausible as soon as one realizes that two other contrasts -- ث : ت and ذ : د -- may have been secondarily restored in precisely the same way; namely, by importing the interdental pronunciation for one of the pair while leaving the other as a dental stop. In other words, we are suggesting that there was a short period of time in which the urban reading traditions in question did not distinguish ث from ت, ذ from د, or ظ from ض, any more than the corresponding urban dialects did. The loss of the three contrasts would have bothered orthoepists, who were concerned with preserving the correct pronunciation of the Qur?ān. Keenly aware, as they were, that their native dialects no longer preserved the three interdentals which still existed in many other dialects (bedouin, sedentary and even urban), it was only natural that they should suppose that the loss of the three contrasts was the direct result of the loss of the three interdentals, ignoring the fact that even in the other, more conservative dialects the contrast between ظ and ض had been lost. The proportion ث : ت :: ذ : د :: ظ : ض which we find reflected in many reading traditions can be explained as the product of such a mistaken belief and need not, therefore, be taken as historically accurate.

Aramaic *ś*

We have followed current practice in transcribing Old Aramaic orthographic ‹š› as *ś* where etymology (or subsequent replacement by ‹s›) dictates. The justification for this practice, i.e., the proof that ‹š› was polyphonous in Old Aramaic (and Official Aramaic as well), comes from the later graphemic split of ‹š› along etymological lines. In other words, the fact that ‹s› later replaced precisely those instances of ‹š› which correspond to MSA ɬ, ESA s^2, Arabic *š*, etc., while ‹š› remained when corresponding to MSA *š* or *h*, ESA s^1, Arabic *s*, etc., indicates that etymological *š* and *ś* must have been phonetically[33] distinct in Aramaic all along. The alternative solution, that they merged unconditionally but later re-split in such a way that they re-created the old word-classes, is impossible, not only for purely statistical reasons but also because the old word-classes show no phonetic conditioning whereas any new word-classes carved out of the *š* word-class by a split would ordinarily[34] have to be phonetically conditioned.

Aramaic q_2

The justification for distinguishing between q_1 and q_2 (i.e. the proof that ‹q› was polyphonous in Old Aramaic) comes, as in the case of ‹š› (see above), from the later graphemic split of ‹q› along etymological lines, in which those instances of ‹q› which came from PS *ḍ* were replaced by ‹ʕ›, and those instances of ‹q› which came from PS *q* remained. The former are labeled q_1, the latter, q_2.

The phonetic identity of q_2 is still an open question (Degen 1969:36) even though the vast majority of Semitists seems to have accepted Nöldeke's rather half-hearted suggestion (1875:73) -- inspired, no doubt, by the similarity between the mergers **ġ* › ʕ (attested in many Semitic languages, including Aramaic) and q_2 › ʕ -- that it was a voiced uvular fricative which differed from q_1 primarily in manner of articulation. That the difference might have been one of place rather than manner was not even considered until recently when an Americanist (Jacobsen 1969:152) pointed out the striking similarity between q_2 › ʕ and Nootka **q'* › *ʔ̣* (where *q'* is a uvular glottalized ejective and *ʔ̣* is a glottal stop with pharyngal constriction resembling Arabic ʕ, ibid., 125), and wondered aloud whether q_2 might possibly have been realized [q']. This theory, of course, presupposes another theory, known to Jacobsen through Martinet 1953, namely that the PS emphatics where very much like their modern Ethiopian reflexes,[35] and, in particular, that q_1 was realized [k']. Taken together, the two theories portray Old

Aramaic as having had a contrast between *k'* and *q'* -- a situation which is not uncommon but which is, nevertheless, suficiently unstable to explain the subsequent shift of q_2 away from q_1 (ibid., 152). It is worth noting that the same picture of Old Aramaic was suggested to the present writer (before he came across Jacobsen's article) by the fact that in the traditional Hebrew of Georgian-speaking Jews, ‹q› is realized [k'] and ‹ʕ› is realized [q'] (Garbell 1954:234-5, Morag 1972:1133).

The advantages of Jacobsen's theory are several. Not only does it provide a functional explanation for the shift of q_2 to pharyngal position (if we may be permitted to focus only on the merger prevented by the shift and ignore the one caused by it), but it also provides an interesting new interpretation[36] of the change *q_2 › *g* in *gḥk* "laugh" and *gʕṭ* "oppress," according to which *g* is the non-emphatic correlate of q_2 and q_2 › *g* is simply a dissimilatory loss of the emphatic feature (cf. Aramaic *zʕr* "be small" ‹ *ṣʕr* ‹ **ṣġr* and *zʕq* "shout" ‹ **ṣʕq*). Finally, Jacobsen's theory is compatible with a post-Old Aramaic date for the merger of **ġ* with ʕ in Aramaic, whereas Nöldeke's theory, as Rosenthal (1936:24fn) has pointed out, is not:

> Das problem des Auftretens von ק fur ursem. **ḏ̣* hat Brockelmann...durch die Annahme gefördert, dass *ḏ̣* bei der nichtsem. Bevölkerung Syriens zu einem *ġ*-laut verschoben sei. Allerdings ist es dann nicht ohne weiters einleuchtend, warum man nicht ע, das damals auch noch den Lautwert *ġ* hatte, geschrieben hat.

Whether or not this difference actually represents an advantage of Jacobsen's theory over Nöldeke's depends in large measure upon the correctness of Rosenthal's assertion that *ġ* was still unmerged in Old Aramaic. The present writer is compelled to admit that he, like Degen (1969:37), has been unable to ascertain what Rosenthal's basis might have been for that assertion. In any event, a new basis for the assertion has now been provided by Ginsberg's discovery (1970:123) that the scribe of the cuneiform Aramaic incantation from Uruk "seems to distinguish *ġ* from ʕ, expressing the former by *ḫ* and leaving the latter unexpressed."

A problem of considerable interest, but one which has been largely ignored by Semitists, is the transition problem: by what route did apical *ḍ* shift to postdorsal q_2? It is obvious that there will be at least as many solutions to this problem as there are theories about the phonetic identity of *ḍ*, but it is worth noting that some of these theories make for an easier solution to the problem than others. In particular, explaining how *ḍ* was able to travel virtually the entire length of the tongue without undergoing a single merger is easier with a theory which posits a lateral *ḍ* than with a theory which posits a central *ḍ*, for the simple reason that the lateral route to the back of the mouth is much less crowded than the central route. Once at the back of the mouth, it would have been a simple matter for *ḍ* to discard its lateral feature and arrive at its Old Aramaic place of articulation. The entire shift, starting from the PS value of *ḍ* reconstructed by Cantineau ([1951-2] 1960:284) and Martinet (1953:71) and ending at Jacobsen's q_2, would look something like this:

tɬ'	›	*qɬ'*	›	*qχ'*	›	*q'*
glottalized alveolar affricate-lateral		glottalized uvular affricate-lateral		glottalized uvular affricate		glottalized uvular stop

A striking parallel to the middle stage of this shift is attested in Zulu (Doke 1926:115):

> There is an interesting variant to the [glottalized velar] lateral affricate; it is used by certain Zulu speakers who always substitute it for *kɬ'*, though its use by the Zulus is not nearly so widespread as the latter.
>
> In this sound, the explosive element is *k*, while the fricative element is the ordinary velar unvoiced fricative *x*. The sound is produced over the center of the back of the tongue and is ejective...*kx'* and *kɬ'* are interchangeable and not phonemically different.

Many other parallels could be adduced from the Northeast Caucasian languages, where the Proto-North Caucasian lateral affricates and fricatives generally yield palatal, velar, and uvular stops and fricatives. This characteristic of the Northeast Caucasian languages has been described in great detail by Trubetzkoy in his study of "Les consonnes latérales des langues caucasiques septentrionales" (1922). In this study (pp. 200-202), Trubetzkoy reconstructed the shift

***tɬ**	›	***kɬ**	›	***kx**	›	*k*
voiceless alveolar affricate-lateral		voiceless velar affricate-lateral		voiceless velar affricate		voiceless velar stop

for much of Northeast Caucasian -- the major exceptions being Archi and the Avaro-Andian[37] languages which preserve *kɬ*. Trubetzkoy's later realization (1930:90) that the diaphoneme in question was a glottalized ejective makes the parallel with Aramaic even stronger.

A second development reconstructed by Trubetzkoy (1922: 202) for the same group of languages

(*dɮ)	>	*ɮ	>	*ʟ	>	γ
voiced alveolar affricate-lateral		voiced alveolar fricative-lateral		voiced velar fricative-lateral		voiced velar fricative

brings us back to Nöldeke's q_2 and shows us that the latter could easily have developed out of a velarized voiced fricative-lateral *ḍ*[38]. A development from a glottalized fricative-lateral *ḍ*, i.e. [ɬ’], would require only one additional step: the spontaneous de-glottalization of *ḍ*, where the voicing of the resultant phone could be attributed to the fact that the glottal stricture required for glottalization is closer to that required for voicing than to that required for voicelessness (Ladefoded 1971:17). The fact that no other Aramaic emphatic underwent this change does not necessarily argue against this reconstruction because [ɬ’] would certainly have been the least audible of all the emphatics. In any event, the fact that the MSA languages shifted [ɬ’] to [ɮ] (Fresnel 1838b:546, Yushmanov 1930:384, Johnstone 1970a:296fn) while retaining all the other glottalized emphatics except [θ’] (Johnstone 1975a:156)[39] proves that such a development is entirely possible. A development from Cantineau's affricate-lateral *ḍ*, i.e. [tɬ’], is less likely, but cannot be excluded in view of the marginally attested shift of [tɬ’] to [γ] in Dargwa (Trubetzkoy 1930:90), a Northwest Caucasian language of the Lakk-Dargwa group.

Hebrew *ś*

It is generally accepted today that Biblical Hebrew had a phoneme /ś/ contrasting with both /š/[40] and /s/[41], even though the Hebrew alphabet had no special sign for this phoneme until the Masoretes, a thousand years after the Biblical period, created one. Moscati's discussion (1964b: 33) is typical:

> This consonant appears in Hebrew and in Biblical Aramaic, but without a graphic sign of its own (the symbol for š is used, and a diacritic mark was introduced at a late date as part of the Masoretic pointing). Hence it may be thought that it is merely a secondary differentiation of š; yet an examination of the correspondences in the other languages suggests its original autonomy...

In other words, unless the perfect one-to-one correspondence of Masoretic שׁ with Arabic š and with ESA s^2 is to be written off as a mere coincidence, the only possible conclusion is that שׁ stands for something which goes back not merely to Biblical Hebrew but all the way to Proto-West Semitic. Moreover, says Moscati (ibid., 35):

> There are...indications of an autonomous *ś* in the Tell Amarna glosses and in the Egyptian transcriptions of North-West Semitic names.

The present writer feels that Moscati presents a fairly strong case for the existence of a *ś*-phoneme in Biblical Hebrew and in Canaanite -- or at least the Moscati of sections 8.29 and 8.33 does. The Moscati of 8.34 seems to be a new man:

> As for Hebrew, it is, of course, well known that the Masoretes indicated a graphic distinction between *ś* and *š* by placing a point either above the left side of the letter (for *ś*) or its right (for *š*), the same symbol having always served for both consonants. The distinction may be based on ancient tradition, but we have no reliable evidence for this: the indications furnished by the Tell Amarna letter from Jerusalem are insufficient (§8.33), and the famous passage in *Judges* 12,6, according to which the Ephraimites pronounced *š* as *s*, probably points to a dialectal differentiation rather than to the existence of an independent phoneme *ś*. In any case, the phenomenon which formed the basis of the Masoretic distinction must have been of fairly limited extent, since by and large *ś* and *š* appear to have coalesced in one single consonant (just as they possessed one graphic symbol only). It has, therefore, been conjectured that the Masoretes may have generalized a purely dialectal differentiation. Indeed, the Akkadian, Greek, and Latin transcriptions of Hebrew names do not distinguish between *ś* and *š*; and St. Jerome, in a well-known passage (*Onomastica sacra*, p. 36), shows that he knows of *s*, *ṣ*, and *š*, but not of *ś*.

This passage is puzzling, not only because of the contradictions between it and the preceding passages, but also in its use of "Akkadian, Greek and Latin transcriptions of Hebrew names." Kutscher (1965:39) has dealt with this subject in a devastating critique of Garbini 1960 (without, however, noticing a footnote where Garbini cites Moscati's *Preistoria e storia del consonantismo ebraico antico* as his source):

> Garbini's views on p. 45 are incomprehensible: "The Akkadian transcriptions do not distinguish between /ś/ and /š/, and the same holds true of the Greek and Latin transcriptions." After all Akkadian had only *one* phoneme /š/ paralleling Proto-Semitic /ś/ and /š/ of Hebrew and Aramaic. How, then, could Akkadian differentiate in notation between the two? Garbini's words concerning Greek and Latin transliteration are even more bewildering; after all these languages could not express even a Semitic /š/, since they did not have a proper sign for it, *s* and σ respectively being their means of denoting all sibilants in any foreign language. Therefore, how can any conclusion be drawn from the fact that they had no notation for the /ś/? Would Garbini try to prove on the basis of these transcriptions that Semitic /š/ has never existed?

Moscati's use of Jerome to impeach the credibility of the Masoretic testimony is another weak link in his argument, since, as Sperber pointed out forty years ago (1937-8:115, 150), Jerome's teachers may have been heirs to a tradition of Hebrew different from that of the Masoretes -- specifically, a tradition influenced by the dialect of the northern kingdom of Israel. Sperber's assumption, based (not too solidly) on Judges 12:6, that ש had only one value in northern Hebrew, is corroborated by the Samaritan reading tradition (Ben-Ḥayyim 1961:16), which has a good many northern traits, some of which (but only some) were noted by Sperber himself (op. cit., 151-2). And since northern Hebrew often agrees with Phoenician,[42] additional corroborating evidence for Sperber's assumption may be deduced from that language -- assuming, of course, that Harris' arguments for a monovalent ש in that language (1936:22, 1939:33-4) are sound.

It need hardly be added that the present writer agrees with Sperber's assumption concerning northern Hebrew ש, and yet he cannot help wondering why it is necessary to go to such great lengths to explain Jerome's failure to mention the dual pronunciation of ש. It was difficult enough for Jerome to explain to his non-Jewish readers that the reason why the "same" Hebrew word (i.e. the same in Jerome's Latin transcription) may sometimes be translated in different ways is that Hebrew has three letters for *s*. Should he also have explained that one of the Hebrew letters represents two sounds? This would have required a good deal of explaining in a period when letters and sounds were not always distinguished. Why add this confusing detail to an already confusing picture?

Moscati speaks of a "purely dialectal differentiation" be- between *ś* and *š* which the Masoretes "may have generalized."

From the slightly fuller discussion in Moscati 1954 (p. 54), it seems clear that he means by this that the Masoretic reading tradition had its origins in a dialect of ancient *Hebrew* different from the one(s) in which the Bible was written. Interpreted in this way, Moscati's[43] proposal is at least intelligible, if not convincing.[44] In Garbini's hands (1960:48), however, Moscati's proposal undergoes a subtle but fatal change.[45] The "dialect" in which the Masoretic distinction between שׂ and שׁ originated turns out to be -- Aramaic:

> [I primi segni sicuri di un'autonomia di ś] nascono verosimilmente in seno all'aramaico...In seno a tale dialetto, provocato probabilmente da fattori esterni, mi sembra vada ricercata l'origine della distinzione tra š e ś, distinzione poi estesa anche alla lettura dell'ebraico biblico.[46]

This identification of Aramaic as the source of Masoretic שׂ provides further grist for Kutscher's mill (1965:40):

> Still, assuming for the moment that Hebrew did not have a /ś/ phoneme, it had somehow mysteriously developed in Aramaic and under the impact of Aramaic the Masoretes decided to introduce it into Hebrew. This may be acceptable in roots containing /ś/ which are found both in Hebrew and Aramaic; for example, בשר ; folowing Aramaic, the Masoretes chose בשׂר with /ś/. But what about the many roots with /ś/ which are not found in any Aramaic dialect, for example words like שמלה , שמח , שיש
> שרד , שרר and so many others? Why did the Masoretes read those ש graphemes as /ś/?

To fully understand this aspect of Garbini's theory, one must view it in its historical context, that is, as an outgrowth of the views of Paul Kahle. Kahle saw the Masoretes as reformers who, based on their knowledge of Aramaic and Arabic, attempted to restore long-lost phonological and morphological features of ancient Hebrew to the official reading tradition. In Kutscher 1965, the arguments advanced by Kahle in support of this theory are considered together with Garbini's contributions, and, like the latter, are thoroughly refuted. In the present writer's view, a similar fate awaits any theory which credits the Masoretes with having played any sort of active role in shaping the reading-tradition which they recorded, for, as Schramm (1964:64) has pointed out:

> ...all levels of analysis would seemingly lead to the observation that the Massoretes could not have sat down to their task by deciding which reading made the

most sense at a given point. If they had worked this way, then a highly regularized patterning would have been likely. It would seem much more probable, then, that the Massoretes simply reduced to a writing system the pronunciation of biblical Hebrew that was traditional for them, i.e., that one generation had learned by rote from the prior generation.

Kutscher's final rejoinder (op. cit., 41) to Garbini is worth quoting in full as a summary of the traditional view:

> Garbini's view in the matter is so far-fetched, and creates so many problems, that one wonders why he conceived it in the first place. The accepted view regarding this matter has long been quite simple. Canaanite, Hebrew and Aramaic had adopted the alphabet used by a certain Canaanite nation (or city) in whose language the Proto-Semitic phonemes /š/ and /ś/ had merged. (This happened in several Semitic languages, for example Ugaritic, Akkadian, etc.) It was only for lack of choice that the grapheme for /š/ was employed to represent /ś/ as well (the realization of /ś/ at that period apparently was closer to that of /š/ than of /s/). This process is quite frequent when one language borrows its alphabet from another.
>
> This view is an uncomplicated one and Garbini himself is quite familiar with it (see, for example, p. 34 regarding Aramaic inscriptions). It is for this reason that the Aramaeans were forced to use the sign ז also for Proto-Semitic /ḏ/ (in the Aramaic inscriptions). The Arabs, when they adopted the Aramaic alphabet, also had to employ a single grapheme for two or more phonemes, for example ح /ḥ/ and /χ/. The diacritical marks came only later (just as the Masoretes later differentiated between שׁ and שׂ). Could Garbini, on the basis of the above, argue that these various phonemes had never existed in Arabic? Obviously, as mentioned above, /ś/ was originally closer to /š/, therefore the grapheme of /š/ = ש was chosen to represent it, but it tended later to develop towards /s/, until it finally merged with it. The same happened in Aramaic as well. *This* development in Hebrew might be due to Aramaic influence.

For all its brilliance, Kutscher's response to Garbini is flawed by his failure to see what is bothering Garbini (and Moscati). Indeed, he admits this failure at the beginning of the passage just quoted. To him, "the accepted view regarding the matter has long been quite simple." But is it? After all, Kutscher himself states that examples of ס for ש in the

Bible "clearly prove that the shift /*ś*/ › /s/ took place towards the end of the Era of the First Temple." How, then, did the Masoretes, a thousand years later, still know about the *ś*-phone(me)? Could it have been preserved by tradition after disappearing from colloquial Hebrew (and Aramaic)? How could tradition have preserved an exact list of the words which were pronounced with this unusual sound rather than with *š*? These questions, based though they are on a misunderstanding, form the unspoken background of the Italian school's doubts about the reliability of the Masoretic *ś*-tradition.

The misunderstanding referred to above is the assumption made by Moscati (1964b:35-6; quoted above) and Garbini (1960: 48) that the Masoretes intended their שׂ grapheme to represent a *ś*-phoneme distinct from *š* and *s*. As Schramm(1964:19) has pointed out:

> It is quite certain that for the Tiberians, ‹ ś › was nothing more than another way of writing ‹ s ›, since, in the passage cited above in connection with the pronunciation of ‹ r ›, the letter ‹ s › is cited among the environments for the lenis articulation, but the examples illustrating this point are spelled with ‹ ś › as well as ‹ s ›, and ‹ ś › itself is not listed separately as one of the environmental factors.

Further evidence for Schramm's interpretation comes from the Babylonian and (some of) the Palestinian pointing systems where we find $\overset{ס}{ש}$ instead of שׂ (and $\overset{ש}{ש}$ instead of שׁ.) This symbol suggests a kind of *kĕṯiḇ-qĕre* -- *kĕṯiḇ* ש, *qĕre* ס "*š* is written but *s* is read" (cf. Yoma 75b: *ktyb šlyw wqrynn slyw)* -- and like the *kĕṯiḇ-qĕre* proper, it has to be understood against the background of an established reading tradition (Kutscher 1959:35) which was relatively independent of the received consonantal text (cf. the Talmudic distinction between the *miqrå(ʔ)* and the *måsorɛṯ*) and which the Masoretes endeavored to preserve alongside the latter.[47]

It is highly probable that the same is true of the Tiberian שׂ, and that it should be seen as an allograph of ס rather than as a representation of a remembered *ś*. Does this mean that Garbini is right in denying that Biblical Hebrew had a phoneme *ś*?

It is paradoxical that our interpretation of שׂ as a sign for *s* does not diminish its value as evidence for an ancient Hebrew *ś*, at least in the eyes of those who take the comparative method seriously. It is true that the existence of Masoretic שׂ can be explained simply and directly -- without positing the existence of *ś* in ancient Hebrew -- by the assumption of a conditioned merger of *š* with *s*,[48] if we are willing to ignore the peculiarity of a conditioned sound-change which shifts the š of

> *šåḥaq, šaʕar, šåḥaṯ, šåḵar, šåḵur, šårim, šĕḏe, šoreq, nišbaʕ, hišbiaʕ, maškil, maššå(?), hišši(?), šiḇro, šum, šåm, nåšim, mišrå(h), ḥɛrɛš, gɛrɛš, pɛšaʕ*

when they mean (respectively)

> "laughed," "hair of," "squeezed," "he hired," "hired," "officials," "field(s) of," "choice vines," "we shall become satiated," "he caused to become satiated," "skillful," "burden," "he caused to bear," "his hope," "to put," "he put(s)," "we shall put," "dominion," "earthenware," "grits," "step"

but not when they mean

> "pulverized," "gate of," "slaughtered," "he became intoxicated," "intoxicated," "singers," "breasts of," "is hissing," "he swore," "he caused to swear," "bereaving, miscarrying," "lending on interest," "he beguiled," "its interpretation, the breaking of it; his grain," "garlic," "there," "women," "juice," "secretly," "crop," "sin."

But how can we ignore the peculiarity of a conditioned sound-change which affects only those instances of š which correspond to MSA ɬ, ESA s^2, etc. (plus a number of etymologically indeterminate cases) and leaves all the others untouched?

The answer is that we cannot, and that Masoretic שׂ still provides evidence for the existence of ś in ancient Hebrew, even if it does not *represent* it. It is important to realize, however, that the evidence provided by Masoretic שׂ is no different from the evidence provided by the late-Biblical and post-Biblical replacement of ancient שׂ by ס where MSA has ɬ, ESA has s^2, etc.[49] The thread which binds שׂ to ś is strong,[50] but it is visible only through the lens of the comparative method.

Hebrew ṣ

There is a serious possibility that etymological ḍ and ṣ were not merged in Biblical Hebrew, as is usually assumed, but that they simply shared the same (polyphonous) grapheme. This possibility is explored at the end of chapter xiv.

Ugaritic š

Since Ugaritic š is the reflex of the two PS phonemes -

š and *ś* -- most scholars assume that Ugaritic has carried out a merger of those two phonemes. However, in view of the widespread practice in the Syria-Palestine area of writing *š* and *ś* with the same sign, the possibility that two phonemes lie concealed behind the Ugaritic ‹š› grapheme (Rin 1968:12) should be kept in mind.

Ugaritic *ṣ*

In the standard dialect of Ugarit, *ḍ* is merged with *ṣ*; however, it has been suggested (Harris 1939:35) that Ugaritic has a second, more archaic dialect in which *ḍ* was still a distinct phoneme. The evidence for this dialect comes from the famous UT 75, a text in which etymological *ḍ* appears several times as *ẓ* rather than *ṣ*. According to Harris (loc. cit.):

> ...the writer of [this tablet] seems to come from an area of speakers among whom the phoneme [ḍ] still existed and was, for lack of a sign, represented by the sign for [ḏ].[51]

Another possibility is considered by Harris (loc. cit.) in a footnote:

> The alternative explanation would be that in the dialect of [this tablet] too the phoneme [ḍ] no longer existed, but that here it had merged with [ḏ̣].

A third interpretation has been proposed by Blau (1970: 43) according to which the appearance of *ḏ̣* for etymological *ḍ* reflects nothing more than scribal archaizing. As evidence for this scribal practice, Blau adduces two apparent hypercorrections in UT 77, a text closely related to UT 75 which, by chance, has no examples of etymological *ḍ*. Another piece of evidence comes from the word *darṣ* at the beginning of UT 75. If the customary (Gordon 1949:53, Driver 1956:71, Rin 1968:255) interpretation of this word (*d-arṣ* "of the earth") is correct, we have here an isolated but telling example of *ṣ* for PS *ḍ* in UT 75. (Gordon's statement (1965:27) that "in 75 every reflex of ض appears as *ẓ*" is puzzling.) This example would seem to show that the Ugaritic dialect spoken by the scribe of UT 75 was no different (in this respect, at any rate) from the standard dialect of Ugarit.

Akkadian *š*

Like most sound laws, the law which states that PS *ś* appears in Akkadian as *š* has its share of troublesome exceptions. There are cases where *s* appears to be the Akkadian reflex of PS *ś*, and, in fact, our chart contains two of them: *bus(s)urtu* "tidings" and *kabsu* "young (male) sheep." The latter is not attested until the Neo-Assyrian period (CAD s.v.) and even then it is rare; it may therefore be a loanword. The former, however, cannot be explained away so easily, since it is already attested, with an *s*, in the Old Babylonian period period (2000-1500 BCE). In fact, the root of *bus(s)urtu* has been cited (Harris 1936:22) as an example of the rule that:

> Every word in a language has its own history, and single cases cannot be made the basis of phonetic discussion.

Today, forty years later, we cannot claim to have advanced far beyond this "explanation," but we do have a better idea of the dimensions of the problem, thanks to a brilliant dialectological study by Goetze (1958).

Goetze's study established that in the Southern and Middle Euphrates dialects of OB, the sibilant of *bu-Su-ur-tum* was neither *s* (always expressed by the set ZA ZI ZU) nor *š* (always expressed by the set ŠA ŠI ŠU) but a third sibilant, s_x, expressed by SA SI SU. This sibilant appears consistently in a rather small set of words:

s_x*ebe* "seven"	s_x*ūmum* "redness, red spot"
s_x*adīdum* "?"	*bus*$_x$*urtum* "good tidings"
s_x*adārum* "arrange in rows"	*tabs*$_x$*irtum* "good tidings"
s_x*alīmum* "peace"	*mans*$_x$*ūm* "ruler"
s_x*āmum* "red"	*šas*$_x$*ūm* "shout, call"

and replaces *š* at the beginning of the third person suffixes (*šu, ša, šunu, šina*) when they are attached to a word ending in *š* (e.g. *reš* + *ša* → *res*$_x$*s*$_x$*a* "her head").

The obvious question to be asked at this point is whence this sibilant came and whither it went. In answer to the second half of the question, it is generally agreed that by the Middle Babylonian period (1500-1000 BCE) s_x was merged with *s*, even in southern Babylonia and the Middle Euphrates region (Goetze 1958:148, Aro 1959:331). The first half of the question is much more difficult. According to Goetze (1958:140) the answer boils down to a choice between two possibilities:

> Either [it] developed under special conditions which are to be defined from one of the known sibilants, or it represents an unknown sibilant inherited from PS but not yet otherwise recognized.

Actually, there is a third possibility, but we shall for the moment accept the choice which Goetze offers us.

It should be stated at the outset that we cannot expect any help from the writing system in making this choice. The Old Akkadian syllabary had only three contrasting sets of signs available to express the entire range of sibilants, and, thus, the lack of orthographic evidence of contrast between s_x and *ś* in Old Akkadian is not in any way conclusive.

That being the case, we are forced to turn with Goetze to inferences of a very tenuous nature to resolve the issue. Goetze argued (ibid., 40) that s_x must go back to PS since "no special conditions are observable" in the distribution of s_x -- special conditions which would have justified the alternative view (later adopted by Aro (1959:331)) that s_x was a conditioned retention of Old Akkadian *ś*. The fact that Goetze's theory creates a PS phoneme which suffered the same distinctive fate (namely, merger with *š* in the words for "seven" and "peace," merger with *ś* in the word for "tidings," and merger with *ś* or *s* in the word for "arrange") in all of the Semitic languages except Akkadian (ibid., 149) seems not to have bothered him; and, given the prevailing assumption by Semitists that Akkadian by itself constitutes one of the two major branches of the Semitic family, there is no reason why it should have. What should have bothered him, however, is the fact that the Assyrian dialect of Akkadian, as represented by the Kültepe tablets (Hecker 1968:117,52,65), has a *š* in the words for "seven" and "peace" (and in the *š* + pronoun combination) rather than s_x or *s*, thus agreeing with West Semitic and proving that s_x is a Babylonian innovation.

Another objection to Goetze's solution is that it is more complicated than the evidence requires; for, although the correspondence of OB s_x to both *š* and *ś* in West Semitic can theoretically be attributed to a split of s_x in the latter (Goetze's solution), it can also be attributed to a merger of *š* and *ś* in the former -- a solution which is far more economical in that it exploits the fact that a merger of *š* and *ś* in Akkadian has been established on other grounds. In other words, s_x corresponds to both *š* and *ś* in West Semitic because it is a chip off the Old Akkadian phoneme (namely, *ś*) which was created through the merger of PS *š* and *ś*.

Our final criticism of Goetze's solution is that his argument-by-elimination is based upon a false choice:

> Either [it] developed under special conditions which are to be defined from one of the known sibilants, or it represents an unknown sibilant inherited from PS but not otherwise recognized.

This statement ignores the possibility that OB s_x developed from *more than one* of the Old Akkadian sibilants, no doubt because Goetze, like Aro (1959:331), did not realize that one of the OB s_x-words -- *šasūm* -- appears in Old Akkadian with an *s* (Gelb 1957 s.v. *ŠS?*; cp. Old Assyrian *šasāʔum* with an *s*[52]). This possibility cannot be eliminated by noting that the s_x word-class as a whole does not exhibit any "special conditions." It can be eliminated only by showing that the etymological subdivisions of the s_x word-class (e.g., the s_x‹*ś* word-class, the s_x‹*s* word-class, etc.) do not exhibit such conditions. At present, the question is academic since our knowledge of Old Akkadian is not yet full enough to enable us to set up these etymological sub-divisions. But the evidence we have considered thus far gives reason to believe that when the facts are known, they will show that s_x -- if it actually is a phoneme rather than an allophone of /s/[53] -- was an OB innovation.

Proto-Semitic *ś*

It has long been an established tenet of Semitic linguistics that PS had three contrasting voiceless unemphatic sibilants : *š, ś,* and *s*. Each of these proto-phonemes has been preserved unmerged (but not necessarily unaltered phonetically) in a number of Semitic languages.

Thus, for example, PS *ś* is preserved unmerged in MSA, ESA, Ethiopic, Arabic, Old and Official Aramaic, and Biblical Hebrew. In order not to pre-judge the question of the existence of *ś* in PS, we can re-formulate this last statement as a purely empirical observation: The MSA, ESA, Ethiopic, Arabic, Old Aramaic and Biblical Hebrew phonemes which enter into correspondence set A at the beginning of this chapter do not enter (regularly) into any other correspondence set.

All of these facts are well known and would not require repetition if it were not for a recent claim by Garbini (1971: 34) that "the very existence of a Semitic phoneme /*ś*/ is highly questionable." It is somewhat premature to refute this claim since Garbini has promised (ibid., 32fn) a paper defending it, but the broad outlines of his argument can already be seen. Having discredited, or so he believes, all of the evidence for Hebrew *ś*[54] and Aramaic *ś* (Garbini 1971:34,37), he is now free to claim that *ś* is a South Semitic innovation, created by secondary split out of PS *š*. As evidence, Garbini can point to the fact that in all languages outside the South Semitic group -- namely, Akkadian (including Old Akkadian), Old and Official Aramaic, Biblical Hebrew, Phoenician, and Ugaritic -- etymological *ś* is orthographically indistinguishable from etymological *š*. Nevertheless, even if we ignore (as does Garbini) the persuasive evidence that, for Hebrew and

Aramaic at least, orthography does not tell the whole story,[55] we can still show, by means of reconstructed minimal pairs, that the contrast between š and ś evidenced in South Semitic definitely goes back to PS.

One such reconstructed minimal pair is PS *šakūrum* "intoxicated" : *śakūrum* "hired" (although the first vowel -- *a* -- is uncertain[56]). The reconstruction is particularly solid since it rests on minimal pairs in two widely separated languages: Hebrew *šå̄kur* "intoxicated" : *śå̄kur* "hired" and Geez *səkur* "intoxicated" : *šəkur* "hired." Furthermore, the roots alone are attested in various forms in a number of other Semitic languages: Akkadian *šakru* "intoxicated," Ugaritic *škr* "become intoxicated," *škr* "hire," Syriac *šḵar* "become intoxicated," Arabic *sakira* "become intoxicated," *šakara* "thank,"[57] Mehri *śkor* "thank." It should especially be noted that our reconstruction is solid even if we accept Garbini's thesis that Hebrew *ś* was artificially differentiated from š by the Masoretes. In that case, the words for "intoxicated" and "hired" would be homonyms in Hebrew, while contrasing in Geez. The standard procedure in such a situation is to assume that the homonymy is an innovation and the contrast, a retention (Hoenigswald 1960:121-2).

Another minimal pair which can be reconstructed with some confidence is PS *šabʕ(at)um* "seven"[58] : *śabʕ(at)um* "satiety." This time, our evidence comes from a wider variety of languages: Shahari *š(i)béʕt*[59] "seven" : *śebʕét* "satiety," ESA *s¹bʕ* "seven" : *s²bʕ* "satiety," Arabic *sabʕ* "seven" : *šabʕ* "satiety," Syriac *šḇaʕ* "seven" : *sḇaʕ* "satiety," Hebrew *šɛḇaʕ* "seven" : *śå̄ḇå̄ʕ* "satiety" (not a minimal pair, of course[60]) and Ugaritic *šbʕt* "seven" : *šbʕt* "satiety." We might also mention Akkadian *sebe* "seven" (with *s* instead of the expected *š*[61]) and *šēbu* "to satiate oneself."

Another minimal pair worth mentioning is PS *šaraqa* "he stole" : *śaraqa* "he combed." Unlike the others we have dealt with thus far, this one cannot be reconstructed solely from minimal pairs in the daughter languages, since actual minimal pairs are attested only[62] in Shahari, where we find *šeróq* "he stole": *śeróq* "he combed," and in Socotri, where we find *héraq*[63] "he stole" : *śéroq* "he combed." Nevertheless, both members of the pair seem to have, individually, a good claim to PS pedigree:

(1) "he stole": Shahari *šeróq*, Mehri *hirôq*, Socotri *héraq*, ESA *s¹rq*, Geez *säräqä*, Arabic *saraqa*, Akkadian *šarāqu* (inf.)

(2) "he combed": Shahari *śeróq*, Socotri *śéroq*, Syriac *sraq*, Hebrew *śå̄riq* (pass. part.)

Our last minimal pair is PS *parašа* "horse (accus. cstr.[64])" : *paraśa* "he spread," reconstructed from Arabic *farasa* "horse, mare (accus. cstr.)": *faraša* "he spread" and Hebrew *påråš* "horse" : *påraś*[65] "he spread." Evidence for this reconstruction comes from Mehri[66] *firhin* "horse, mare," ESA *frs*[1] "horse," Geez *färäs* "horse," Syriac *parāšā* "horseman," *pras* "spread," and, according to Brockelmann (1928 s.v. *pras*), Akkadian *rapāšu* "become wide."

Any of the minimal pairs we have discussed suffices to show that PS already had a phoneme *ś* distinct from *š*. Garbini's final assault on the *ś*, if it is to have any chance of success, will have to be directed against these minimal pairs.

[1]Note that we occasionally find *š* for *k* before front vowels in Socotri.

[2]Cf. Leslau 1958 s.v. *śåpå(h)*.

[3]For an explanation of the unusual correspondence, see the section entitled "Akkadian *š*" in this chapter.

[4]For an explanation of the unusual correspondence, cf. Leslau 1937:215 and Beeston 1951:8.

[5]Note the *s* in this word, presumably reflecting the rather early merger of *š* with *s*; see the section entitled "Ethiopic *š* and *ḍ*" in this chapter.

[6]The metathesis here is probably at least partially the result of contamination with *sbar* "hope."

[7]For an explanation of the unusual correspondence, see the section entitled "Akkadian *š*" in this chapter.

[8]Cf. Leslau 1938 s.v. *śíom*.

[9]Old Akkadian *śaʔāmum* and Old Assyrian *šaʔāmum*.

[10]Cf. Leslau 1958 s.v. *śårap̱*.

[11]Note that ʕ › *ḥ* after consonants or in final position in Socotri (Leslau 1938:19).

[12]"In M and H the sound change *š* › *h* › *ḥ* is not infrequent" (Johnstone 1973:100). Actually, two independent sound-changes are involved here, both of which are discussed at the beginning of chapter ii.

[13]This form is from Johnstone 1975b:10.

[14]This is probably a mistake; see chapter ii, fn. 35 and chapter xiv.

[15]Note the *ṣ* in this word, presumably reflecting the rather early merger of *ḍ* with *ṣ*, see the section entitled "Ethiopic *š* and *ḍ*" in this chapter.

[16]Note that ʕ › ʔ in the vicinity of ʕ in Syriac; cf. the discussion of Mandaic *ahk* in chapter xiv.

[17]Cognates in some of the modern Ethiopian languages (Gafat, Selti-Wolone and Zway) preserve the meaning "wash" (Leslau 1958 s.v. *råḥaṣ*).

[18]This is probably a mistake, see chapter xiv.

[19]For an explanation of the unusual correspondence, see chapter xiv.

[20]For the analogical process which produced this form, cf. Barth 1902:1.

[21]See chapter xiv, fn. 15.

[22]Actually, Fresnel thought that *yz* had developed from a palatalized geminated *l*, but Yushmanov ignored this minor detail and rightly so, since the same sequence appears in Thomas' *ghoyži* (alongside *ghuži*) "dear" as the reflex of a simplex *l* (cp. the cognates cited above). Moreover, the optional nature of the *y* in the word for "dear" seems to suggest that it is a nonphonemic on-glide to a palatalized fricative-lateral rather than the reflex of the first half of a geminated *l* as Fresnel believed. Note that the optional *i* in the word for "indigo" is synchronically identical with the *y* of

ghoyźi and that, even though it is to some extent historically motivated, it is not exactly the reflex of the *y* of **niyl* › **nayl*. One could say that the original glide (of **niyl* › **nayl*) was "stored" in the neighboring segment (the fricative-lateral) in the sense that it palatalized it, and that it is free to reappear (non-phonemically) whenever it likes.

[23]/š/ has a variant (or variants?) which Fresnel transcribes *ch* or *si*, e.g., *lichîn* "tongue" (cp. PS *lišānum*) and *chîro* "navel" (cp. PS *šurrum*); /k/ has a variant *tch* or *tsy*, e.g., *-tsi* "you both, we both" (cp. Mehri, Harsusi, Socotri *-ki* (Johnstone 1970b));/g/ has a variant *dz* or *dj*; and /q/ has a variant *ttch* or *tss* (note that the gemination in these two allographs denotes glottalization), e.g., *ttchîn* "scorpion" = Thomas' *ichiʔin* (1937:282) (cp. Mehri *qubãin* (Thomas 1937), *qabîn* (Jahn 1902), *kabeen* (Carter 1847)) and *schoutssi* "he drank" = Thomas' *shidzi* (cp. PS *šaqā*).

[24]"*l* › ǯ in the contiguity of close front vowels;" cf. also 1970a: 305fn.

[25]See chapter ii.

[26]This may be due to the fact that some of Jahn's informants came from Mahra-land (west of Ẓufār) where the influence of Arabic is very strong (von Maltzan 1873:253, quoted in chapter ii, above) or it may be simply due to the fact that Thomas elicited less sophisticated lexical items.

[27]The use of this Arabic name (rather than some reflex of the ancient name *S¹aʔkalhan*) by all of the MSA-speaking tribes does not necessarily mean that they are new-comers to the region. In fact, there is another place-name -- *Hanun* -- which suggests the contrary. Hanun is a spot just north of the Qara Mountains of Ẓufār where Bait Kathir tribesmen go during the harvest season to pick frankincense and where pre-Islamic frankincense storage bins have been uncovered (Phillips 1966:196-7). An ESA inscription at the spot gives the ancient name of Hanun as *S¹ʔnn*, or *S¹aʔnân* as vocalized by Jamme (cf. Hebrew *šaʔănan* "untroubled," used several times in the Bible of "abodes" and "resting-places"!). It has not hitherto been noted that *Hanun* is the expected outcome of *S¹aʔnân* in Mehri, where š (the reflex of ESA *s¹*) is weakened to *h* between a word-boundary and a vowel (also intervocalically), and etymological ā is raised to ū. Arabic mediation between ESA and MSA is of course conceivable here, assuming that the ESA place-name passed into Arabic after the sound-change *š* › *s* had ceased to operate in the latter (otherwise, ESA *S¹aʔnân* = [šaʔnân] would have been transformed into **Saʔnân* in Arabic, a form which could not have yielded *Hanun* in Mehri), but it would be gratuitous to assume such mediation since no Arabic form of the name (i.e. with š rather than *h*) has been reported.

[28]In other areas, these two phonemes merged, but there is no reason to assume that in all such areas the merger product was realized [š] rather than [ś].

[29]In order to avoid confusion, I have substituted [ɨ] for Beeston's [s̩].

[30]Blau (1970:59fn) writes that "Sibawaihi's description, on which Beeston relies..., might, *pace* Beeston, well exhibit š..." Blanc (personal communication) is even more sceptical: "That Sibawayhi meant his description of *š* to convey an *ich-Laut* seems highly unlikely."

[31]See chapter iv.

[32]Cf., for example, Cantineau [1941] 1960:56, Moscati 1954:31, and the reference cited by the latter.

[33]And probably, but not necessarily (Labov, Yaeger and Steiner 1972: 255), *functionally* distinct as well.

[34]Chen and Wang (1975:259,263) have found unconditioned splits in Chinese and Swedish, but it remains to be seen how general this phenomenon will turn out to be.

[35]See chapter ii, fn. 5.

[36]The traditional interpretation is that the presence of two postdorsal fricatives in these roots violated Semitic incompatibility rules and led to dissimilation (Yushmanov 1926:44).

[37]It should be noted, however, that one dialect of Avar (the Jar dialect) has carried out the same shift (Gudava 1964:133,135).

[38]Cf. the realization of Old Arabic *ḍ* discussed in chapter iv.

[39]According to Johnstone (1975:156fn), only Shahari preserves [θ’].

[40]Minimal pairs (for the meanings, see below in this section): *šåḥaq : śåḥaq, šaʕar : śaʕar, šåḥaṭ : śåḥaṭ, šåkar : śåkar, šåḵur : śåḵur, šårim : śårim, šēḏe : śēḏe, šoreq : śoreq, nišbaʕ : niśbaʕ, hišbiaʕ : hiśbiaʕ, maškil : maśkil, maššå(ʔ) : maśśå(ʔ), hišši(ʔ) : hiśśi(ʔ), šiḇro : śiḇro, šum : śum, šåm : śåm, nåšim : nåśim, mišrå(h) : miśrå(h), ḥɛrɛš : ḥɛrɛś, gɛrɛš : gɛrɛś*. We must, of course, keep in mind that when the history of Hebrew is better known, many of these minimal pairs will be judged anachronistic, either because their members come from different periods or because they did not become minimal pairs until after *ś* merged with *s*. The minimal pair *śårim* "officials" : *šårim* "singers" may be an example of the latter type of anachronism since the word for "officials," unlike the word for "singers," originally had a geminated *r*.

[41]Minimal pairs: *śar, śårå(h)* "official" : *sar, sårå(h)* "sullen," *niśkar* "was hired" : *niskar* "was shut up," *niśtar* "broke out" : *nistar* "hid" (Ben-Ḥayyim 1959:15), *śåp̱aq* "sufficed" : *såp̱aq* "slapped, clapped," *hiśkil* "acted prudently" : *hiskil* "acted foolishly," *romeś* "creeping": *romes* "trampling."

[42]Cf. the forms *yn* "wine" and *št* "year" in the Samaria ostraca, and the *kĕṯiḇ bhśdh* "in the field" in II Kings 7:12.

[43]The proposal really is Moscati's although one would not know it from the formulation in Moscati 1964b ("It has therefore been conjectured"); cp. the original Italian formulation in Moscati 1964a:38 and 1954:54. We might add that a similar idea was considered by Schramm (1964:19): "...it may be that the manuscript tradition, where Tiberian ‹ ś › and ‹ š › are both represented by the same skeletal letter, was based on a dialect of Hebrew in which, as in Samaritan Hebrew, the sound values of ‹ ś › and ‹ š › fell together, while the oral tradition stemmed from another dialect, where the sound values of ‹ ś › [and] ‹ s › instead, merged."

[44]Since the Biblical text itself already shows *s* for etymological *ś* and vice versa.

[45]Garbini's close adherence to Moscati's presentation makes it easy to see where Garbini has re-interpreted an idea of Moscati's.

[46]"The first certain signs of an autonomous *ś* probably appear in Aramaic...It is in this dialect, it seems to me, probably under the influence of external stimuli, that we must look for the origin of the distinction between *š* and *ś*, a distinction which was then extended to the reading of Biblical Hebrew."

[47]The present writer's view of the *kĕṯiḇ-qĕre* system thus coincides with that of Morag (1960:121-2, 1963a:xxiv-xxvfn, 1969:183-4), Goshen-Gottstein (1963:94), Schramm (1964:64-5), and Revell (1970:6-7), rather than that of Orlinsky (1960) or the "general consensus of scholarly opinion" criticized by the latter (ibid., 185).

[48]In fact, this is precisely the way Garbini (1971:34) interprets the partial replacement of שׂ by ס in Aramaic after the Persian period -- a problem which, as we shall see in a moment, is the same as the problem of the Masoretic שׂ.

[49]Cf. our discussion of the parallel phenomenon in Aramaic in the section entitled "Aramaic *ś*" (this chapter) and the arguments presented there.

[50]Nevertheless, it is entirely conceivable that there were sporadic cases of *š* › *s* in Hebrew due to dissimilation, contamination, or what-have-you. These would also show up as שׂ in the Bible. Consider, for example, the hypothetical case of a Yiddish-speaking Masorete assigned the task of pointing the word שמש in the Mishnah. Originally, this word was pronounced [šammåš] but in Eastern Europe the word became [šaməs]. Thus, our hypothetical Masorete -- faithful to his oral tradition -- would have to produce the form שַׁמָשׂ.

[50]Nevertheless, it is entirely conceivable that there were sporadic cases of *š* › *s* in Hebrew due to dissimilation, contamination, or what-have-you. These would also show up as שׂ in the Bible. Consider, for example, the hypothetical case of a Yiddish-speaking Masorete assigned the task of pointing the word שמש in the Mishnah. Originally, this word was pronounced [šammåš] but in Eastern Europe the word became [šamas]. Thus, our hypothetical Masorete -- faithful to his oral tradition -- would have to produce the form שַׂמָּשׂ.

[51]For simplicity's sake, I have substituted *ḍ* and *ḏ* for Harris' *ḏ* and *ṯ*, respectively.

[52]This form (Hecker 1968:65) confirms that the s_x of $\check{s}as_x\bar{u}m$ is a reflex of *s*, since s_x ‹ OAkk *ś* shows up as *š* in OA, as we saw above.

[53]The latter possibility is suggested by the fact that the Akkadian word for "call" contained an /s/ before and after the OB period. The assumption that the OB word for "call" also had an /s/ (i.e. that s_x was an allophone of /s/) would make for a simpler historical picture, but this consideration is not necessarily decisive.

[54]See the section entitled "Hebrew *ś*" in this chapter.

[55]See the sections entitled "Aramaic *ś*" and "Hebrew *ś*" in this chapter.

[56]Since Geez *ə* does not ordinarily come from PS *a*.

[57]The semantic change from "wages" to "reward" (cf. Hebrew *śåkår* "wages, reward") to "thanks" (= "verbal reward") is transparent.

[58]We should, however, admit the possibility that the first vowel of this word was *i*.

[59]The metathesis of *e* and *ʕ* in this form may be non-phonemic.

[60]The probable proto-forms -- **šabʕ* and **śabaʕ* -- come much closer to being a minimal pair.

[61]See the section entitled "Akkadian *š*" in this chapter. Old Assyrian, however, has *š* (Hecker 1968:115).

[62]Arabic does have a minimal pair *saraqa* "he stole" : *šaraqa* "he split" but the latter meaning is not close enough to the required one.

[63]Note that *š* › *h* in Socotri between an initial word boundary and a vowel, and intervocalically (Leslau 1938:32-4). Cp. the conditioning of the corresponding Mehri merger in footnote 27, above.

[64]From Arabic and Akkadian we reconstruct the fact that, in PS, nouns dropped their final nasal in the construct state. This rule can also be internally reconstructed from the Hebrew alternations of *ʔåḇ, ʔåḥ, ḥåm* (absolute) with *ʔăḇi, ʔăḥi, ḥămi* (construct and suffixed).

[65]This is not quite a minimal pair in the Tiberian vocalization due to a difference in the V_2 position. Since this difference is apparently the reflex of a contrast between verbal and nominal stress in Hebrew (Nyberg 1952: 33-4, but cf. Blau 1972:65 for a different interpretation) which could be very old, we cannot simply side-step the issue by appealing to the Sephardic reading tradition or the Palestinian vocalization. And if the accentual contrast between verbs and nouns turns out to be a PS feature, we may have to exclude this pair from our list of PS minimal pairs.

[66]The Shahari form, according to both Bittner (1917:27) and Thomas (1937:302) is *ferhín*. This is one of the few Shahari forms which have *h* as a reflex of PS *š*.

IV.
Evidence from the Arab Grammarians for Lateral ض in Arabic

Our search for fricative-laterals outside of Modern South Arabic quite naturally begins with Arabic -- first, because Arabic is geographically and genealogically close to MSA; second, because Arabic preserved almost the entire stock of Proto-Semitic phonemes until comparatively recent times; and third, because we possess some excellent native decriptions of the Arabic sound-system in the eighth century and later.

The targets of our investigation are ض *ḍād* and ش *šīn*, for, as we have seen, they are the Arabic phonemes which correspond to MSA ɮ̣ and ɬ. In the case of ض we do not have far to look. It is widely accepted today that the normative Arabic ض described by the grammarians was a voiced emphatic fricative-lateral or lateralized fricative (the difference will be discussed later). The list of scholars who subscribe to this view is as impressive for its quality as for its quantity:

Bosworth (1974:135)
Fischer (1968:56)
Blanc (1967a:296)
Fleisch (1965:75, 1968:16)
Gaudefroy-Demombynes and Blachère (1952:25)
Rabin (1951:33)
Cantineau ([1941] 1960:55, [1951-2] 1960:284)
Leslau (1938:30)
Bravmann (1934:53)
Colin (1930a:92)
Bergsträsser ([1928] 1963:135)
M. Cohen (1927:173)
Yushmanov (1926:42, [1938] 1961:9)
Růžička (1909:171)
Vollers (1893:145, 1906:13)
König (1877:33)
Lepsius (1861:136)

It is one of the ironies of scholarly history that Richard Lepsius -- a brilliant linguist whose bibliography includes books on Ethiopic, Egyptian history and hieroglyphics, Nubian and the classification of African languages, Persian cuneiform and the Zend alphabet, and Oscan and Umbrian -- has gotten no credit for his idea. Leslau, for example, called it "l'idée de Vollers" (1938:30), no doubt because Vollers himself was less than consistent in citing the source of this idea. Yushmanov (1926:42) quoted König's definition of *ḍād* as an "emphatisch assibiliertes *ḷ*" (1877:33) without realizing that it had been taken word for word from Lepsius (1861:136) without acknowledgement. And despite Yushmanov's citation, Fischer (1968:55) was able to claim that:

> Zweifel an dem Ansatz ض = *ḍ* äusserte zuerst N. Jušmanov... 1926 wobei er die laterale Realisation *ḍ̦* als für ض ursprünglich ansetzt.

The same erroneous attribution (stated somewhat ambiguously, however) is found already in Moscati 1954 (p.31).

Lepsius' accomplishment cannot be fully appreciated unless one realizes the great handicaps under which he worked, more than a century ago. Sībawaihi's *Kitāb*, which contains the earliest (eighth century), fullest, and most reliable discussion of ض, was not yet known in Europe. (The first European edition of the relevant portion (book 2) did not appear until 1889.) Similarly, Zamaxšarī's *Mufaṣṣal* and Ibn Yaʕīš's commentary on it (vol. 2) did not appear until 1879 and 1886 respectively. Instead of these classics, Lepsius worked with two late digests of the Arab grammatical tradition. The study of phonetics was also in its infancy. The first edition of Sievers' *Grundzüge* did not appear until 1876 and Sweet's *Handbook* was not published until 1877. Most remarkable of all is that Lepsius made his discovery without any help from MSA (although Fresnel's description of the fricative-laterals in Shahari had already been published and, moreover, was quoted in Wallin 1858, one of Lepsuis' sources). In other words, he had absolutely no reason to expect to find a lateral ض when he first approached the grammarians -- on the contrary, he had every reason to expect to find a description which would fit one of the two "classical" pronunciations of ض current in his time. In spite of these handicaps, his presentation (1861:135-6) of the case for lateral ض has never been surpassed:

> Am meisten Schwierigkeit dagegen hat jederzeit der dem Zeichen nach entsprechende weiche Laut ض z̲ gemacht, auf dessen richtige Aussprache die Araber soviel Gewicht legten, dass, wie Fleischer zu Wallin bemerkt,[1] *Juwainī* den *S̲āfiʾī* "den am reinsten redenden derer, die das z̲ aussprechen," d.h. der Araber, nannte; und es vom Kalifen ʾUmar besonders angemerkt wird, dass

er zwischen ظ $\underline{\delta}$ und ض $\underline{z}$ keinen Unterschied machte.[2] Es scheint nicht nöthig, auf alle die Erklärungen und Vermuthungen einzugehen, welche von den neueren Gelehrten über diesen Buchstaben aufgestellt worden sind. Auch hier sind die Orthoepisten unsre untrüglichen Leiter. Sie rechnen den Buchstaben zu den tönenden[3] Frikativen.[4] Darüber herrscht keine Ungewissheit. Die Schwierigkeit liegt vielmehr in dem Orte der Friktionsbildung.

Schon *Xalil* rechnet diesen Buchstaben zu den *Intermaxillares*, d.h. zu denen, welche in dem Raume zwischen den Backzähnen gebildet werden. Der Verfasser,[5] der dies anführt, trennt ihn von den beiden andern, die *Xalil* dazu stellt, nämlich von ǰ und š, und *verbindet ihn mit l zu einer Klasse*...Die Maroniten[6] nennen $\underline{z}$ eine *littera extensionis, quia sese extendit usque ad organum litterae l*, eine unklare Bestimmung, welche aber gleichfalls auf die Nähe der *l*-Bildung hinweist. Diese letztere wird noch genauer so angegeben (Sacy p. 32): "Es wird gesprochen von dem Zungenrande [حافّة لسان *latus, ora, margo linguae*. Sacy übersetzt statt dessen ***partie antérieure de la langue***], aber von dem Theile des Zungenrandes, welcher der Spitze am nächsten liegt." Nach Wallin (p. 634) wird der Artikulationsplatz des ض $\underline{z}$ als "zwischen dem Anfange der Zungenränder und den diese Stelle der Zunge berührenden Backzähnen liegend" angegeben. Von den Orthoepisten wird gesagt (W. p. 633[7]) dass die östlichen Araber den Laut wie ein emphatisches *l* aussprechen, und dass diese Aussprache als die normale gelte, während einige die der westlichen Araber vorzögen.[8] Aus allen diesen Zeugnissen geht unverkennbar hervor, dass der Laut ض $\underline{z}$ ein emphatisches assibilirtes *l* war, was sich nun...unschwer und sehr genau aussprechen lässt. Man formire ein *l* mit gleichzeitiger Gutturalstellung der hintern Zunge, und lasse den Hauch an den Augenzähnen zur tönenden Reibung gelangen, so spricht man das vorgeschriebene normale $\underline{z}$.

We see here a five-point argument for a voiced fricative-lateral ض:

1. Its place of articulation is said to be the edge of the tongue (*ḥāffatu l-lisān*), and it is said to be voiced and a fricative.
2. The place of articulation of *lām* is also said to be the edge of the tongue, and no other consonant is so described. (This provides a check on the literal meaning of *ḥāffatu l-lisān* and shows that the Arab phoneticians did not mistakenly identify as lateral any phonemes which we know to be central.)

3. It has the property of *ʔisti*ṭ*āla* which has something to do with *l* (an explanation will be offered below).
4. It was pronounced as an emphatic *ḷ* in some areas of the Arab world.
5. It was a very unusual sound -- so unusual that it characterized not only the Arabic language but the Arab nation as well.

There is not much one can add to Lepsuis' brilliant interpretation of the grammarians except in the one area where he himself admits to bewilderment: the problem of *ḍād*'s *ʔistiṭāla*. Before dealing with this problem, however, we must deal with a related problem.

Lepsius and the scholars who followed him concentrated on explaining the *similarity* between the *muxraj*[9] "place of articulation" of *ḍād* and that of *lām*, without attempting to interpret the *difference* between them. That there is a difference is obvious from a comparison of Sībawaihi's descriptions (reproduced in the later digest used by Lepsius) of the two places of articulation (p. 453). The *muxraj* of *lām* is:

> *min ḥāffati l-lisāni min ʔadnāhā ʔilā muntahā ṭarafi l-lisāni mā baynahā wa-bayna mā yalīhā mina l-ḥanaki l-ʔaʕlā wa-mā fuwaiqa ḍ-ḍāḥiki wa-n-nābi wa-r-rabāʕiyyati wa-ṯ-ṯaniyya*
>
> between the tongue's edge, from front to tip, and the corresponding section of the palate together with the area just above the first premolar, the canine, the lateral incisor, and the central incisor.

The *muxraj* of *ḍād,* on the other hand, is:

> *min bayna ʔawwali ḥāffati l-lisāni wa-mā yalīhi mina l-ʔaḍrās*
>
> between the beginning of the tongue's edge and the corresponding molars.

It is clear that "this beginning is to be taken as starting from the root of the tongue" (Fischer 1965:75) since

a) the corresponding teeth are called "molars."
b) *ḍād* precedes *lām* in the order of the places of articulation (from back to front).
c) Zamaxšarī's paraphrase of Sībawaihi actually reads *ʔṣl* "root" instead of *ʔwl* "beginning."[10]
d) the beginning of the tongue's edge at the opposite end seems to be called *ʔadnā ḥāffati l-lisān*.
e) according to Zamaxšarī (*Al-Mufaṣṣal* p. 188), *lām*'s place of articulation is the tongue's edge up to its

tip but minus its beginning (*mā dūna ʔawwali ḥāffati l-lisāni ʔilā muntahā ṭarafihi*) -- this implies that the beginning is in the back.

Assuming that Lepsius was right in concluding that *ḍād* was an "assibilated *ḷ*" (i.e. a fricative-lateral), we can easily explain why *ḍād* was made further back on the edge of the tongue than *lām*. We need only quote Doke's description (1926:100) of the Zulu voiced fricative-lateral:

> As has been noticed already, ɮ differs from *l* in that the side of the tongue is raised sufficiently to produce friction with the palate. The air escapes unilaterally, but somewhat further back in the mouth than for *l*.

In other words, the raising of the side of the tongue to produce friction blocks the passage of air over the front of the tongue's edge, making it impossible for air to escape in the vicinity of the incisors, the canine or the first premolar.

With this in mind, we can attempt to interpret the mysterious term *ʔistiṭāla*. Many interpretations have already been offered. According to Yushmanov (1926:42), *ʔistiṭāla* means "à passage latéral," but this cannot be right (Cantineau [1951-2] 1960:284), since it makes no sense in the relevant contexts and since *šīn* also has *ʔistiṭāla* (Sībawaihi pp. 462, 467,471,477)[11], a fact ignored by most modern scholars. Fleisch (1965:75) follows Wallin (1858:634) in taking *ʔistiṭāla* as *temporal* length indicating "not...a great extent for the place of articulation but rather a dwelling on it, a special prolongation of it."

Most scholars, however, take *ʔistiṭāla* as a *spatial* property, referring to the long *muxraj* of ض (e.g. Jahn 1900: 854,876,882, Schaade 1911:74, Cantineau [1941] 1960:55). These scholars are certainly on the right track since, in one place (p. 462), the noun *muxraj* occurs as the subject of the verb *ʔistaṭāla* (*liʔanna š-šīna staṭāla muxrajuhā*); but they seem to think that Sībawaihi was talking about an unusually long *muxraj* (*ʔistiṭāla* = length). Sībawaihi's own description (p. 452), however, seems to refer to a *muxraj* that gets longer and longer (*ʔistiṭāla* = lengthening):

> *wa-ʔinnahā tuxāliṭu muxraja ġayrihā baʕda xurūjihā fa-tastaṭīlu ḥīna*[12] *tuxāliṭu ḥurūfa l-lisān.*
>
> And it merges into the area of articulation of other consonants after it is articulated, and gets longer and longer until it merges into [the area of articulation of] the consonants of the tongue.

This passage states quite explicitly that the *ʔistiṭāla* does not take place until "after articulation" or, more literally, "after [the air used in producing] it passes out [of its *muxraj*]." Presumably, the *muxraj* is of normal length during articulation; it is only later, in passing or "gliding" to the following vowel (or consonant), that it becomes long.

Since Sībawaihi's next point is that ض can easily be articulated on the left side of the tongue by simply performing the same articulatory motions on the left side as one usually does on the right, he repeats his description of the off-glide in describing (p. 453) the left-sided ض:

> *fa-sahula taḥwīluhā ʔilā l-ʔaysari liʔannahā taṣīru fī ḥāffati l-lisāni fī l-ʔaysari ʔilā miṯla mā kānat fī l-ʔayman; ṯumma tansallu mina l-ʔaysari ḥattā tattaṣilu bi-ḥurūfi l-lisāni ka-mā kānat ka-ḏālika fī l-ʔayman.*
>
> And deflecting[13] it [i.e. the airstream of *ḍād*] to the left is easy, because it goes to the same part of the tongue's left edge as on the right edge. Then it slips away from the left until it joins the consonants of the tongue, just as on the right.

Here again we see the two stages: first it is articulated, then it glides. But where? Schaade's guess (1911:70) that "bei *ḥurūf al-lisān* (II, 453, 1) denkt Sībawaihi hier wohl in erster Linie an Laute wie *d*, *ḏ*, u. dgl." only points up the vagueness of the above descriptions. Fortunately, these descriptions are not the only sources of information about *ḍād*'s *ʔistiṭāla* which we possess. The same feature is discussed twice more by Sībawaihi (as Schaade 1911:74 points out, cf. also the *Grammatica Arabica Maronitarum*, cited by Lepsius above), once to explain why *lām* is assimilated by *ḍād* (p. 467) and a second time to explain why *ṭāʔ*, *tāʔ*, and *dāl* are assimilated by *ḍād* (p. 470). The first of these passages uses the verb *ʔistaṭāla* explicitly:

> *wa-l-ʔaḥada ʕašara ḥarfan an-nūnu wa-r-rāʔu wa-d-dālu wa-t-tāʔu wa-ṣ-ṣādu wa-ṭ-ṭāʔu wa-z-zāyu wa-s-sīnu wa-ẓ-ẓāʔu wa-ṯ-ṯāʔu wa-ḏ-ḏālu wa-l-ladāni xālaṭahā ḍ-ḍādu wa-š-šīnu liʔanna ḍ-ḍāda staṭālat[14] li-raxāwatihā ḥattā ttaṣalat bi-muxraji l-lāmi wa-š-šīnu ka-ḏālika ḥattā ttaṣalat bi-muxraji ṭ-ṭāʔ.*
>
> And the eleven consonants of the tongue-tip are: *nūn*, *rāʔ*, *dāl*, *tāʔ*, *ṣād*, *ṭāʔ*, *zāy*, *sīn*, *ẓāʔ*, *ṯāʔ*, and *ḏāl*; and the two which merge into them are *ḍād* and *šīn*, because *ḍād* gets longer and longer on account of its weak con-

tact[15] until it joins the place of articulation of *lām*, and the *šīn* does likewise, joining the place of articulation of *ṭāʔ*.

One is immediately struck by the fact that in this passage Sībawaihi names *lām* rather than the "consonants of the tongue" as the target of *ḍād*'s off-glide, and one is led at first to suspect that the substitution was motivated by Sībawaihi's need to explain why *lām* is totally assimilated by *ḍād* (Sībawaihi's principle being that total assimilation should take place only between consonants which are already somewhat similar). That such a suspicion is unfounded is proved by the description of *šīn* in the same passage, and by the last of Sībawaihi's descriptions of *ḍād*'s *ʔistiṭāla* (p. 470):

> *wa-qad tudġamu ṭ-ṭāʔu wa-t-tāʔu wa-d-dālu fī ḍ-ḍādi liʔannahā ttaṣālat bi-muxraji l-lāmi wa-ṭaʔṭaʔat ʕani l-lāmi ḥattā xālaṭat ʔuṣūla mā l-lāmu fawqahu mina l-ʔasnān wa-lam taqaʕ mina t-taniyyati mawḍiʕa ṭ-ṭāʔ li-nḥirāfihā liʔannaka taḍaʕu li-ṭ-ṭāʔi lisānaka bayna t-taniyyatayn.*
>
> *Ṭāʔ*, *tāʔ*, and *dāl* are sometimes assimilated by *ḍād* because it joins the place of articulation of *lām* and then turns away from *lām* until it merges with the roots of the teeth which *lām* is above. It does not fall upon the part of the central incisors which is the place of articulation of *ṭāʔ*, because of its [vertically? horizontally?] displaced tongue-tip, and because for *ṭāʔ* you place your tongue *between* the central incisors.

It is quite obvious that the reference to *lām* in this description is not motivated by any *ad hoc* considerations. Moreover, there is an additional detail here which seems to explain why chapter 565 speaks in general terms of the "consonants of the tongue," instead of simply saying "*lām*."

The passage describes in great detail how the laterally-deflected airstream which is characteristic of *ḍād* returns to its normal course (along the median line of the palate) as the articulators are separated. First the side of the tongue is lowered, allowing the air to escape further forward -- from the *muxraj* of *lām*. Then apical contact is broken, allowing the air to escape between the tongue-tip and the front teeth, slightly above or to the side of the *muxraj* of *ṭāʔ*, *tāʔ*, and *dāl*. It is clear, then, that Sībawaihi needed a term general enough to cover both of these stages; his use of the term "consonants of the tongue" must be judged in the light of that need.

LATERAL OR LATERALIZED?

In discussing the MSA fricative-laterals, we encountered Thomas' description of them as "lateralized consonants or lisped sibilants" and Murtonen's paraphrase "lateralized variants."[16] Cantineau, who seems to have been unaware of Thomas' work, used the same term to describe Arabic ض ([1946] 1960:169,200, [1951-2] 1960:285), and like Thomas, he used it, in place of the traditional term "lateral spirant" (Yushmanov 1926:42, [1938] 1961:9, Bergsträsser [1928] 1963:135), to convey his view of lateralization as something secondary or tacked on -- a "travail accessoire" (Cantineau [1946] 1960: 169).

Some scholars have accepted this new term (Fleisch 1965: 75, 1968:16, Bosworth 1974:135); others have explicitly rejected it (Martinet 1953:77) or quietly ignored it (Gaudefroy-Demombynes and Blachère 1952:25). However, it is difficult to avoid the impression that most scholars have failed to grasp the full import of the term (as used by Cantineau, at least) and, specifically, the fact that a lateralized fricative is not simply a fricative-lateral seen from a different perspective.

Cantineau views lateralization as the "marque" of a "rapport d'opposition privative" ([1946] 1960:169), which means that it is superimposed on consonants without replacing any of their primary features ([1941] 1960:155-6). Consequently, when lateralization is added to a consonant, the central passage of air has to be retained along with the lateral passage (ibid., 139):

> Les consonnes *latérales* ou *latéralisées*, et surtout *labiovélaires* ou *labiopostpalatales*....sont des consonnes ayant en somme deux points d'articulation: un point d'articulation principal apical, postpalatal ou vélaire, et un second point d'articulation latéral ou labial; la rupture de ces deux obstacles se produit à peu près en même temps.

Or again, earlier in the book, where ض is first described (ibid., 55):

> ...la pointe de la langue s'approchait des incisives supérieures comme pour un *ḏ* et le souffle expiratoire s'échappait non seulement par la pointe, mais aussi par le côté de la langue.

These descriptions reveal a profound but easily overlooked difference between Cantineau's lateralized fricative $\underline{d}^{l}$ and the fricative-lateral ɮ. No air escapes "par la pointe" in the production of ɮ or any other lateral. Given this interpretation, it is highly unlikely that ض was a lateralized fricative since

a) the *muxraj* of ض, as described by Sībawaihi, does not include the tongue-tip.
b) to the best of the present writer's knowledge, no such phone is attested in any other language.
c) the existence of such a phone is physiologically unlikely because of the great effort that would be required to produce friction at the tip of the tongue if the sides of the tongue were lowered.

Blanc's restatement (1967:296) of Cantineau -- "ḍ (*ḍād*) was an emphatic spirant with lateral release" -- eliminates the last of these objections by making the central passage of air and the lateral passage consecutive rather than simultaneous, but does nothing for objections (a) and (b).

It is clear then that we must reject Cantineau's conception of ض. It is a conception which was designed to explain the alleged compatibility of *ḍād* and *lām* in Arabic roots by distinguishing the primary lateral articulation of the latter from the allegedly secondary lateral articulation of the former (Cantineau [1946] 1960:200). But are *ḍād* and *lām* really compatible? The present writer's own investigation, summarized in chapter xiii, indicates that they are not. If so, it follows that Cantineau's characterization of ض is not only untenable but unnecessary as well.

[1]Wallin (1858:633).

[2]Zamaxšarī has a different tradition about ʕUmar's pronunciation of ض in his Qurʔanic commentary *Al-Kaššāf* (*Sūrat al-Takwīr*, verse 24). According to this tradition ʕUmar was able to execute ض on both sides (i.e. either side) of his tongue because he was ambidextrous. The connecting link between the two traditions may have been one which associated ʕUmar with the *ḍād ḍaʕīfa* "weak *ḍād*," which originally referred to some unknown variant of ض (possibly a left-sided ض if the expression *wa-huwa ʔaxaffu* "it is weaker" in Sībawaihi, p. 452, refers to execution on the left side) and later came to refer to the ض which had shifted to ظ.

[3]More recently, the traditional equation *majhūra* = voiced has been called into question by several scholars (cf. Blanc 1967) because of the appearance of ṭ, *q* and especially ʔ in Sībawaihi's list of the *majhūra*. Still, for our purposes, it is not necessary for *majhūra* to actually *mean* "voiced." It is sufficient that when this feature occurs in fricatives, it is always accompanied by voicing. The latter is a fact which has not, to my knowledge, been questioned.

[4]Actually, the term *rixwa* is not exactly equivalent to our term "fricative," since the latter is basically an acoustic term referring to the noise of friction, while the former is an articulatory term for the second of three degrees of stricture: *šidda* "firm closure," *raxāwa* "weak closure," *līn* "feeble closure." This interpretation is based not only on the literal meaning of the words and the lists of consonants in each class, but also on Sībawaihi's explicit statements (e.g. p. 454) that the characteristic of the

rixwa which distinguishes them from the *šadīda* is that they "shun, shy away from" (*tatajāfā* ʕ*an*) their place of articulation. The fact that Sībawaihi classifies *m, n,* and *l* as *šadīda* is further evidence for the articulatory nature of this system. It is worth noting that some modern phoneticians (e.g. Abercrombie 1967:44-5, but cf. Ladefoged 1971:55) also speak of three degrees of stricture: "complete closure" (characterizes all stops including the nasals), "close approximation" (characterizes all fricatives), "open approximation" (characterizes the semivowels and *l*). The only difference between this system and that of Sībawaihi is in the classification of *l*, and even here we see from Abercrombie's language (ibid., 50) how close *l* is to the category of complete closure: "A lateral is a type of segment produced by a stricture of complete closure in the center of the vocal tract..."

[5]The anonymous author of a treatise on the pronunciation of the Arabic consonants published by de Sacy (1813).

[6]The two Lebanese authors of *Grammatica Arabica Maronitarum* (1716).

[7]Lepsius has "p. 663" here but the statement in question appears on p. 633.

[8]This does not seem to be an accurate summary of the tradition cited by Wallin. See chapters vii and viii for a discussion of this tradition and a similar tradition, reported in Ibn Jinni's *Kitāb al-Tanbīh*, about the Zayāliʕ.

[9]This is the vocalization found in the manuscripts of Sībawaihi; nouns of place derived from the "derived" forms of the verb are identical in form with the passive participles (Wright [1896] 1967:129).

[10]*Fa-ʔinna ḍāda min ʔaṣli ḥāffati l-lisāni wa-mā yalīhā mina l-ʔaḍrāsi min yamīni l-lisāni ʔaw yasārihā.* This statement is cited by Wallin (1858: 635) from the Qurʔanic commentary of Baiḍāwī but Professor Haim Blanc was kind enough to inform me that Baiḍāwī has here, as elsewhere, followed Zamaxšarī's commentary Al-Kaššāf (Sūrat al-Takwīr, verse 24) word for word. Professor Blanc also points out the curious fact that "in Zamaxsarī's *Mufaṣṣal*, where he puts on his grammarian's hat, the wording is exactly that of the *Kitāb*, viz. *min ʔawwal*, etc.; same in Ibn Yaʕīš's commentary on the passage." Now, the word for "root" differs from the word for "beginning" by only one letter, and since Sībawaihi uses *ʔaṣl* (and its antonym, *ṭaraf* "tip") in speaking of the incisors, one might suspect that he used it in referring to the tongue's edge as well (*ʔawwal* does not appear elsewhere as a subdivision of an articulatory organ). But according to Professor Blanc:

> "There is no reason to think that this might be Sībawaihi's wording: the *Kitāb* and all later grammarians, so far as I recall, all have *ʔawwal*; in general, quotes in the later grammarians from the *Kitāb* are remarkably uniform, showing that the text was solidly established quite early. Of course there are occasional elaborations or paraphrasings, and I imagine your quote, or rather Wallin's, is something of the sort."

Another point in favor of the present text is the fact that the phrase *min ʔawwal ḥāffati l-lisān* occurs again in the *Kitāb* (p. 467, line 17).

[11]It is curious, however, that in Ibn Yaʕīš (p. 1461), the *ʔistiṭāla* (or rather *tafaššī*) of *šīn* connects it with *lām* rather than *ṭāʔ* as in Sībawaihi (p. 470, see below): *ʔinna š-šīna tatafaššā fī l-fami ḥattā tattaṣilu bi-muxraji l-lāmi* "*Šīn* spreads in the mouth until it joins the place of articulation of *lām*." I am grateful to Prof. Federico Corriente for bringing this passage to my attention (cf. his forthcoming article in the *Journal of Semitic Studies*: "From Old Arabic to Classical Arabic through the Preislamic Koine: Some Notes on the Native Grammarians' Sources, Attitudes, and Goals"). Prof. Corriente believes that "some earlier grammarian might have heard the lateralized /š/ and reported it in a scarcely circulating work." But even if he is right, *ʔistiṭāla per se* has nothing to do with the lateral feature, because it is mentioned in connection with *ṭāʔ* as well as *lām*.

[12]Schaade (1911:70) emends to *ḥattā*, which is graphically quite similar. The emended phrase makes much more sense and is attested several times

in the *Kitāb*: *ʔistaṭāla muxrajuha...ḥattā ttaṣala* (p. 462), *ʔistaṭālat... ḥattā ttaṣalat* (p. 467), *ʔistaṭālat ḥattā xālaṭat* (p. 477). The same emendation would seem to be necessary on p. 471: *li-stiṭālatihā ḥīna ttaṣalat bi-muxrajihā*.

[13]"Deflecting" rather than "transferring" since *taḥwīl* is also involved in articulation on the right side -- the usual side -- according to 452.20: *liʔannaka tuḥawwiluhā mina l-yasāri ʔilā l-mawḍiʕi l-laḏī fī l-yamīn* "because you deflect it from the left to the place [of articulation] which is on the right." It would not make sense to translate "because you transfer it..." since there would be no need to transfer it to the normal side.

[14]Note the use of the perfect instead of the expected imperfect here and in many other places in the *Kitāb* (e.g. after *liʔanna* in 462.10.15, 467.10.15, 471.7.9, 473.7.10). According to Prof. Haim Blanc (personal communication):

> "The tenses are not exactly in free variation...at least not totally free in all possible cases, but they do alternate rather freely in given verbs describing general properties of sounds and other linguistic elements in the *Kitāb*...
> "Anyway, descriptive statements which are, on the whole, in the *Kitāb* and most of the tradition, synchronic or rather anachronic, can have either tense."

[15]Cf. fn. 4 above, where I translated "weak closure." Sībawaihi apparently believes that weak contact between the articulators leads to slipping, while firm contact keeps them in place. The same phrase appears again on p. 462, line 1.

[16]See the end of chapter ii.

V.
Evidence from Loanwords for Lateral ض in Arabic (I)

ARABIC LOANWORDS IN THE IBERIAN PENINSULA (SPANISH, PORTUGUESE, CATALAN)

Lepsius' revolutionary view of the Arabic ض as an emphatic assibilated *l* was published in 1861. In the same year Willem H. Engelmann published the first edition of his *Glossaire des mots espagnols et portugais dérivés de l'arabe*. Among the loanwords collected in this book are six in which Arabic ض seems to be rendered by Spanish *ld* or *l*:

alcalde[1] "judge"[2] < *ʔal-qāḍī*[3] or *ʔal-qāḍ*[4]
albayalde[5] "white lead, ceruse" < *ʔal-bayāḍ*
arrabal[6] "suburb" < *ʔar-rabaḍ*
Albelda[7] (toponym) < *ʔAl-Bayḍāʔ* "The White"
aldava[8] "latch" < *ʔaḍ-ḍabba*
aldea[9] "hamlet" < *ʔaḍ-ḍayʕa*

The first edition was of course too early to benefit from Lepsius' insight,[10] but the second edition, put out by Dozy (1869), was not. It is therefore not unfair to feel that a great opportunity was missed when one reads the explanations of the *l*(*d*) rendering offered in that edition (p. 23): "Devant le ض ...on intercale un *l* euphonique...Au reste ce *l* sert à exprimer le son emphatique du ض..."

As vacuous as these two explanations seem today, they have managed to infiltrate two of the three most influential subsequent studies of Arabic loanwords in Spanish: Eguilaz 1886 (which reproduces the first explanation on p. xxi) and Neuvonen 1941 (which reproduces the second explanation on p. 282, with an obviously mistaken reference to Steiger 1932: 162). Steiger 1932 is the only one of the three which incorporates Lepsius' insight (though the reference is to Vollers 1893 rather than to the actual discoverer). Arabists, understandably, have a better record in this respect than Hispanists. The first scholar to see the significance of the *l*(*d*) rendering was Ružička (1909:171) -- although we must ignore his assumption that *alcalde*, etc. reflect a sound change *ḍḍ*<*lḍ* -- followed by Yushmanov (1926:42), Colin (1930a:101) and Cantineau ([1941] 1960:56).

In evaluating the importance of this rendering as evidence for lateral ض, it is important to note that several of

Engelmann's examples have been challenged by subsequent scholars. According to Asín Palacios (1944:47) and Malkiel (1950: 115), the toponyn *Albelda* reflects Arabic *ʔal-balda* "town" rather than *ʔal-bayḍāʔ*. *Aldea* and *aldaba* are also problematical as Eguilaz (1886:xxi) points out:

> Esta regla [euphonic *l* is inserted before *ḍ*] no es aplicable, como creen Engelmann y Dozy, a *aldea* y *aldaba*, cuya *l* es, en mi humilde sentir, la del art. ár. que precede al nombre, ó el primer د (*dal*) duplicado por el *texdid*, transformado en la líquida referida. Lo mismo ha de decirse del *lam* que antecede al د (*dal*) de *aldargama* por *ad-dargama*, *aldebaran* de *ad-debaran*, *aldiza* de *ad-diza*, y al ط (*thá*) enfática de *altabaque* de *attabaque*.[11]

In other words, the *l* of *aldaba* and *aldea* seems to reflect the *l* of the Arabic definite article *ʔal* rather than the lateral feature of *ḍ*, for, in spite of the fact that *ḍ* is one of the so-called "sun-letters" which assimilate the *l* of the definite article, we find several examples of loanwords where the sun-letters have not done their job. In addition to the examples cited by Eguilaz, which are taken from Dozy and Engelmann(1869:23), we find: *aldufe* (Steiger 1932:162), *altamía, aldúcar, altramuz* (ibid., 376) *Aldeire, Aldovara, Aldovareta, Aldover, Aldovera* (Asín Palacio s 1944:56-7).

Steiger (1932:162), on the other hand, argues that Eguilaz is wrong in his analysis of *aldea* and *aldaba*:

> Creo muy difícil asentir a la opinión del sabio orientalista. En primer lugar, porque su explicación deja sin abarcar el hecho del paso de ض a *l, ll, ld*, en posición final,[12] y luego porque, al igual de los actuales dialectos magrebíes, la asimilación solar se extiende en hispano-árabe al propio ج. Si la *l* del artículo vuelve a encontrarse en algunos arabismos (*aldufe*, frente a *adufe; aldebarán*, etc.), esto ha de explicarse por analogía con sustantivos que principiaban por letra lunar (*alcántara*, **etc.**); analogía facilitada por la aparente contradicción en el tratamiento del artículo.[13]

Three arguments are presented here:

(a) Eguilaz needs a second explanation to account for the rendering of ض with *l,ll, ld* in final position, while Steiger accounts for ض in all positions with *one* explanation.

(b) Assimilation of the article is *more* extensive in Andalusian Arabic (where initial ج assimilates the *l* of the article) than in classical Arabic (where ج does not assimilate the *l* of the article) -- not less extensive.

(c) The appearance of the unassimilated article in *aldufe, aldebarán,* etc. is due to analogy with words which begin with phonemes which never assimilate the article.

None of these arguments has any force. The economy of Steiger's explanation (Argument (a)) disappears as soon as *aldufe, aldebarán,* etc. are taken into account. Argument (c) fails to explain why the same process of analogy could not be behind *aldea* and *aldaba.* Point (b) is obviously intended to suggest that it would be inconsistent for a dialect to extend the domain of the assimilation rule on the one hand, while restricting it on the other; but this argument is undercut by Steiger's own admission in (c) that the *l* of *aldufe, aldebarán,* etc. represents the *l* of the Arabic definite article. The appearance of *l* in these words is also inconsistent and yet it is a fact. Furthermore, the inconsistency becomes comprehensible once we recall that the immediate source of these loanwords was not the Arabs but the *Mozarabes* (Neuvonen 1941:29-30), the Spanish-speaking Christian population in the areas conquered by the Arabs. These *Mozarabes* (Arabic *mustaʿrabī* "Arabized") did not become native speakers of Arabic for centuries (loc. cit.; Menendez Pidal 1956:416ff) but they must have begun acquiring an imperfect knowledge of Arabic soon after the Arabic conquest of 711. Forms like *aldufe* and *aldebarán* exhibit just the kind of mistake-by-analogy which one would expect to find in the broken Arabic of the first generations of *Mozarabes.* Alternately, the words may have been originally borrowed without an *l* (cf. *adufe* and *addebaran*) only to be later "corrected" by Spanish speakers who recognized them as Arabic loanwords.[14] This latter alternative is recommended by the fact that forms with unassimilated *l* before *d* seem to be rather late. *Aldea* is an exception to this rule -- a fact which suggests that Steiger may be right after all in distinguishing the *ld* of this loanword from the *ld* of *aldufe, aldebarán,* etc. Until the question is settled, however, it is best to omit these problematic examples.

We are left with only three of Engelmann's six examples of *ld* for ض, but they are, as Malkiel (1950:114-5) remarks, "tres palabras de gran importancia" and "de derivación incontrovertible." Part of the evidence that makes the etymology of these words so certain comes from a Spanish-Arabic dictionary published in Granada in the sixteenth century by Pedro de Alcalá ([1505] 1928). This dictionary, the *Vocabulista arauigo in letra castellana,* renders *Spanish Arrabal* with Arabic *Rabăd, arbăd,*[15] and *Spanish Aluayalde* with Arabic *Bayǎd*.[16] *Alcalde* does not appear, but its origin is so transparent (especially since *ʔal-qāḍī* was borrowed by practically every language which ever had contact with Arabic) that it requires no special proof.

CHRONOLOGY AND SOURCE OF THE LOANWORDS

We have very little information on when the lateral realization of ض was replaced by the modern central realizations in various regions, due to the fact that the Arab grammarians did not change their description of the ض when the ض changed. They simply continued to repeat Sībawaihi's words, apparently without realizing that the description no longer fitted.[17] There are of course exceptions to this rule, for example, the eleventh century philosopher Ibn Sīnā (Avicenna), whose completely independent treatise on the speech sounds describes ض as a stop (Blanc 1967a:304); the tenth-century linguist Ibn Jinnī, who reported several colloquial pronunciations of ض in his *Kitāb al-Tanbīh* (*apud* Al-Jazarī, *Kitāb al-Tamhīd*, 43) including [ḍ] ("they make ض into ظ"[18]), and [ḍ] in Egypt and North Africa ("mixed with ṭ"); and the ninth century author Al-Jāḥiẓ, whose *Bayān* contains an anecdote about confusion between ض and ظ in Baṣra (Fück 1955:89). But these are only isolated reports and, moreover, give no idea of how long the lateral realization persisted alongside the colloquial realizations. Thus, any light which the loanwords might be able to shed on this question would be very welcome.

Unfortunately, the loanwords we have gathered are extremely difficult to date because of the strong possibility that their earliest attestations (*alcalde* 1062, *alraual* 1146 but also *arravalde* 950, *albayalde* 1439; Neuvonen 1941 s.v., Corominas 1967 s.v.) in our documents are considerably later than their real dates of entry into the language. This possibility is due not so much to a scarcity of documents or (in the case of *alcalde* and *arrabal*, at least) to any unusualness of the words in question[19] as to the fact that the Spanish documents which we possess come from the Christian kingdoms, whose inhabitants did not begin to use Arabic loanwords on a large scale until the *Reconquista* broke down the political and social barriers which separated them from their fellow-Spaniards, the *Mozarabes*. In other words, *alcalde* may have been in use for centuries among the *Mozarabes* before it began to show up in Castillian documents in the eleventh century, and, thus, we have no assurance that Andalusian ض was still a lateral at that time.

The source of the words, i.e. the dialect from which they were borrowed, is even less certain. Colin (1930a:102) suggested that the words had originated with the large South Arabian segment of the Arab community in Spain, and, indeed, a recent history of the Maghrib (Abun-Nasr 1971:87) states that "the majority of the Arabs who settled in the peninsula were Yemenites." If so, Colin's suggestion is quite plausible, but nothing definite can be said until a thorough investigation of the non-classical features of Andalusian Arabic is made.

[1]Cp. *alcalde* in Old Portuguese and Old Catalan, where it is a Spanish, rather than Arabic, loanword (Neuvonen 1941:110, Batlle Y Prats 1954).

[2]Throughout this chapter, the meaning given for the loanword applies to the Arabic original as well, unless a separate gloss is given for the Arabic word.

[3]Cf. Steiger 1932:341-2 for the rendering of Arabic *i* with Spanish *e*, and ibid., 312 for the Moroccan form *qâḍe*.

[4]Cf. Blau 1961a:94 and 1961b:211-2 for Middle Arabic forms like *ʔal-qāḍ*, and Birkeland 1940:68-9 for the pausal origin of such forms.

[5]Cp. Portuguese *alvaiade* (Steiger 1932:165).

[6]Cp. Old Spanish *ravalde, arrabalde* alongside *arraval(e), arrabal;* Old Portuguese *arravalde;* Old Catalan *(ar)raval* (Malkiel 1950:115).

[7]Alongside *Albaida* (Steiger 1932:165).

[8]Cp. Portuguese *aldrava, aldraba* (Steiger 1932:163). Do these come from **aldlava, *aldlaba* by dissimilation?

[9]Cp. Portuguese *aldeia* (Malkiel 1950:115).

[10]Although the tradition that some Arabs pronounced *ḍād* as an emphatic *lām*, in Wallin 1858:634 (see chapter ii above), would have done just as well.

[11]"This rule [euphonic *l* is inserted before *d*] does not apply, as Engelmann and Dozy believe, to *aldea* and *aldaba*, whose *l*, in my humble opinion is either the *l* of the Arabic definite article which precedes the noun or the first [*d* of the] doubled *d* transformed into the above-mentioned liquid. The same can be said of the *l* which precedes the *d* of *aldargama* for *ad-dargama, aldebaran* from *ad-debaran, aldiza* from *ad-diza,* and the emphatic *ṭ* of *altabaque* from *attabaque*."

[12]Steiger treats *ʔal-qāḍī* as an example of ض in final position, apparently ignoring the final long vowel.

[13]"I find it very difficult to agree with the opinion of the learned Orientalist, in the first place because his explanation does not take into account the shift of *ḍ* to *l, ll, ld* in final position, and then because in Andalusian Arabic, as in the modern North African dialects, "solar" assimilation extended as far as ج. If the *l* of the article happens to appear in a few Arabisms (*aldufe* alongside *adufe* ; *aldebarán,* etc.), this has to be explained as an analogy with nouns that begin with a "lunar" letter (*alcantara,* etc.) -- an analogy facilitated by the apparent contradiction in [the language's] treatment of the article."

[14]Neuvon (1941:285) proposes a similar process to explain why the Arabic definite article seems to have been exempt from the Spanish sound change *al › o/_consonant*.

[15]Alcalá's consistent transcription of ض with *d* or *ḋ* (= ð) as well as the fact that he does not include ض in his lists of letters which have no equivalents in Latin or Castillian (*x, ṯ, ḏ* and ʕ according to *Arte* c iiii side 2; *x, ḏ, ṯ,* ʕ and *ḥ* according to the *Vocabulista* a iii side 2) shows that by his time ض was no longer a lateral.

[16]Strangely, Dozy and Engelmann (1869:70) and Steiger (1932:165) noticed the *Aluayalde* entry but missed the *Arrabal* entry. Perhaps the editions they used omitted this entry by accident.

[17]Cf. the remark of Colin (1930a:92) that "il est assez plaisant de voir de nombreux auteurs arabes modernes continuer de se vanter d'être de

'ceux qui prononcent le ض (ʔan-nāṭiqūna bi-ḍ-ḍād)' et parler avec emphase de leur langue, 'la seule qui possède le ض' (luġatunā ḍ-ḍādiyya)."

[18]This cannot be intended solely as a report that ض was merged with ظ, for if it were, it would apply equally well to the Egyptian and North African ض which is described next. The statement should be understood, rather, as a phonetic description of the ض, and "ظ" should be taken as a phonetic symbol equivalent to [ḏ̣]; i.e., they make ض into [ḏ̣].

[19]According to Neuvonen (1941:309), *alcalde* is the third most common Arabic loanword in the thirteenth century Spanish documents, occurring 1038 times in a sample of 4.4 million words; *arraual* is in the top thirty. *Albayalde*, of course, is much rarer.

VI.
Evidence from Loanwords for Lateral ض in Arabic (II)

ARABIC LOANWORDS IN THE MALAY ARCHIPELAGO (MALAY, MINDANAO, AND SULU)

The first scholar to adduce Arabic loanwords in Malay and the Moro dialects of the Philippines as evidence for the lateral hypothesis was Karl Vollers (1892:145fn):

> I am much indebted to Dr. Rost (India Office Library, London) for the suggestion that in the Malay language the ض of Arabic words is transliterated *dl*, or *l*, and on the Philippine Island Mindanáo by *l* only.

Yushmanov included Malay *kadli* "judge" ‹ *qāḍī* (cf. Spanish *alcalde*), in his summary of the case for lateral ض (1926:42), but Cantineau conspicuously avoided any mention of Malay in his discussions of the lateral hypothesis, despite his acknowledged reliance upon Yushmanov's work. Cantineau [1941] 1960:56, for example, passes directly from a discussion of the Arabic loanwords in Spanish to Landberg's report[1] of a lateral realization of ض in parts of South Arabia.

The reason for this omission is no doubt to be sought in another of Cantineau's sources -- an article by Colin (1930a) which theorizes that Arabic words in Malay like *rela* "consent"[2] ‹ *riḍā(?)* and *lohor*[3] "noon" ‹ *ẓuhr* must have been transmitted by traders from South Arabia. This is a plausible theory, for strong commercial ties existed between South Arabia and Sumatra in the Middle Ages, as we know from the writings of Chau Ju-Kua (Hirth and Rockhill 1911:121,195) and other contemporary authors. Cantineau must have been convinced of the South Arabian origin of the Arabic loanwords cited by Colin and decided that Landberg's description of the South Arabian ض made them redundant. He may not have realized just how redundant they are, for Colin's reference to "traders" ("négociants") suggests that *rela* and *lohor* have been a part of the Malay lexicon since the Middle Ages -- an unlikely assumption, as an examination of early Malay dictionaries reveals. *Rela* (also pronounced *redla* according to Hendershot and Shellabear 1945 s.v.) appears in Marsden's dictionary (1812) as *ridlā*, but is not to be found anywhere in Bowrey 1701, Haex 1693, Houtman [1603?[4]] 1680, or Neck 1601 in spite of the fact that all of these independently composed[5] dictionaries (except Neck 1601) are fairly large and full of Arabic loanwords. *Lohor* does not appear in any of these dictionaries, nor does it appear in the later dictionary by Crawfurd (1852).

The same picture emerges from a study of the other Arabic loanwords with (*d*)*l* for ض - ظ found in recent dictionaries like Winstedt 1962 (=W)[6] and Hendershot and Shellabear 1945 (=H). In the following list, each word is followed by the date of the earliest dictionary (of the eight mentioned above) in which it appears, together with its spelling in that dictionary:

rialat(W) "self-mortification" ‹*riyāḍat* (1962)
melarat(W) "loss, injury" ‹ *maḍarrat* (1812; *medlerat*)
dloha(H), *loha*(H) "forenoon" ‹*ḍuḥā* (1945)
hafal(W), *hapal*(WH), *apal*(H) "memorize" ‹*ḥafaẓa* (1852; *Hafǐl*)
apalkan (H) "memorize" ‹*ḥafaẓa + kan* (1852; *Hafǐlkân*)
lalim(H), *dlalim*(W) "tyrannical" ‹*ẓālim* (1812; *tlālim*)
dlaʔif(H), *laʔif*(H) "weak" ‹*ḍaʕīf* (1812; *dlàīf*)
dlamma (H), *lammah* (H) "vowel points corresponding to *o* and *u*" ‹*ḍamma* (1812; *dlammah*)
dlarurat(W) "compulsion" ‹*ḍarūrat* (1812; *dlarūrat*)
dlil(W) "shadow" ‹*ẓill* (1812; *tlil*)
lahir(WH), *dlahir*(W) "to be born" ‹*ẓāhir* (1812; *tlāhir*)
lafal(W) "correct pronunciation of Qurʔan; word" ‹*lafẓ* (1812; *lefetl*)
hadlir(H), *halir*(H) "present, prepared" ‹*ḥāḍir* (1812; *hādlir*, *hadler*)
hadlerat(H) "royal presence" ‹*ḥaḍrat* (1812; *hadlirat*)

The only one of these examples which may appear in a pre-nineteenth century dictionary is *lalim* "tyrannical" if it is identical with Bowrey's "*Lalim*, to Pervert the Sence of words, Perversion"; however, the definition given by Bowrey makes the identification uncertain.

Thus, one gets the impression that the rendering of ض - ظ with (*d*)*l* is a recent innovation in Malay. This impression is reinforced by the appearance of several loanwords with *d* for ض in the earliest dictionaries. Significantly, one of them -- *hadir*(*kan*) "prepare" -- represents the same Arabic original as *hadlir* "present, prepared" in the list above. This loanword is attested in Bowrey 1701 (*Hādir*, Prepare, Make ready; *Hādirawn*, Preparation; *Hādircan̲*, to Prepare), Haex 1631 (*Hadir. Paratus, veluti cibos apparare*[7]), and Houtman [1603?] 1680 (*toerusten/gereet maken*[8]/*hadirken*). A second loanword with *d* for ض -- *feduli* (Winstedt 1962 s.v.) ‹ *fuḍūlī* "meddlesome" and *fuḍūl* "kindnesses?"[9] -- is attested in Bowrey 1701 (*Fādoolee*, to Meddle, Concern, Regard, Observe, Visit) and Haex 1631 (*Fadouli. Asserere, tutari, alicui ben facere*[10]). Lastly, the name of the ninth month of the Islamic calendar is given by Bowrey (in an appendix) as *Ramasàn* or *Ramadán*.

There is another fact which reinforces our initial impression even more strongly: the presence of a large Arab colony (numbering 70,000 in 1955 according to Phillips 1955: 29) in the Malay Archipelago in recent times. A study of this colony carried out in the 1880's for the Dutch government[11] showed that it was composed almost entirely of natives of Ḥaḍramawt (van den Berg 1886:1) who spoke a dialect in which ض "est un *dh* ou *dl*, articulé avec emphase" and ظ "se prononce presque comme le *Dhad*, et l'on le confond souvent avec cette dernière lettre, même dans la langue écrite" (ibid., 239). The study also concluded that the colony probably did not pre-date the beginning of the nineteenth century (ibid., 104).

It appears, then, that the dictionaries give us an accurate picture of the chronology of the loanwords we are studying and that the Malay Archipelago at the beginning of the nineteenth century saw both an influx of Ḥaḍramī Arabs and an influx of Arabic loanwords with (*d*)*l* = ض - ظ. This conclusion is in perfect accord with the judgement of Ronkel (1904:189) that "the Arabic loanwords which are really part of the Malay lexicon do not come from Arabic but rather from one of the two ... literary languages of Indian Islam, principally Indian Persian," since Arabic loanwords in Persian never have (*d*)*l* for ض - ظ .

It should be noted that our discussion up to this point has centered around Arabic loanwords in *modern* Malay -- specifically, loanwords found in Winstedt 1962 or Hendershot and Shellabear 1945. Once we broaden our investigation to include loanwords which appear in the early dictionaries but not in the more recent dictionaries, we discover that our earlier conclusion represents only one part of the total picture and that the rendering of ض with *l* was not totally unknown before the nineteenth century. Two early examples of this rendering have turned up in the course of this investigation: *hil* "menstruation" ‹*ḥayḍ*[12] and *Ramalan* "the month of *Ramaḍān*." The former appears in Bowrey 1701 (*Hill parampoan*, the Monthly courses of Women) and Houtman [1603] 1680 (*maen stondt der vrouwen/hil parampouan*) but appears to be obsolete now, having been replaced by other forms of the same Arabic original (*haidl, haidz*; cp. Indonesian *haid, hail*). The latter appears only in Houtman [1603?] 1680 (p. 77; *Ramalan, Rammaláen*) out of all the Malay dictionaries consulted, but the fact that it occurs in Bahasa Indonesia (Poerwadarminta and Teeuw 1952 s.v.) and Javanese (Pigeaud 1963:25; Ramĕlan) suggests that it may occur in some modern dialects of Malay as well -- either as a survival or as a re-borrowing.

Much less certain are the supposed examples of *l* for ض - ظ in a sixteenth-century Malay translation of an Arabic religious poem published by G. Drewes (1955). The Arabic graphs[13] in question -- *lfẓ* and *ẓāhr* -- are read *lapal* and *lahir*[14] by Drewes (ibid., 43), which is the way they would be read today by some speakers; however, there is absolutely no guarantee that they were read that way in the sixteenth century. We have already seen that some Arabic words have been borrowed three or four times by the Malay language -- each time in a different form. In fact *lfẓ* and *ẓāhr* are cases in point. Even today, the former Arabic graph can be read *lapal, lafal, lafaz,* and *lafat* (perhaps also *lafatl*) and the latter can be read *lahir* and *zahir* (Poerwadarminta and Teeuw 1952 s.v.). Similarly, there is no way of knowing whether *frḍ* "obligation, obligatory" is to be read *pĕrlu, pĕrdu, fardu* or *farat* (ibid., s.v.) in the Trengganu inscription from the fourteenth century, the oldest Malay inscription in the Arabic script which has yet been discovered in Malaya (Paterson 1924; Rauf 1964: 78 and frontispiece). The Arabic orthography of Arabic loanwords in Malay is no guide since, in all periods, writers have tried to conform to the classical spelling. Of course a writer who used a different alphabet would not be bound by Arabic orthographical traditions and it is therefore with great interest that we examine the Malay poem in Old Sumatran characters inscribed on a tombstone dated 1380 (Stutterheim 1936; Marrison 1951). Unfortunately, though it has several Arabic words and even phrases, it has no words containing ض or ظ .

It is clear, then, that the native inscriptions and manuscripts do not and cannot be expected to provide any unequivocal answers about the history of the Arabic loanwords in Malay. Another possibility might be to date the loanwords by their (phonological or morphological) shape. This method, of course, depends upon a knowledge of the linguistic history of the Arabic dialects from which the words were borrowed. Thus, for example, we may assume that words with *l* for ظ were borrowed after the merger of ظ with ض in South Arabia. As it turns out, this criterion is not too helpful, since we have evidence that the above-mentioned merger had already taken place by 1225, when Chau Ju-Kua wrote his treatise on international trade. We learn from this work that "Ju-hiang [frankincense[15]] comes from the three Ta-shi [Arab] countries of Ma-lo-pa [Mirbaṭ, Murbaṭ], Shi-ho [Shiḥr], and Nu-fa [Ẓufār]" (Hirth and Rockhill 1911:195; cf. also pp. 116,121). The commonly accepted identification of Nu-fa with Ẓufār (called Tsu-fa-êrh, Tso-fa-êrh[16] by later geographers[17]) must be considered virtually certain, if only because frankincense was (with one exception) produced nowhere else *but* Ẓufār[18] (van Beek 1964:103-4 and cf. also the description of Dufar and its frankincense industry by Marco Polo, II, 441). The problem of the rendering *n* = ظ was solved long ago, in a brilliant book-review, by Gabriel Ferrand (1925:309):

> ...si, en outre, on se rappelle que les Chinois emploient assez souvent un caractère à *n* initial pour les mots étrangers présentant un *l* à initiale, on peut ainsi poser: chinois *nu-fa* ‹ancien **nu-far* = *lu-far*. L'emphatique arabe ظ *ẓ* sonne quelquefois comme un ض *ḍ* dans la langue parlée de l'Arabie méridionale; les Malais rendent ce phonème graphiquement par un ض qu'ils pronouncent *dl*, et ici apparait la liquide que les Chinois ont pu entendre également et noter par un caractère à *n* initiale. Soit *Ẓufār* ›**Ḍufār* ›**Dlufar* › **Lufar* ›*Nu-far*.

This explanation, which, incidentally, was accepted by Colin (1930:102), provides us with a *terminus ante quem* for the merger of ظ with ض in Ẓufār; however, since the *terminus* pre-dates the spread of Islam in the Malay Archipelago and hence (presumably) also the spread of Arabisms, it is even less useful as a tool for dating than are the inscriptions and manuscripts. We are left, then, with the European dictionaries and our original conclusions: a) the Arabic loanwords in modern Malay with *(d)l* for ض - ظ were borrowed within the last two centuries from the Ḥaḍramī dialect spoken in the Malay Archipelago's Arab colony; b) earlier contacts between Malay and the Arabic dialects of South Arabia left a few traces in seventeenth century dictionaries in the form of loanwords with *l* for ض which are today largely obsolete.

Turning now to the second half of Vollers' footnote, concerning the Philippine Island Mindanao, we find that this evidence has been completely ignored by later scholars, perhaps because the vagueness of the reference makes it difficult to substantiate. Vollers' informant may have been refering to the Moro (Spanish for "Muslim") dialect spoken by the Magindanao of Southwest Mindanao,[19] which has Arabic loanwords with *l* for ض - ظ:

> *lad* "the letter *ḍād*" (Porter 1903:73)
> *la* "the letter *ẓā?* (ظ)" (loc. cit.)
> *Ramedlan, Ramadlan* "the month of *Ramaḍān*" (Juanmarti 1893 s.v.)
> *lapal* "word" (loc. cit.) ‹*lafẓ*

The same is true of the Moro dialect spoken by the Sulu of the nearby Sulu Archipelago:[20]

lād "the letter *ḍād*" (Cameron 1917:20)
lāʔ (alongside *sāʔ*) "the letter *ẓāʔ* (loc. cit.)
Lamalan "the month of *Ramaḍān*" (ibid., 34)
luhul "noon" (ibid., 35) <*ẓuhr*

These loanwords cannot, it seems, be considered independent witnesses to the pronunciation of Arabic ض - ظ since, according to Cameron (1917:131), they were not borrowed directly from Arabic (just as *alcalde* in Old Portuguese and Old Catalan probably did not come directly from Arabic):

> The (modern) Malay element, which came in with Islam [five centuries ago (p.1)] has furnished the terms referring to days of the week, months of the year, religious, governmental, and many abstract terms, social titles, compliments, terms relating to writing and agriculture, and in general those new words required by a people developing along commercial and agricultural lines. Most of the words from non-Philippine languages have come through Malay.

Nevertheless, they may some day turn out to be useful in separating the older stratum of Arabic loanwords in Malay from the more recent borrowings, if it can be established that Cameron's dating of the Malay loanwords in the Moro dialects is accurate.

[1]See above, chapter ii.

[2]Colin translates "satisfaction" but most dictionaries translate "consent, approve, willing."

[3]The *l* in this word represents classical ظ rather than classical ض but this does not mean that ظ was also a lateral. It simply means that in the Arabic dialect from which *lohor* was borrowed, ظ and ض were merged, as they are in every modern Arabic dialect (ibid., 92).

[4]Although the book is dated 1680, the card catalogue of the New York Public Library gives the date of Houtman's death as 1627 and mentions another book by him called *Spraek ende Woorboeck in de Maleysche ende Madagarskarsche talen,* Amstelredam 1603. There seems to be some connection between this book and the one I used, since the latter, in explaining the Islamic calendar on page 77, talks about the years 1600, 1601 and 1602.

[5]Another dictionary, Howison 1801, turned out to be dependent upon Bowrey 1701, and it has therefore been excluded from the discussion.

[6]I have avoided, wherever possible, citing examples of *dl* for ض from Winstedt 1962, since this dictionary uses *dl* as a conventional Romanization of ض (but not ظ, which is written *tl*) in any Malay word, whether or not ض is actually pronounced [dl] in that word by Malays of non-Arabic origin. The method adopted by Hendershot and Shellabear (1945:14) is much better suited to our needs:

> "Malay lexicographers have usually romanized words of foreign origin in harmony with the spelling of the language from which such words are derived rather than with the way in which they are pronounced by Malays.

This plan of having a different system for romanizing foreign words ... has been avoided as far as possible in this work. Such words will be found spelled according to the Malay pronunciation."

[7]Prepared, as, to prepare food.

[8]Prepare/make ready.

[9]*Fuḍūl* is one of the plurals of *faḍl*, but the plural generally used for the *faḍl* which means "(act of) kindness" is *ʔafḍāl*.

[10]Assert, observe, do good to someone.

[11]Cf. also van der Meulen and von Wissman [1932] 1964, commissioned by the Dutch government half a century later.

[12]The change *ay* › *i* is also reflected in *salamat-alicum* ‹ *salāmat ʕalaykum* (Houtman [1603?] 1680 s.v. *vaert-vel*). Note that Hausa *hayla* "menstruation" and Somali *hāyl* "*id*." represent the same Arabic original.

[13]Malay has of course been written with the Arabic alphabet since the conversion of the Malays to Islam.

[14]Cf. *lafal* and *lahir* in the list at the beginning of this chapter.

[15]Literally, "milk-incense;" cf. Arabic *lubān* "frankincense" from the same root as *laban* "milk." Ju-hiang is quite possibly a loan translation.

[16]These spellings may reproduce the name Ẓufār as it sounded in a dialect which did not have lateral ظ; cf. Marco Polo's *Dufar* and Barbosa's *Dofar* (Pelliot 1903:637).

[17]Ma Huan (c. 1430) and Fei Sin (1436). For references, cf. Pelliot 1963:637.

[18]I.e., the *region* which is today known as Ẓufār and which contains the modern village of Mirbaṭ or Murbaṭ (-- the city of Shiḥr is 400 miles to the west, outside of the frankincense producing region but no doubt one of the ports from which frankincense was exported). Chau Ju-Kua and Marco Polo were referring to the medieval *city* of Ẓufār (cf. Guest 1935 for its history) which gave its name to the region and then disappeared.

[19]No doubt the Lanao of Central Mindanao also have such loanwords, but I was unable to obtain Charles Elliot's *A Vocabulary and Phrase Book of the Lanao Moro Dialect*, Manila 1913, or any other description of their dialect.

[20]This area has been in the news in recent years as the center of a Moslem insurrection against the Philippine government.

VII.
Evidence from Loanwords for Lateral ض in Arabic (III)

ARABIC LOANWORDS IN WEST AFRICA (CENTRAL SUDAN: HAUSA, SONGHAY, KANEMBU, KANURI, TEDA, DAZA; WEST SUDAN: DYULA, MANDINKE, TEMNE, WOLOF, FULA, ẒNAGA) AND NORTH AFRICA (BENI-SNOUS, KABYLE)

The first scholar to adduce Arabic loanwords in an African language as evidence for lateral ض was N.V. Yushmanov (1926:43). The language was Hausa, the *lingua franca* of much of West Africa, and the evidence was the *l* = ض rendering which we have encountered so many times. Yushmanov did not give examples, but twenty years later Greenberg made a study of the Arabic loanwords in Hausa, in which he gave two examples of this rendering (1947:88):

> *ʔalká·lí* "judge" < *ʔal-qāḍī*
> *háyla* "menstruation" < *ḥayḍa*

Other examples appear scattered throughout the literature:

> *lódi* "the letter *ḍād*" (Krause 1884:38)
> *alwal(l)a* "ablution" < *ʔal-waḍāʔa* (Robinson 1899 s.v.)
> *lullo* "purification" < *l-wuḍūʔ* (loc. cit.)
> *fululuwa* "exaggerated, superfluous" < *fuḍūl* (loc. cit.)
> *liyafa* "hospitality" < *ḍiyāfa* (Bargery 1934 s.v.)[1]
> *lahiya, layya* "the Moslem festival of the 10th day of Muharram [=the Feast of Immolation]" < *ḍaḥiyya* "immolation" (loc. cit. and Delafosse 1955 s.v. *lahiya*)
> *Ramalan* "the month of Ramaḍān" (Dianoux 1962-3:610)
> *laʔīfi* "sexually impotent man" < *ḍaʕīf* (Abraham 1962b s.v.)
> *lamīri* "personal pronoun" < *ḍamīr* (loc. cit.)
> *larūra* "necessity" < *ḍarūra* (loc. cit.)
> *liddi* "opposite" < *ḍidd* (Hiskett 1965:25)
> *larli* "country" < *l-ʔarḍ* (Lacroix 1967[2]:197)

The only other study of Arabic loanwords in an African language which has hitherto appeared in the Semitist literature is a paper given by Dianoux (1962-3) at the Twenty-fifth International Congress of Orientalists in 1960 containing three examples of the *l* = ض rendering in Songhay (spoken in Mali, Niger, Upper Volta, Dahomey and Nigeria):

> *alwala* "faire les ablutions" (verb) < *ʔal-waḍāʔa* "the ablutions" (noun)
> *alkali* "le juge" < *ʔal-qāḍī*
> *alfalilla* "prière surerogative" < *ʔal-fāḍila*

However, other studies have been available in African language journals and grammars. Gouilly's list (1952:216) of Arabic loanwords in West African languages includes *alkali* "juge" in Dyula (a dialect of Mandinke on the Atlantic coast of Senegal) and *alikali* "chef du territoire de Poto-Lokko" in Temne (Sierra Leone). Mouradian's study (1940:278) of Arabic loanwords in Wolof, today a close neighbor of Dyula but originally spoken in Mauritanian Adrar (Trimingham 1962:13,164), gives *ḥali* (for *ḳali*?) as a borrowing of Arabic *qāḍī*. The same Arabic word appears as *ʔalkāli* or *ʔalgali* "judge" (Labouret 1952: 248; Lacroix 1967:191) in Fula (spoken almost everywhere in West Africa; cf. Dunstan 1969:57), as *al'kāli* "magistrat, juge, cadi, chef de police, agent de police" in Mandinke (Delafosse 1955 s.v.), and as *ləgáḷì* "judge" (Lukas 1937: 221) in Kanuri (spoken west of Lake Chad in the Bornu Province of Nigeria).

Fula has other examples as well. Krause (1884:30) reports that the letter *ḍād* is called *vā́di* (with *v* perhaps rendering velarized *l*) or *lā́di*. A search through two Fula dictionaries (Taylor 1932 and Labouret 1955) turned up the following additional examples:

> *lāfa* "be in construct state, annex, join to" < *ʔaḍāfa* (verb) or *ʔiḍāfa* (verbal noun)
> *lamēri, lamīri* "personal (or impersonal) pronoun; conscience" < *ḍamīr*
> *liddi* "opposite" < *ḍidd*
> *luha* "forenoon" < *ḍuḥā*
> *mulāria* "the present tense" < *muḍāriʕ*
> *farilla* "dîme Coranique" < *farīḍa* "religious duty" (Labouret 1955 s.v. *dîme*)

Examples from Mandinke (Delafosse 1955 s.v.) include (in addition to *al'kali*):

> *Ramalāna* "mois de Ramaḍān"
> *lahiya* "mouton offert en sacrifice" < *ḍaḥiyya*
> *sòlātuwalua* "prière de la matinée" < *ṣalātu aḍ-ḍuḥā*

The Arabic loanwords in the language of the Káidi-Kanembú

(in Kanem, east of Lake Chad) have been treated by Lukas (1931:22) and include one example of *l* for ض: *wo̱ló̱nī́*, *wo̱lo̱ī̂* "to wash oneself (before prayer)" < *wuḍūʔ*. Finally, the Kanuri language has (in addition to *ləgáḻì*, mentioned above):

> *armalán* "the month of *Ramaḍān*" (Lukas 1937:215)
> *wólò* "the religious ablutions" (ibid., 248) <*wuḍūʔ*
> *yílla* "menstruation" (ibid., 250) <*ḥayḍ*

and the related dialects of Teda and Daza have *lehille*, *lefille* "silver" <*l-fiḍḍa* (Greenberg 1960:212; cf. perhaps Kanuri *ḻifillā*).

It is remarkable that, *pace* Greenberg,[3] no genuine examples of *l* for ظ have turned up in any of the languages of West Africa -- a fact which sharply distinguishes them from the languages of the Malay Archipelago. Thus, the Hausa name of the letter ظ is not *lā* as in Magindanao and Sulu, but *s̄ádi* (contrast the Hausa name of the letter ض above); and in Fūla, ض is called *vá̄di* or *lá̄di*, while ظ is called *s̱ódi* (Krause 1884:30,38). This fact should be of great interest to historians of the Arabic language once the words in question have been traced back to their dialectal source, especially if that source turns out to be one of the (South Arabian) dialects in which ظ later turns up as a lateral (i.e., merged with ض).

CHRONOLOGY OF THE LOANWORDS

The problems we encountered in dating the Arabic loanwords in Spanish and Malay are mild in comparison with the problems we encounter here. Arab authors tell us that the spread of Islam among the black peoples of West Africa began early in the eleventh century (Trimingham 1962:28, Gouilly 1952:47), but there are no native documents from this early period in which we could look for Arabic loanwords; and when the native chronicles finally begin, in the sixteenth century (Trimingham 1962:5), they are in Arabic and therefore even less useful for our purposes than the Malay documents were. The latter, since they are written in a language other than Arabic, at least reveal to us the *identity* of the early Arabic loanwords, even if, being written in the Arabic script, they do not reveal their phonetic shape; the former, since they are in Arabic, can naturally tell us nothing about Arabic loanwords.

In the absence of evidence on the loanwords themselves, we might adduce evidence on the diffusion of Islam. The date of islamization of each people could be taken as a *terminus post quem* for the Arabic loanwords in its language. But these dates would be of dubious value for the history of Arabic, since, as we shall see shortly, many of the Arabic loanwords we have examined did not come directly from Arabic.

SOURCE OF THE LOANWORDS

The first scholar to deal with this question was Greenberg (1947). Greenberg posited a North African origin for the *older* Arabic loanwords in Hausa, and in view of the geographical (not to mention historical and linguistic) facts, it is difficult to imagine any alternative.[4] Indeed, the present writer would go further than Greenberg and claim that even the later loanwords, for which Greenberg posited a bookish origin, could not have assumed phonetic shape without a reading tradition, which once again must have been ultimately of North African origin. (I say "ultimately" because Greenberg (1960) and Hiskett (1965) have shown that this reading tradition and/or the loanwords did not come to the Hausa directly from North Africa but rather by way of other West African peoples).[5] Hiskett's theory (1965) that all of the Arabic loanwords in Hausa have a bookish origin is naturally subject to the same qualification, namely, that the phonetic shape of loanwords, unlike their phonological shape, cannot have a bookish origin.

It would seem, then, that the Arabic loanwords with *l* for ض spread thoughout West Africa are evidence for the existence of a lateral ض (probably an approximant rather than a fricative)[6] in some North African reading tradition or colloquial. Further evidence pointing in the same direction comes from the ض-isogloss tradition discussed in chapter ii and repeated here for convenience:

> The Master (ʕUmar?) used to say: It is the *ḍād* of the westerners which is the true *ḍād* -- the *ḍād* of the easterners is an emphatic *l*. Sheikh ʕĪd differed with him and said: It is the *ḍād* of the easterners which is the true *ḍād*. The consensus of the scholars favors this latter opinion.

In utilizing this tradition, it is important to realize that the two conflicting views presented are really two conflicting versions of *one* tradition -- otherwise one may fail to see that the view of Sheikh ʕĪd is not presented in its entirety. Sheikh ʕĪd holds that it was the easterners who had the genuine ض *and conversely* that the *l*-like ض was the property of the westerners (i.e.the North Africans excluding the Egyptians). Sheikh ʕĪd's version, which was the one accepted by native scholars and which is really the only logical one (since the grammarians who set the standards in the first place were easterners with little interest in the North

African dialects), *seems* to confirm the existence of a lateral approximant ض in some North African reading-tradition or colloquial. And yet, several questions remain. Why is there no trace of this lateral ض today? Why does Ibn Jinnī, whose dialect survey of the various realizations of ض includes North Africa,[7] know nothing of this lateral ض? Worst of all, why don't the many Arabic loanwords in the Berber dialects of North Africa reflect this lateral ض? The dialect of the Beni-Snous (Destaing 1914 s.v.), for example, has *ḷûḍů* "ablutions" (cp. Hausa *lullo*), *ḍḍîfeθ* "hôte" (cp. Hausa *liyafa* "hospitality") and *eḍʕāf* "faible" (cp. Hausa *laʔīfi* "weak") but no examples of *ḷ* for ض. A search through a dictionary of the dialect of Kabyle (Ministère de la Guerre 1844) in Algeria was likewise fruitless.

It appears, then, that the lateral North African ض, assuming that it actually existed, was not nearly as widespread as the present-day distribution of the *l* = ض rendering in the Sudan leads us to believe, and that we will not get far by searching at random through the dictionaries of the various Berber dialects. Let us, instead, focus our attention on the dialect of the first Muslim missionaries to the blacks of West Africa.

Historians tell us that the islamization of West Africa is due in large part to the efforts of the Almoravids (*ʔal-murābiṭūn*). Gouilly (1952:47), for example, writes that "l'islamization ne commence en effet dans ces régions qu'avec les Almoravides." The Almoravids were not an ethnic group but rather members of a militant Islamic movement founded in the eleventh century in Mauritania by ʕAbd Allāh ibn Yāsīn. They were recruited almost entirely from among the Ṣanhāja Berbers, in particular the Lamtūna tribe of Mauritanian Adrār (Gouilly 1952:48, Trimingham 1962:23). The first goal of these Berber warriors was to convert their own people by means of persuasion and *jihād*. The movement then turned its attention to Morocco and Spain, and conquered both under the leadership of Yūsuf ibn Tāshufīn (1061-1106). At the same time, Abū Bakr ibn ʕUmar, after losing control of the movement to Ibn Tāshufīn, went back south to wage holy war against the blacks of the Sudan until the powerful black state of Gāna was subjugated. As a result, "the Soninke of Gāna were compelled to adopt Islam and they not only did so *en masse* but began to spread it amongst the many peoples over whom they still ruled. ...Its acceptance by the peoples of the Sāhil and Māsina is due primarily to their efforts. Their traders converted and blended with the commercial and industrious Mande Dyula who carried it to the edge of the equatorial forest" (Trimingham 1962:30-1). About a century and a half later, these same Mande Dyula (called Wangāra by the Kano Chronicle) brought Islam to the Hausa city-states (ibid., 32, 54fn).

It is clear, then, that the Ṣahāja Berbers played a decisive role in the islamization of West Africa through the Almoravid movement -- especially its southern branch under Abū Bakr. But when we examine the Arabic loanwords in the Berber dialect of their modern descendants -- the Ẓnāga (= Ṣanhāja) of Mauritania -- we find no trace of a lateral ض. According to Basset's treatment (1909:17) of the Arabic loanwords in Ẓnāga:

> Le <u>dh</u> [ض] se maintient: *tabiodh* "plume de la flèche, ar. باض Par affaiblissement, il peut devenir un *d'*: *etchfarad'* "obligation" de l'ar. الفرض

A search through Nicolas 1953 turned up three undoubtedly old loanwords with ḍ for ض:

> *əǰwăḍă* "ablutions" (p. 127) ‹ *ʔal-waḍāʔa*
> *əčfarăḍă* "obligation" (loc. cit.) ‹ *ʔal-farḍ*
> *uḍḍăṭ* "the letter *ḍād*" (p. 117)

but no loanwords with *l* for ض. Nor does it do any good to point out that Arabic *l* is rendered by ǰ or its voiceless counterpart, č, in these and in many other loanwords due to a Ẓnāga sound-change *l* › ǰ (Nicolas 1953:24), for there are no examples of ǰ or č for ض either.

The literature on the Arabic dialect of Mauritania has a little more to offer, but not much. Cohen (1963:12) reports that the merger product of ض and ظ is a voiced emphatic interdental fricative in Mauritania today but adds the following footnote:

> Il faut signaler l'existence en Mauritanie d'une tradition tendant à réaliser le ض comme une latérale emphatique. Telle que nous avons pu l'entendre, elle répond parfaitement à la description qu'en donnait Cheikh Sidia au début de XXe siècle: l'extrême bord de la langue touche les molaires "sans toucher aux dents de devant. Le milieu de la langue doit venir s'appliquer au milieu [des incisives de la mâchoire supérieure]..."

All of the hedging (e.g., "tendant," "telle que nous avons pu l'entendre") makes one reluctant to rely on this report. The reference to Sheikh Sidia's *Wasīṭ* compounds this reluctance since, according to Colin (1930b:138), that work describes ض as an emphatic د (*dāl*). However, Cohen's report is not isolated. Kamffmeyer (1899:204) has pointed out that "ض vielleicht = *l*" in the word *mārāla*, which the *Polyglotta Africana* (Koelle 1854:149) gives as the word for "sick" in the Arabic dialect of Ádirar. Ádirar is, of course,

Mauritanian Adrār, the old homeland of the Lamtūna tribe mentioned above. Kamffmeyer could have omitted the "perhaps" since there is another example of *l* for ض in the Polyglotta's Ádirar column: *lafáda* pl. *lúfdu* "frog" (Kamffmeyer's #210 = Koelle 1854:141) ‹*ḍafdaʕ*. Of course, this is only one of several different renderings of the Adrār ض in the Polyglotta, including *d, r, ṛ* (=ġ) and *dṣ* (=č). And other sources give *mrīdh* as the word for "sick" in Mauritanian Arabic (Basset 1909:306, Faidherbe 1887:126-7).

It must be admitted that we have not had much success in our attempt to show that the Berber tribes from which the Almoravid warriors were recruited pronounced ض as *l* in reciting the Qurʔān. But not all of the Almoravids were Ṣanhāja Berbers -- some of their leaders, in particular their religious leaders and teachers, were brought in from the outside. We know, for example, that the founder of the movement himself, Ibn Yāsīn, was brought from Morocco by the Ṣanhāja ruler Yaḥyā ibn Ibrāhīm to "teach his semi-pagan tribesmen the true doctrine" (Trimingham 1962:22). Similarly, when the Ṣanhāja chieftain Abū Bakr ibn ʕUmar returned to the desert from Morocco, he brought with him a man who had already established himself as a teacher of theology in the Maghreb: Muḥammad ibn al-Ḥasan al-Ḥaḍramī (Moraes Farias 1967:855). This Almoravid teacher and holy man is mentioned in several medieval works and he is a major figure in the legends and historical traditions of many Mauritanian tribes today. These traditions associate the "Imām al-Ḥaḍramī" with Abū Bakr's battles against the Negroes, and one of them states that he came from Morocco to the Sahara with Abū Bakr "to islamize the Negro and white unbelievers" (loc. cit.). In light of these traditions, Moraes Farias (ibid., 861) believes that the Imām al-Ḥaḍramī "may have been as important as Ibn Yāsīn, as far as religious teaching and proselytism are concerned," especially among the blacks.

The Imām's *nisba* -- al-Ḥaḍramī -- refers of course to his (or his parents') place of origin in South Arabia. A second *nisba* reported by a medieval source (ibid., 855) -- al-Murādī -- refers to a tribe known to have lived in South Arabia (Levi Della Vida 1933). Has the loanword-trail led us back once again to South Arabia and the lateral Ḥaḍramī ض? Naturally it seems fantastic to attribute so many loanwords in so many languages to one man (although, in actual fact, we may be dealing with the diffusion of one reading tradition rather than many loanwords).

On the other hand, we must keep in mind that the Imām al-Ḥaḍramī lived at a turning point in the religious history of West Africa -- a turning point marked by the fall of the Soninke empire of Gāna. He may even have presided over the mass conversions that ensued. These forced conversions, as we have seen, set off a great chain reaction in the Sudan, for the Soninke became missionaries themselves, and their converts in turn converted others (Trimingham 1962:31).

Thus, it is just barely possible that one very active teacher in the right place at the right time could have left his dialectal imprint on a huge number of converts who had known nothing of Arabic before their conversion. Certainly, there is at least one loanword which can be plausibly traced back to him: the omnipresent *ʔal-kāli*. This is by far the most widespread of all the loanwords we have collected with *l* for ض and therefore probably one of the earliest. It may be only a coincidence that, according to both of the extant medieval sources about the Imām al-Ḥaḍramī, his position was that of *qāḍī*, or, as he himself would have pronounced it, *qāḷī*. But it seems more likely that the name of this high religious office, in its present phonetic shape at least, was given to it by one of its first and most famous occupants.

Appendix

During the time when the above chapter was being written, the present writer was unaware of Kampffmeyer's theory (1899: 16) that "nach Centralafrika hin eine Einwanderung von Südarabien her stattgefunden hat, die von dem Einfluthen der Araber in Nordafrika ganz und gar zu trennen ist." This theory, brought to the writer's attention by Prof. Federico Corriente, seems to account for many of the facts discussed in this chapter (especially the abundance of evidence for lateral ض in the Sudan versus the absence of such evidence in North Africa), but more facts are needed before any firm conclusions can be reached.

[1]Bargery did not, however, recognize the Arabic origin of *liyafa*.

[2]I am greatly indebted to Professor Haim Blanc for this reference and for the reference to Gouilly further down on this page.

[3]The one example that was cited by Greenberg (1947:88) -- Hausa *muliddi* "envious person" ‹ *muẓidd* -- does not hold water since no root *ẓdd* occurs in the Arabic dictionaries. Greenberg apparently copied this etymology from Bargery 1934, his acknowledged (Greenberg 1947:9) source, without realizing that Bargery transliterates ض with *ẓ* instead of *ḍ* (cf. *aẓ-ẓuhay* in Bargery 1934 s.v. *layya*). Interestingly enough, he was not as faithful to Bargery's gloss: "a cantankerous person, one with whom it is hard to get on." This translation, given also by Abraham 1962 (s.v.), makes a relationship between *muliddi* and *liddi* "opposite" (‹ *ḍidd*) almost certain. Most of the standard dictionaries do not give *ḍdd* in the fourth form, but Dozy 1967(s.v.) has three references for *muḍidd*, the most pertinent of which is a reference to Alcalá's Vocabulista ([1505] 1928). Alcalá uses Arabic *didd* (‹ *ḍidd*) to render both *porfia en mal* "stubbornness in a bad sense, pig-headedness" and *porfia en bien* "stubbornness in a good sense, perseverence," but the participle *mudĭd, mudidĭn* seems to mean "stubborn" only in the bad sense, for it

renders *porfiado en esta manera* "stubborn in this way" which comes immediately after *porfia en mal*. It is well known that Andalusian Arabic was closely related to the Arabic spoken in Africa, and so there can be no doubt that *muliddi* "cantankerous" = *mudǐd* "stubborn in a bad way" = *muḍidd*.

[4]But cf. the appendix to this chapter.

[5]Cf. also Lacroix 1967:188.

[6]I know of no instance where foreigners have transcribed a fricative-lateral with a simple *l*.

[7]See the beginning of chapter viii.

VIII.
Evidence from Loanwords for Lateral ض in Arabic (IV)

ARABIC LOANWORDS IN EAST AFRICA (GEEZ, GURAGE, HARARI, TIGRE, SWAHILI, SOMALI)

After all the examples of *l* for ض in West Africa, the absence of such examples in East Africa is very striking. Several languages of Ethiopia, both ancient (Geez) and modern (Gurage, Harari, Tigre), have been combed for Arabic loanwords by Leslau (1956a,b,c; 1958)[1] but no examples of *l* for ض have turned up (the usual rendering is with *d*).

The Arabic loanwords in Swahili have been treated many times (e.g., Krumm 1932, Růžička 1953, Wald n.d.; cf. also Snoxall 1938) but, so far as I know, no genuine[2] examples of *l* for ض have been discovered.

The only East African language for which I have found a report of Arabic loanwords with *l* for ض is Somali. Reinisch (1903:12) has a list of twelve examples, including:[3]

> *árli* "country" <*ʔarḍ*
> *hȁyl* "menstruating" <*ḥayḍ* "menstruation"
> *ráalli* "content" <*rāḍī*

Unfortunately, these loanwords have little independent value as evidence for lateral ض in view of the proximity of Somaliland to South Arabia.[4] The same is true of the report, contained in a remarkable mini-dialect survey by the tenth century linguist Ibn Jinnī[5] (*Kitāb al-Tanbīh apud* Al-Jazarī, *Kitāb al-Tamhīd*, 43) that the Zayāliʕ pronounced ض as an emphatic *l*:

> *mina l-ʕarabi man yajʕalu ḍ-ḍāda ẓāʔan muṭlaqan fī jamīʕi kalāmihim...wa-minhum man lā yuwaṣṣiluhā ʔilā muxrajihā bal yuxrijuhā dūnahu mamzūjatan bi-ṭ-ṭāʔi l-muhmalati lā yaqdarūna ʕalā ġayri ḏālika wa-hum ʔakṯaru l-miṣriyyīna wa-baʕḍu ʔahli l-ġarbi wa-minhum man yuxrijuhā lāman mufaxxamatan wa-humu z-zayāliʕ wa-man ḍāhāhum.*

> Some of the Arabs make *ḍād* into *ẓāʔ* unconditionally in all of their utterances...And some of them do not make it at its place of articulation; rather they articulate it elsewhere mixed with *ṭāʔ*, being incapable of doing otherwise. These are the Egyptians and some of the

Westerners. And some of them articulate it as an emphatic *lām*. These are the Zayāliʕ and people like them.

Several scholars[6] have quoted this passage without identifying the Zayāliʕ; Professor Haim Blanc was kind enough to inform me that the Zayāliʕ are the people of Zaylaʕ,[7] and that they are discussed at some length by Yāqūt in *Muʕjam al-Buldān* (s.v.). Zaylaʕ was a little state "formed and ruled generally by local dynasties of Somalized Arabs or Somali strongly influenced by Arabic culture" (Cerulli 1927:468). A distinctive Zaylaʕ culture emerged in the course of time as well as a Zaylaʕ dialect "which was a blend of Arabic, Somali and ʕAfar"(Lewis 1960:218). Its port -- one of the chief ports of early Abyssinia -- was still in use in the early part of this century (Grohmann 1933b:1198) and the name Zeila still appears on the map (near the western border of the Somali Republic, facing South Yemen across the Gulf of Aden), but "today Zeila is deserted, an empty place of crumbling mosques and saints' tombs and its ancient population has almost completely disappeared" (Lewis 1960:218).

Could this ancient outpost of Arabia have been the source of the Arabic loanwrods in Somali with *l* for ض? Now that the people of Zaylaʕ have disappeared, and with them their dialect, we may never know.

[1] I wish to thank Professor Haim Blanc for providing me with the references to these articles by Leslau.

[2] By a curious coincidence (if it is indeed a coincidence), F. Stuhlmann, *Beiträge zur Kulturgeschichte von Ostafrika*, Berlin 1909:112, derives *sermala* "Zimmermann" from a non-existent Arabic *sirmaḍḍ*, according to Krumm (1932:27). Like Krumm, I have been unable to find this word in the dictionaries (*Lisān al-ʕArab, Tāj al-ʕArūs*, etc.), but I still feel that there must be some kernel of fact, however small, in Stuhlmann's derivation.

[3] These are three of five examples whose meaning I was able to verify using Abraham 1962a. The other two were *nòol* "alive" and *lába* "two."

[4] One receives the impression from modern travel accounts that natives of the two areas often visit and reside in each other's countries. Thus, Krapf collected his Mehri and Shahari word-lists from native South Arabians living on the Somali coast (Ewald 1846:310), while Phillips describes in several places (1966:164,166,203,230) his contacts with Somalis in Ẓufār.

[5] Bravmann (1934:53) and Bouvat (1913:307) quote the same text -- the former citing Muḥammad Makī as his source, the latter citing Abū Moḥammad Sayyid ʕAlī Al-Nūrī. I am greatly indebted to Professor Haim Blanc for informing me that the text also occurs in Al-Jazarī's *Kitāb al-Tamhīd* and for sending me a photostat of the text.

[6] Cf. the preceding footnote.

[7] *Zayāliʕ* is, of course, the broken plural of *Zaylaʕī*.

IX.
Evidence from *Ruldayu* - *Rḍy* for Lateral ض in Arabic

By far the oldest piece of evidence for lateral ض dates from the reign of the Assyrian king Esarhaddon (680-669 BCE). This king restored to the Arabs of Adumatu (Biblical Dumå(h), the Dūmat al-Jandal of the Arab geographers, modern Jawf) deities which his father, Sennacherib, had taken from them. The deities are actually named in a contemporary royal inscription (Borger 1956:53, Pritchard 1969:291): Atarsamayin (A-tar-sa-ma-a-a-in), Day, Nuḫ̌ay (Nu-ḫ̌a-a-a), Ruldayu (Ru-ul-da/ṭa-a-a-u), Abirillu, Atarquruma.

It was probably obvious from the start that Atarsamayin was ʕAttar (earlier ʕAṯtar) of Heaven, known throughout the Semitic world under the names Ištar and ʕAštart (Astarte). But it was not until 1956 that Jacques Ryckmans (1956:5) and Riekele Borger (1956:53) identified more of them.

According to Ryckmans, Ruldayu and Nuḫ̌ay are the same as Rḍw or Rḍy[1] and Nhy, pre-Islamic deities who are often invoked in Thamudic[2] and Safaitic inscriptions. This identification was strengthened by the fact that Rḍw-Rḍy had already at the beginning of the century (Dussaud 1903:60) been equated with the Rabiʕite and Tayyite deity Ruḍā[3] (Lane [1874] 1968 s.v., Wellhausen 1961:58) whose vowels are nearly identical with those of Ruldayu -- the one difference being the result of a well-known sound change in Arabic, *ayu* › *ā*.

Borger's 1956 rendering of *Ruldayu* as *Ruḍâu* (p. 53, line 11) makes it clear that his discovery of the *Ruldayu* = *Ruḍā*[4] equation was independent of Ryckmans', but it was not until 1957 that he published an article explaining his rendering. He went further than Ryckmans in adducing this equation (1957:10) as a proof that "*ḍ* damals, wenigstens in Nordarabien, lateral ausgesprochen wurde."

Other scholars have been noticeably cautious in reporting this discovery (Fischer 1968:56, Winnett and Reed 1970: 76). It will not be superfluous, therefore, to present further evidence in favor of the equation.

First, there is the rendering of ض with *ld* or *lt*. This is paralleled in the Spanish and Portuguese borrowings from Arabic:[5] *alcalde* ‹ *ʔal-qāḍī* "the judge," *arrabalde* ‹ *ʔar-rabaḍ* "the suburb" and *albayalde* ‹ *ʔal-bayāḍ* "white lead."

It is also paralleled in transcriptions of the MSA *ḍ* made by field workers over the last century. Bent (1900:441), for example, gives *Kaldi* as the word for "judge" in Socotri. The word for "guest" in Mehri is *ldif* (or *dlif*) according to von Maltzan (1873:259). Matthews (1969:23) reports a name ʔAldi in Shaḥari which is obviously identical with the Shahari name Aẓ́i (ẓ́ = ḍ) reported by Thomas (1937:281).[6] It is clear then that *ld* is a perfectly normal way for foreigners to represent ض and that the equation Ruldayu = Rḍy = Ruḍā is phonetically unimpeachable.

In addition to the linguistic evidence, there is epigraphic evidence which strongly supports the Ruldayu = Rḍā (Rḍw) equation. Winnett and Reed (1970:75,80) have published four inscriptions from the Jawf area which invoke Rḍw. The reader will recall that it was from Jawf (ancient Adumatu) that Sennacherib carried off Atarsamayin, Nuhay, Ruldayu, etc.

One of the four inscriptions, found only thirty miles from Jawf (in Sakākah) and written in the Jawfian script, reads (according to Jamme 1972:524) as follows:

hrḍw wnhy wʕtrsmn sʕd nʕl wddy
O Rḍw and Nhy and ʕtrsmn, help Nʕl and Ddy.

In this remarkable text it is clear that ʕtrsmn and Nhy are Assyrian Atarsamayin and Nuḫay. There can be no doubt, then, that the third deity invoked in this inscription, Rḍw, is also one of the deities carried off by Sennacherib from this very area.

[1]"The Safaitic Arabs worshipped the god under two aspects, RḌW and RḌY, possibly the evening and morning stars respectively." (Winnett and Reed 1970:75.) Only Rḍw occurs in Thamudic inscriptions.

[2]More precisely, Thamudic inscriptions of the Najdī type as opposed to Ḥijāzī and Tabukī (Winnett and Reed 1970:76,80).

[3]There are two spellings of this name in Arabic: رضى Rḍy (with historical *y* still preserved in the orthography but not pronounced), corresponding to Ruldayu and Safaitic Rḍy, and رضا Rḍā (with *ā* reflecting original final *-awu*) corresponding to Safaitic Rḍw.

[4]Borger spells the name Ruḍāʔ but I have been unable to find this spelling in the sources.

[5]See above, chapter v. I should point out, however, that the Spanish examples may not be exactly comparable to Ruldayu if *ld* in the former comes from *dl* by metathesis as Martinet (1953:74) supposes. As Martinet points out, *dl* › *ld* is a regular Spanish sound-change. It converted Vulgar Latin sequences like *dul, til, ttul, tul* and *thul* into Old Spanish *ld* instead of the expected *dl* (Malkiel 1950:105,110). Germanic *dil* was also metathesized into *ld* in *Tuelda* ‹ *Theodila* (ibid., 112). Most important of all for Martinet's argument, but overlooked by him, is the treatment of Arabic *ṭl* and *ṭil* in Old Spanish: *arrelde* ‹ *ʔar-raṭl* "a weight -- 4 1/2 grams in modern Egypt" and *balde* ‹ *bāṭil* "(in) vain" (Neuvonen 1941:296, Griffin 1961:57, Malkiel 1950:116).

It is also interesting to note, for the purposes of comparison, that Arabic *l* is on rare occasions also rendered by *ld* in Spanish and Portuguese: Old Spanish *galdifa* (alongside the more common *(al)califa)* ‹ *xalīfa* "Caliph"; and Old Portuguese *cabilda* (alongside *cabila* in Old Portuguese and Old Spanish) ‹ *qabīla* "tribe " (Malkiel 1950:116). This is a very marginal rendering, however.

[6]Both men report that the name is the Shahari equivalent of Arabic ʕAlī. This is comprehensible in light of the Shahari sound-change *l* › ɮ / *i*; see the section entitled "Shahari ɮ" in chapter iii.

X.
Evidence from *Qišda* - *Qilda* for Lateral ش in Arabic

We have already pointed out that the Arabic phoneme which corresponds etymologically to MSA /ɬ/ is ش. Though pronounced [š] today, and [š] or [ç] in the standard Arabic of Sībawaihi's day[1], there is evidence that at an earlier period (or in a different dialect) Arabic ش was a fricative-lateral.

The evidence comes from a pair of doublets reported in *Lisān al-ʕArab* s.v.*qilda* on the authority of the ninth-century grammarian Al-Kisāʔī:

> *yuqālu li-tufli s-samni l-qildatu wa-l-qišdatu wa-l-kudādah.*
>
> The sediment of clarified butter is called *qilda* or *qišda* or *kudāda*.

Brockelmann included these doublets in his *Grundriss* (1908: 235) but it was not until Cantineau's masterful *Cours* ([1941] 1960:63) that the doublets were adduced in support of the lateral hypothesis.[2] The doublets were of crucial importance for Cantineau's argument since he had no other evidence for the existence of a voiceless fricative-lateral in Arabic, or, for that matter, any other Semitic sub-group besides MSA. Strangely enough, in spite of the crucial importance of this evidence, he failed to exploit it fully.

As an isolated phenomenon, a pair of doublets like *qišda* - *qilda* may be interpreted in many ways, not all of which strengthen the lateral hypothesis. But taken together with two other pairs of doublets (one of which is cited by Cantineau in another connection), it provides compelling evidence for the existence of a lateral ش at some undetermined[3] time in the history of Arabic or even Pre-Arabic:

> *ʔiḍṭajaʕa* - *ʔilṭajaʕa*[4] "he lay down (on his side)"
> *jaḍd*[5] - *jald* "hard"

At first glance, *jaḍd* - *jald* seems different from *ʔiḍṭajaʕa* - *ʔilṭajaʕa* and qišda - qilda -- so different in fact that Brockelmann dealt with it separately and Cantineau ignored it completely. In *ʔiḍṭajaʕa* - *ʔilṭajaʕa* the change was clearly *to l*, since the root which appears in all other environments is *ḍjʕ*. The same is true of *qišda - qilda*, where the root of *qišda* appears in the form *qušāda* while the root of *qilda* appears nowhere else. In *jaḍd - jald*, on the other hand the doublet with *l* seems to be original, judging from the synonym *jalīd* "hard" and plural forms like *ʔajlād* and *jilād* and from the lack of such forms corresponding to *jaḍd*. Accordingly, native grammarians and modern scholars present *jaḍd* and *ʔilṭajaʕa* as the products of two different sound-changes.

Actually, the difference is only apparent. Assuming that the direction of the sound-change is ض > *l*, we can easily explain *l* > ض as a hyper-correction. Whether *jaḍd* is only a hyper-correct *spelling* (and is to be read [jald]) or whether it represents a hyper-correct *pronunciation* (and is to be read [jaḍd]) cannot be decided.

Again, at first glance, *ʔiḍṭajaʕa - ʔilṭajaʕa* and *jaḍd - jald* do not seem all that similar to *qišda - qilda*, since they involve ض and *l* rather than ش and *l*. Closer examination, however, reveals that they are tied to *qišda - qilda* by the fact that in all of them the free variation occurs before apical stops.[6] The importance of this similarity cannot be exaggerated, for it is only this link which allows us to explain the more obscure doublets involving ش and *l* in the light of the other, better understood doublets with ض and *l*. I say that the doublets with ض and *l* are better understood because Sībawaihi's description of the ض as a fricative-lateral provides a clear phonetic rationale for the change from ض to *l* before homorganic (i.e. apical) stops: since ض was basically a velarized *l* plus audible friction, a shift from ض to *l* involved only a loss of friction. Such a change is perfectly in order before a homorganic non-fricative.

This is where the link established by the apical stops comes into play; for if loss of friction is the operative mechanism in ض > *l*/_*apical stop*, it is reasonable to suppose that it is the operative mechanism in ش > *l*/_*apical stop* as well. Now, a loss of friction will not ordinarily turn *š* into *l*, but it *will* turn ɬ into *l̥*, which could then easily become voiced to *l* before *d*.

Thus, seen in the context of ض > *l*/_*apical stop*, the sound-change ش > *l*/_*apical stop* becomes a convincing argument for the lateral hypothesis. Cantineau failed to point out that context, thereby leaving the *qišda - qilda* doublets open to many other interpretations.

Cantineau also overlooked crucial evidence from what may be[7] the only living Arabic dialect which has preserved ض as a fricative-lateral, apparently because he was unaware that such a dialect existed.[8] Rhodokanakis' description (1911:82) of the (North) Arabic dialect of Ẓufār contains the following remarkable statement.

> Vor nichtspirantischem Dental (*t*) wird *ḍ* zu *l*, z.B. *elṭöget* 72,10 *yalṭâg* 109,21 (Brockelmann 85aζ, in unserem Falle s.o. wohl nur, indem schon *ḍ* die Zungenstellung von *ṭ*,*t* vorbereitet); meist wird aber *eltöget*, *yaltag* gesprochen.

Here we see precisely the same alternation of ض with *l* that we found in *ʔiḍṭajaʕa* - *ʔilṭajaʕa*, in precisely the same environment. The parallel was also noticed by Rhodokanakis, as we see from his reference to Brockelmann.

Another example of this alternation is found in Socotri where the root *ḍbʕ* occurs unchanged in *šeḍábʕek* "j'ai considéré comme peu nombreux" but alternates with *lbʕ* in *cltábeʕen* "j'ai une petite part" (Růžička 1909:171, Leslau 1938:360). Surprisingly, Socotri has the same alternation of *ḍ* with *l* before *s* and *š* as well:

> **lirhaḍ* "to wash" (literally: "that he may wash") ~ *lirhal-s* "to wash her" (Leslau 1938:30)
> **imeroḍ* "il a soigné" ~ *imerol-s* "il l'a soigné" (loc. cit.)

Socotri also has an alternation of *ś* with *l*, a parallel we would have taken up sooner had it not been for the fact that this alternation apparently takes place only before *s* and *š*:

> **iʔoś* "il pousse" ~ *iʔol-š* "il le pousse" (ibid., 32)
> **iḥeś* "il aide" ~ *iḥel-s* "il l'aide" (loc. cit.)

Leslau gives no examples of *ś* › *l*/_*apical stop* and a search through his *Lexique* reveals only counter-examples: *miśtihi* "triste" (‹ *śéʔe* "se soucier" ibid., 423-4) and *miśtef* "qui a la lèvre fendue" (ibid., 428).

All of these parallels overlooked by Cantineau and *mutatis mutandis* by Leslau give *qišda* - *qilda* great weight as evidence for lateral ش. They also have an interesting by-product: a possible explanation for the Arabic doublets *rakaḍa* - *rakala* "kick (esp. a horse, to make it run)" (Lane [1874] 1968 s.v.) and *markaḍ* - *markal* "the place on a horse's body which the rider kicks to make it run" (loc. cit.).

Let us assume that originally only *rkḍ* existed. When this root was conjugated in the perfect, where half of the suffixes begin with *t*, it was no doubt affected by the sound-change (*ḍ* › *l*/_*apical stop*) which we have discovered. If so, the following paradigm resulted:

rakaltu	*rakaḍnā*
rakalta	*rakaltum*
rakalti	*rakaltunna*
rakaḍa	*rakaḍū*
rakaḍat	*rakaḍna*

Thus *rkl* (which today occurs in all environments) may have been created out of forms like *rakaltu*, etc. On the other hand, it is just as possible (and simpler) to assume that *rakala* originated in one of those dialects which merged *ḍ* with (velarized) *l*.[9]

[1]See chapter iii, fn. 30, and chapter xi, fn. 2.

[2]Both Brockelmann and Cantineau give the meaning of *qišda - qilda* as "a kind of plant full of milky sap" but *Lisān al-ʕArab* has this meaning only for *qišda*. The meaning common to both *qišda* and *qilda* is "sediment of clarified butter."

[3]Al-Kisāʔī's life-time provides, of course, a *terminus ante quem* for the change *qišda › qilda*, but no *terminus post quem* can be given.

[4]This form occurs in a verse by Manẓūr ibn Ḥabba al-Asadī (Cantineau [1941] 1960:55), presumably of the tribe of Asad located near the Euphrates (Caskel 1960:684).

[5]According to Al-Suyūṭī's *Muzhir* (p. 228), this form occurs in the *Dīwān al-Adab* of Al-Fārābī, who may be identical with the famous Turkish philosopher of the same name.

[6]The grammarians who reported these doublets differ from the present writer concerning the conditioning of ض › *l* or *l* › ض, e.g. Sībawaihi (p. 480):

> *wa-miṯlu ḏālika qawlu baʕḍi l-ʕarabi lṭajaʕa fī ḍṭajaʕa ʔabdala l-lāma makāna ḍ-ḍāda karāhiyata ltiqāʔi l-muṭbaqayni fa-ʔabdala makānahā ʔaqraba l-ḥurūfi minhā fī l-muxraji wa-l-ʔinḥirāfi wa-qad buyyina ḏālika.*
> Similar to that is the utterance (*ʔilṭajaʕa* for *ʔiḍṭajaʕa*) of some Arabs who put *lām* in place of *ḍād* out of an aversion for the meeting of two emphatics [i.e., in sequences like *ḍṭ*], replacing *ḍād* with the consonant closest to it in place of articulation and "deviation" [from the median line of the palate] -- this has already been explained.

We need not worry about contradicting Sībawaihi on this point. It is true that Sībawaihi had an intimate acquaintance with the fricative-lateral ض, but he seems to have had no evidence for a sound-change ض › *l*/ _ *emphatic* beyond the word *ʔilṭajaʕa* taken from a poem. As a result, we are justified in wondering whether the supposed aversion of Arabs or Arabic to a sequence of two emphatics is not in reality an *ad hoc* explanation. For Al-Suyūṭī's *ad hoc* explanation of *jaḍd - jald* see chapter xi, fn. 3.

[7]But cf. chapter ii, fn. 32.

[8]Cf. his statement (1960:56): "En dehors de ces deux dialectes [Andalusian Arabic and Daṯīnī Arabic], il ne reste plus de traces de la prononciation latérale du *ḍād*. En conclusion, qu'il soit passé à *ḏ̣* ou à *l*, on peut dire que le *ḍād* a disparu des dialectes arabes modernes."

[9]Cf. chapter ii.

XI.
Evidence from a Ninth-Century Grammarian for Lateral ش in [Pre-] Arabic

We have seen that there is evidence that ش was a lateral at some undetermined time in the history of Arabic or even Pre-Arabic. Additional evidence for lateral ش, this time of a more historically concrete nature, comes from a hitherto neglected statement attributed to Al-Kisāʔī (born c. 805), Sībawaihi's famous contemporary and rival.[1]

Sībawaihi himself knows nothing of a lateral ش. In his "approved" phonetic system, *šīn*, like *jīm* and *yāʔ*, is produced between the middle of the tongue and the middle of the palate[2] (Sībawaihi, p. 453) -- not between the edge of the tongue and the corresponding adjacent teeth as in the case of *ḍād* and *lām*. Sībawaihi also reports an approved voiced variant (the *šīn* which is like *jīm*, p. 452) but no lateral variant, approved or unapproved. It is important to realize, however, that this omission does not in any way damage the credibility of the tradition we are about to cite, since what the tradition reports is a dialectal pronunciation and Sībawaihi was not particularly interested in the Arab dialects (Rabin 1951: 7).

The tradition in question, reported by Kofler (1940:92) from *Tāj al-ʕArūs* (s.v. *muḍṭ*), is in the form of a commentary on the word *muḍṭ*:

> *Qāla l-Kisāʔī: hiya luġatun li-rabīʕata wa-l-yamani yajʕalūna š-šīna ḍādan bayna š-šīni wa-ḍ-ḍādi ġayra xāliṣatin, ʔay laysat bi-ḍādin ṣaḥīḥatin wa-lā šīnin ṣaḥīḥatin; wa-yaqūlūna ʔayḍani ḍṭari lī miṯla štari lī.*
>
> Al-Kisāʔī said: It is a dialectal variant of Rabīʕah and the Yemen(ites) who make *šīn* into a *ḍād* which is between *šīn* and *ḍād* (and is) impure, i.e. neither a real *ḍād* nor a real *šīn*; they also say *ʔiḍṭari lī* = *ʔištari lī* "buy for me."

Now, statements like *yajʕalūna š-šīna ḍādan* "they make *šīn* into *ḍād*" in medieval works on Arabic grammar cannot invariably be accepted at face value, for, though they sound like general rules, based on empirical data which the author has simply neglected to report, they can at times be *ad hoc* rules (Blanc 1967a:299) possessing no more empirical value than the doublet they were made up to explain.[3]

This is evidently not true of our passage, however, for it goes beyond what anyone could reasonably have inferred from the *muḍṭ* - *mušṭ* doublets. One cannot help but notice that the author of this passage was trying his best to describe a phone which he had heard with his own ears -- a phone which did not exist in standard Arabic but which was close to ض. That phone can only have been [ɬ], as I shall now try to show.

We know that ض was 1) emphatic, 2) voiced, 3) fricative, 4) lateral in Al-Kisāʔī's time from the description of his contemporary, Sībawaihi. If the Rabīʕite and Yemenite ش sounded to Al-Kisāʔī like an "impure" ض, it must have lacked one or two of these features -- but not just any one or two. It cannot have lacked the lateral feature for, if it had, Al-Kisāʔī would have said, "they make *ḍād* into *ẓāʔ*."[4] It cannot have lacked the fricative feature, for in that case, he would have said, "they make *ḍād* into *lām mufaxxama* (velarized *lām*)."[5]

The point is that these two features are essential ingredients of the ض and any phone which did not have them both would not be aptly compared to the ض. Voicing and the emphatic feature, on the other hand, are redundant in the ض, for no other Arabic phone is classified as both *rixwa* "fricative" and *min ḥāffati l-lisān* "lateral" -- de-voice or de-emphasize a ض and it will remain recognizable as a ض[6] albeit an "impure" ض. It follows that Al-Kisāʔī must have been reporting a voiceless and/or unemphatic fricative-lateral.

This also follows from the phrase "between *šīn* and *ḍād*." Since both of these are fricatives, anything between them would certainly be a fricative. Combining the other features we get [ž] (emphatic or unemphatic) and [ɬ](emphatic or unemphatic) as possibilities. The former phone is an unlikely choice, however, since it would have been easily and more clearly described as *ʔaš-šīnu l-lati ka-l-jīm* "the *šīn* which is like *jīm*" (Sībawaihi, 452).

The reference to Yemen clinches the point, for Yemen, which classically included Ẓufār and the Mahra country (Grohmann 1933a:1250), is precisely the area where ش is realized [ɬ] until this very day. Of course, it is not *Arabic* ش which is so realized but MSA ش -- or rather the MSA phoneme which corresponds to Arabic ش and is written with the same symbol by MSA speakers (e.g. Carter's informant). But the ancestor of MSA may have been intelligible to Arabs in the ninth century C.E. Even if it wasn't, individual cognates are and were easily recognizable, so the correspondence of MSA ɬ to Arabic š must have been widely known, especially to bilinguals. It is even possible that native speakers of MSA used ɬ in their Arabic as well.

We see, then, that Al-Kisāʔī's description of the Yemenite ش, when interpreted as above, accords with what we know of ش in that area today. If the Mesopotamian tribe of Rabīʕah had the same ش, it follows that the realization of ش as [š] is an innovation, since the common ancestor of MSA and the Rabīʕah dialect must be the ancestor of every Arabic dialect, and in that ancestor ش was realized [ɬ].

[1]Cf. also the passage from Ibn Yaʕīš quoted in chapter iv, fn. 11.

[2]Many students of Sībawaihi have interpreted this description as referring to [ç] (i.e., a sound like Spanish ç, Polish ś or the German "ich-Laut") rather than [š], but two leading experts (Blanc and Blau) are sceptical, see chapter iii, fn. 30. Everyone agrees, however, that since it contains no reference to ḥāffatu l-lisān, it does not describe a lateral. Furthermore, Sībawaihi tells us explicitly that ض has no non-emphatic counterpart, although this is not decisive since voiceless ɬ would not be the exact non-emphatic counterpart of the voiced ض.

[3]A good example is found in Al-Suyūṭī's *Kitāb al-Muzhir* (p. 228):

> *wa-fī dīwāni l-ʔadabi li-l-fārābī rajulun jaḍdun ʔay jaldun, yajʕalūna l-lāma ḍādan maʕa l-jīmi ʔiḏā sakanati l-lām.*
> And in the *Dīwān al-ʔAdab* by Al-Fārābī: *rajul jaḍd*, that is *jald* 'a hard man'; they make *lām* into *ḍād* in the vicinity of *jīm* when the *lām* is not followed by a vowel.

This very detailed rule seems tailored to fit the doublets *jaḍd* - *jald* and no other. It cannot even be considered a general rule about the doublets (i.e. "they habitually pronounce *jald* as *jaḍd*") for, by Al-Suyūṭī's own admission, he found the form *jaḍd* in an older literary work. In conclusion, it is interesting to note that the Arab grammarians had the terminology for distinguishing a general rule from an *ad hoc* one, as we see in the following passage by Ibn Jinnī, quoted by Al-Jazarī in *Kitāb al-Tamhīd* (p. 43): *mina l-ʕarabi man yajʕalu ḍ-ḍāda ẓāʔan muṭlaqan fī jamīʕi kalāmihim* "Some of the Arabs make *ḍād* into *ẓāʔ* unconditionally in all of their utterances."

[4]Cp. Ibn Jinnī's statement quoted in the previous footnote.

[5]Cp. Ibn Jinnī's statement quoted in chapter viii, the anonymous tradition quoted in chapter vii, Al-Suyūṭī's statement quoted in fn. 3 of this chapter, and Sībawaihi's statement quoted in chapter x, fn. 6.

[6]Sībawaihi, who was interested mainly in standard pronunciations approved for Qurʔān readers, says that it "goes out of the language" (p. 455), i.e. ceases to exist.

XII.
Evidence from Arabic ش - ض Doublets for Lateral ش in [Pre-] Arabic

We have already considered two pieces of evidence for lateral ش in (Pre-) Arabic. We now turn to a third piece of evidence for lateral ش which is similar to the first (Al-Kisāʔī's statement that the Rabīʕite ش sounded like an impure ض) in that it depends on a prior demonstration that ض was a lateral, and to the second (*qišda* - *qilda*) in that it consists of doublets. Specifically, we will be examining pairs of ض - ش doublets, collected by Kofler (1940), Rabin (1951), Fischer (1968), and Kurylowicz (1973), for the purpose of showing that, if ض was a lateral, ش must have been one as well.

Kofler's doublets *mušṭ* - *muḍṭ*, have already been discussed. In the light of Al-Kisāʔī's explanation (whether our interpretation of it is right or not) it is questionable whether there ever was such a form as *muḍṭ*. Al-Kisāʔī (or someone else) may simply have written this word with a ض in an attempt to render the Rabīʕite-Yemenite phone which was between ض and ش, even though this phone was etymologically a ش. On the other hand, Al-Kisāʔī may have just been guessing about the origin of this word. If his guess was wrong, and *mušṭ* - *muḍṭ* are genuine doublets, the sound change which produced them was probably ش > ض /_emphatic.[1] This would strongly suggest that ض was the emphatic counterpart of ش at some time in history.

Two more pairs of ض - ش doublets were discovered by Rabin (1951:33): *ʕillawḍ* - *ʕillawš* "jackal" (Ibn Durayd, s.v.) and *nāḍa* - *nāša* "carry" (Našwān s.v.). Both *ʕillawḍ* and *nāḍa* are Yemenite forms, according to Rabin's sources, but we need not be unduly concerned about the possibility that the ض in these words is a rendering of the lateral Yemenite ش, for the simple reason that *ʕillawš* and *nāša* (unlike *mušṭ*) are also given as Yemenite forms. Unless the ض of *nāḍa* and the ش of *nāša* both represent ش as it was realized in two different dialects or as it was transcribed by two different field workers -- which is quite unlikely[2] -- we must assume that it is not ض but ش which represents the voiceless lateral fricative in this pair. The same is true of *ʕillawḍ* - *ʕillawš*. Moreover, only a non-Yemenite would be likely to render the lateral ش with a ض, because only a non-Yemenite would make acoustical similarity the sole criterion for his choice of a rendering. A native South Arabian like Našwān would know that the lateral ش was simply a dialectal form of the standard non-lateral ش and would probably represent it accordingly. On the other hand, it should be kept in mind that, even if these doublets are genuine, they can tell us only about the North Arabic dialects of South Arabia, which may have been subject to South Arabic influence.

Another collection of ض - ش doublets, and a rather extensive one, was published by Fischer (1968:59-60):

šarr "Böses"	*ḍarr* "Schaden, Schädigung"
mašā "(zu Fuss) gehen"	*maḍā* "hindurchgehen, vergehen"
šummaxr "hochmütig"	*ḍummaxr* "hochmütig"
šallat yaduhu "seine Hand möge verdorren, verschwinden"	*ḍalla* "verloren gehen"
bayyaša l-lāhu wajhahu "Gott möge sein Antlitz glänzend machen"	*bayyaḍa* "weiss machen"
xafaš "krankhafte Verengung der Augenlider"	*xafaḍa* "(die Lider) senken"
ġamaš "Schwachsichtigkeit"	*ʔaġmaḍa* "die Augen schliessen, blinzeln"
ḥašara "(zum letzten Gericht) versammeln"	*ḥaḍara* "anwesend sein, ansässig sein"
xašaʕa "demütig sein"	*xaḍaʕa* "demütig sein"
raʕaša "zittern"	*raʕaḍa* "zittern, beben, sich winden"
naġaša "wackeln, sich bewegen"	*naġaḍa* "hin- und herwackeln, unruhig sein"

This is also a collection of uneven quality. The best doublets in the list are naturally those reported by the native lexicons themselves (*šummaxr* - *ḍummaxr*[3]; note also the very distinctive shape and length of the two words) or at least hinted at by them (*bayyaša* - *bayyaḍa*[4]). Most of the word-pairs, however, were matched up by Fischer on the basis of dictionary definitions, and they range from near-perfect synonyms (*xašaʕa* - *xaḍaʕa*) to words whose meanings have been subtly distorted to make them match (*xafaš* - *xafaḍa*[5]).

The largest collection of ض - ش doublets is that of Kurylowicz (1973:28):

bašaka "to cut"	*baḍaka* "to cut off"
ḥašaʔa "to set fire"	*ḥaḍaʔa* "idem"
xašaʕa "to be humble, subservient"	*xaḍaʕa* "idem"
šabiṯa V (*sic*, for *šabaṭa*?) "to sieze"	*ḍabaṯa* (*sic*, for *ḍabaṭa*?) "idem"
šaxaza "to tear out one's eye"	*ḍaxaza* "idem"
šafaza "to kick"	*ḍafaza* "idem"
ġaššā "to cover"	*ġaḍā* "idem"
fašā "to spread"	*faḍā* "to be spacious"
qašaʕa V "to be scattered"	*qaḍaʕa* V "idem"
mašaġa "to chew"	*maḍaġa* "idem"
našifa "to be sucked up"	*naḍafa* "to suck dry (the udder)"
hašama "to break"	*haḍama* "idem"
waššaḥa "to comment a text"	*waḍḍaḥa* "to make clear"

The following ض - ش doublets are rejected by Kurylowicz (loc. cit.) on the grounds that root-final ض and ش "could represent independent 'determinatives' (enlargements of biconsonantal roots)":

bayyaša "render one's face fair"	*bayyaḍa* "idem"

jahaša "flee"	*jahaḍa* IV "make flee; hasten"
ḥaraša II "edge on, instigate"	*ḥaraḍa* II "idem"
qaraša "cut off"	*qaraḍa* "idem"
qaʕaša "bend"	*qaʕaḍa* "idem"
naġaša "be loose, shake"	*naġaḍa* "idem"
jašša "noise"	*jaḍḍa* "idem"

It is very difficult to evaluate this list, because many of the items on it do not appear in standard dictionaries like Wehr 1966 and Lane [1874] 1968. It is a pity that the author did not cite his sources. Suffice it to say that Kurylowicz's use of so many rare and unusual words and his readiness to exploit derivative meanings are danger signals, which lead one to wonder whether he has heeded the admonitions of Kopf (1954) concerning the proper use of the native Arab dictionaries.

Finally, my own independently collected list includes:

ḥarraḍa "goad, prod, incite"	*ḥarraša* "instigate, prod, incite"
qaraḍa "sever, nibble"	*qaraša* "gnash teeth, nibble"
nāqaḍa "contradict, oppose"	*nāqaša* "argue with"
ḍaʕʕafa "double"	*šafaʕa* "double"

It must be admitted that, taken as a group, the doublets we have examined exhibit no regularity, no coherent set of environments pointing to a conditioned sound-change. Nevertheless, there are enough unassailable doublets to justify a claim that ض and ش were phonetically similar -- probably emphatic/unemphatic correlates -- at some time in the Pre-Islamic period. If so, the fact that ض was a lateral would seem to imply that ش was a lateral. But there is one loophole here. It is still possible to hold that ض became a lateral after, or as part of the process by which, ض and ش ceased to be paired -- indeed this is precisely what Fischer holds (cf. also Brockelmann 1908:129).

Fischer believes that ض was realized as an emphatic [ẓ̌]

during the period before it became a lateral, and that his doublets were created during that same period. This solution would certainly make ض and ش phonetically similar (especially since he makes the ancestor of ش an unemphatic ž) and would furthermore, as Fischer himself points out, greatly increase the symmetry of the Proto-Semitic sound-system (PS š would in that case possess voiced and emphatic counterparts, and there would no longer be a gap in the *ḍ-ś-?* triad).

Unfortunately, this solution, though superficially attractive, raises more questions than it answers. If PS *ś* was voiced, why are all of its modern reflexes voiceless? Why, for example, did *ś* merge with *s* in Hebrew and Aramaic rather than *z*? Secondly, if PS *ḍ* was realized [ẓ̌] and PS *ś* was realized [ž], why are these phonemes so extremely unstable in the Semitic languages? -- after all, ž (‹ classical *j*) is not unstable in the modern Arabic dialects. Why should a *ś* realized [ž] be any less stable than its voiceless counterpart *š*?

Even the gain in symmetry turns out to be more of a liability than an asset, once we attempt to explain the asymmetrical treatment of the interdentals in Hebrew and Phoenician (*ṯ › š but *ḏ* › *z*[6]). Why didn't the voiced interdental follow the lead of the voiceless interdental and merge with ž if, as Fischer claims, Proto-Semitic had this phone?[7] As much as the idea of a symmetrical Proto-Semitic system appeals to our esthetic sense, it seems that the simplest explanation for the asymmetry of the above-mentioned mergers is that the sound-system was not symmetrical to begin with.

Finally, Fischer's hypothesis seems to ignore the fact that, while there is as yet no evidence that the lateral realization of ض goes as far back as Proto-Semitic, the occurrence of lateral ض in both Arabic and MSA *does* seem to constitute evidence for a lateral *ḍ* in Proto-South Semitic -- evidence that is corroborated by the transcription *Ruldayu* from the first half of the seventh century BCE. Since it is unlikely that the doublets we have collected, including Fischer's, are older than Proto-South Semitic (if only because most of them have no cognates outside of the South Semitic languages) it follows that they were probably created in a Pre-Arabic dialect with a lateral ض. If so, we have one more reason for believing that Pre-Arabic ش was a lateral.

Appendix

A pair of *ḍ*-s^2 doublets from ESA (*ḍqr*-s^2*qr* "cover") reported by Beeston (1962a:15) could similarly be used to show that ESA s^2 was a lateral. Doublets are apparently to be found in MSA as well (Leslau 1938:30-1; Thomas 1937 passim), but they have no particular value for us since we have direct information about both of the MSA phonemes involved.

[1]The fact that *mušṭ* has a by-form *mušuṭṭ* with the š separated from the ṭ, whereas *muḍṭ* has no by-form, is evidence that the ش is original. Cf. also Akkadian *mušṭu* "comb."

[2]Since Našwān was a Yemenite, there is no reason to doubt that he himself heard and transcribed both forms. And if the ض of *nāḍa* and the ش of *nāša* both represent ش as it was realized in two different dialects, how is it possible that a native South Arabian lexicographer was not aware of the hundreds of other pseudo-doublets to be found by comparing these two dialects.

[3]Cf. *Tāj al-ʕArūs* and *Lisān al-ʕArab* s.v. *šummaxr*.

[4]Cf. *Tāj al-ʕArūs* s.v. *bayyaša*: *bayyaša ḷ-ḷāhu wajhahu wa-sarrajahu bi-l-jīm ʔay bayyaḍahu wa-ḥassanahu* (but cf. also *Lisān al-ʕArab* which has the same definition minus *bayyaḍahu*). It seems that the *bayyaša* which means *bayyaḍa* occurs only in this formula and that the change ḍ › š is conditioned here by the presence of emphatic ḷ. We are reminded of Al-Jazarī's warning (p. 43) that one should be especially careful in pronouncing the ض of *ʔarḍu l-lāhi* "Allah's land" because of the emphatic *lām* which follows. On the other hand, Al-Jazarī gives so many examples with other consonants following that the parallel is less striking than it looks.

[5]Cf. Wehr's definition (1966) of *xafaš* -- "dayblindness, hemeralopia" -- and *xafaḍa* -- "to lower" (i.e., in position, magnitude, loudness, etc.).

[6]I omit the merger ḏ › ṣ since it is not known whether the Pre-Canaanite ḏ merged first with ṣ or with ḍ.

[7]If the question is asked in the opposite direction ("Why didn't ṯ merge with *s*?") an answer is readily available: the pitch of ṯ is closer to that of š than to that of *s*.

XIII.
Evidence from Incompatibility for Lateral ش and ض in Pre-Arabic

The compatibility of PS *ḍ* and *ś* with *l*, as reflected in the lexica of daughter languages like Hebrew and Arabic, has been investigated more than once. Cantineau ([1946] 1960:200), Greenberg (1950:173) and Koskinen (1964:45-7) have all tried their hand at some aspect of this problem.

All of these scholars started with the reasonable assumption that a lateral *ḍ* or *ś* would tend to avoid the company of lateral *l*, just as dental *t* avoids dental *d*, pharyngal *ḥ* avoids pharyngal ʕ, and so on. Unfortunately, most of them failed to use statistical techniques to evaluate the data they had collected, and it is therefore necessary for us to re-examine their conclusions.

We have already[1] discussed Koskinen's claim (loc. cit.) that Hebrew *ś* and *l* are incompatible and pointed out that Koskinen's data do not provide compelling evidence for that claim. Conversely, Cantineau's (no doubt reluctant) admission (loc. cit.), cited approvingly by Fischer (1968:59), that neither *ḍ* nor *š* is incompatible with *l* in Arabic, and his unsuccessful attempt to explain away this difficulty[2] are both rendered entirely superfluous by considerations like the ones that follow.

Greenberg's tables (1950:164-6) show that, of 3775 triliteral Arabic roots, 163 have initial *š*, 108 have medial *š*, and 86 have final *š*, while 229 have initial *l*, 160 have medial *l*, and 249 have final *l*. Based on these data, the number of roots containing both *š* and *l* which we would expect if *š* and *l* were totally lacking in aversion for each other is 163x160/3775 (*šl-*) + 163x249/3775 (*š-l*) + 108x249/3775 (*-šl*) + 229x108/3775 (*lš-*) + 229x86/3775 (*l-š*) + 160x86/3775 (*-lš*) = 40.2. This must be compared with an observed frequency of only 19. The χ^2 formula yields $(21.19735099)^2/40.19735099 + (21.19735099)^2/(357-40.19735099) + (21.19735099)^2/(638-40.19735099) + (21.19735099)^2/(3775-638-357+40.19735099) = 13.5$. This is an extremely high value of χ^2 for one degree of freedom -- so high, in fact, that it is beyond the range of the χ^2 tables consulted by the present writer. It is, thus, almost inconceivable that the difference between the expected number of roots containing *š* with *l* and the observed number is due to chance alone. We conclude that the existence of incompatibility between *š* and *l* is virtually certain.

The figures for *ḍ* and *l*, while less dramatic, are nevertheless quite significant. Greenberg's tables show 75 roots with initial *ḍ*, 68 with medial *ḍ*, and 57 with final *ḍ*. (The figures for *l* are given above.) The number of roots containing *ḍ* and *l* which we would expect if *ḍ* and *l* were totally lacking in aversion for each other is 75x160/3775 (*ḍl-*) + 75x249/3775 (*ḍ-l*) + 68x249/3775 (*-ḍl*) + 229x68/3775 (*lḍ-*) + 229x57/3775 (*l-ḍ*) + 160x57/3775 (*-lḍ*) = 22.6. The observed number is 11. The χ^2 formula yields $(11.60980132)^2/22.60980132 + (11.60980132)^2/(638-22.60980132) + (11.60980132)^2/(200-22.60980132) + (11.60980132)^2/(3775-638-200+22.60980132) = 7.0$. This value of χ^2 corresponds to a probability of less than .01 and is, thus, quite significant. Our conclusion is that we may, for all practical purposes, exclude the possibility that the difference between the expected number of roots containing *ḍ* with *l* and the observed number is due to chance rather than incompatibility.

This conclusion is different from the one reached by Greenberg (1950:173) using the same data. According to Prof. David Segal (personal communication), the main reasons for this discrepancy are the following:

> Greenberg's percentages refer only to a normally distributed variable and only to a two-tailed test. In calculations of incompatibility, one encounters variables which are only approximately normal, so there is some slight imprecision here. Our problem will be two-tailed if we are testing for both affinity and aversion simultaneously, without an a priori assumption as to which form of non-randomness should be present if the process is in fact non-random. If we are testing only for aversion (versus absence of aversion), we can halve Greenberg's probabilities. It must be stressed that, in such problems, the one-tail versus two-tail choice will depend on the exact hypothesis to be tested and the background information of the researcher. The net effect of the above remarks is that Greenberg is slightly conservative in his assignment of significance level.

In conclusion, we might mention an intriguing fact about the incompatibility of *ḍ* and *l* which emerges when we divide the six different permutations of *ḍ* and *l* which are possible within the triliteral root into two groups according to the order in which *ḍ* and *l* appear. The group in which *l* precedes (*lḍ-*, *l-ḍ*, *-lḍ*) shows strong evidence of incompatibility with a χ^2 of 8.7, but the group in which *ḍ* precedes (*ḍl*-, *ḍ-l*, *-dl*), with a χ^2 of only .6, shows none. This difference of χ^2 values, assuming that it actually corresponds to a difference in incompatibility,[3] may some day provide insight into the nature of the processes which created *ḍ* in Pre-Proto-Semitic.

[1]See the section entitled "The Problem" in the introduction to this book.

[2]See the end of chapter iv.

[3]This is impossible to prove however, since (as Prof. Segal reminds me) the χ^2 test, by its very nature, never provides evidence *against* incompatibility but only a *lack* of evidence *for* it.

XIV.
Evidence from Doublets that PS Ḍ and Ś were Phonetically Similar: Semitic Words for "Laugh"

In the preceding chapters, we have presented evidence in support of Cantineau's contention that the lateral realizations of ḍ and ś attested in MSA and (Pre-) Arabic go back to PS. In this chapter and the one that follows, we shall attempt to prove (using doublets, etc.) a weaker claim: that the phonological pairing (i.e. phonetic similarity) of ḍ and ś in MSA and (Pre-) Arabic goes back to PS. If we succeed in proving this weaker claim, then the burden of finding evidence for Cantineau's thesis will be greatly lightened: we will need only to find evidence that one of the PS phonemes in question was a fricative-lateral and the other one will follow automatically.

Hebrew *ṣḥq-śḥq*

This pair of doublets has been discovered and rediscovered by alert students of Hebrew through the ages. Menaḥem ibn Saruq (10th century) gives the roots as synonyms[1] in his *Maḥbereṯ* (s.v.), and Yonah ibn Janāḥ (11th century) in his *Seper ha-Riqmah* (p. 113) uses them to show how "letters interchange" in Hebrew. The dictionaries of Gesenius ([1915] 1962 s.v.) and Koehler (1953 s.v.) call *śḥq* a "Nebenform zu *ṣḥq*," while Bergsträsser (1918:88) labels the roots "Doppelformen." Similar statements are found in Brockelmann 1908 (pp. 238-9), Haupt 1909 (p. 361fn), Nyberg 1952 (p. 23), Kutscher 1961 (p. 104), Moreshet 1968 (passim), Rin 1968 (p. xlv) and Hetzron 1972 (p. 37), just to name a few. And yet, in spite of all the attention which these doublets have received, their potential as evidence for the lateral theory has been noticed only recently (by Diakonoff (1965:22), Hetzron (1972:37), Kurylowicz (1972:29), and the present writer). In the past,[2] the dissimilatory change which created *śḥq* was formulated in terms of Hebrew *ṣ* and *ś*, in spite of the fact that the usual non-emphatic alternant of *ṣ* in Biblical Hebrew is *z*,[3] and the problem inherent in this supposedly ambivalent behavior of Hebrew *ṣ* was almost totally ignored. Several solutions to this problem are possible,[4] but the only convincing one is Ben-Hayyim's observation (1959:15) that all of the examples of *ṣ* which alternate with *z* are derived form PS *ṣ*,[5] while the *ṣ* which alternates with *ś* is the reflex of PS *ḍ*.[6] Naturally, this does not mean that *ḍ* somehow remained distinct from *ṣ* even after merging with it. If, as it seems, one of the doublets was not created until the Biblical period, the single grapheme ‹ *ṣ* › must conceal at least two phonemes -- one of which was the emphatic counterpart of *z* (and the reflex of PS *ṣ*) and the other of which was the emphatic counterpart of *ś* (and the reflex of PS *ḍ*). If, on the other hand, both doublets already existed in PS, as Diakonoff (op. cit.) and Hetzron (op. cit.) believe, we would not have to posit the polyphonous use of ‹ *ṣ* › in early Hebrew. We shall return to this subject at the end of this chapter. Here it suffices to raise the question and to point out the answer, though crucial to an understanding of the development of the Hebrew sound-system, has little bearing on the main point of this chapter.

Hebrew *lʕg*

The startling similarity between this root and *ṣḥq* - *śḥq* was pointed out to the present writer by Mrs. Rachel Bernstein Ebner. The meaning of *lʕg* with the prepositions *lĕ* or *ʕal* is the same as that of *ṣḥq* - *śḥq* with those prepositions, namely, "laugh at." In fact, *lʕg* occurs parallel to, or cojoined with, *ṣḥq* - *śḥq* six times in the Bible. Must we, then, reckon with *three* Hebrew reflexes of PS *ḍḥq* (or *ḍḥk*)? This would still be fewer than the number of Aramaic reflexes of this dissimilation-prone root. Or if *lʕg* originally meant "stutter" (a meaning attested in Aramaic as well as Hebrew), did it acquire the second meaning "laugh at" through contamination with the phonetically similar *ṣḥq* - *śḥq*? Either solution would presuppose a lateral realization for *ḍ* and/or *ś* in Pre-Hebrew.

Geez *šḥq* - Gafat *ṣaqä*, Gurage *daqä*

It has long been recognized that the Geez root for "laugh" -- *šḥq* -- corresponds not to Hebrew *ṣḥq* but rather to Hebrew *śḥq*.[7] Not until recently, however, was it discovered that *ṣḥq* also has an equivalent in Ethiopian Semitic: Gafat *ṣaqä* "laugh" (Leslau 1958:44). One is tempted to write off this form as a late derivation from *saqä* (the expected outcome of *šaḥaqa* in Gafat and the form actually attested in East Gurage and Amharic) as Leslau (1956:27) does, but assimilations of this type, so common in other Semitic languages, are virtually unknown in Ethiopian Semitic.[8] If so, the initial emphatic segment of Gafat *ṣaqä* must represent a survival from a very ancient period.

A second Ethiopian cognate of Hebrew *ṣḥq* has been identified by Hetzron and Habte Mariam (1966:19): Gurage *daqä* (> *daʔä* in Ennemor). According to these scholars, Western Gurage has several examples of *d* for older *ḍ* (and of course older *d*) but "no clear example where *d* in Chaha would stand for PS *ṭ* or *ṣ* except the one for 'hair' which is problematic for many reasons."[9] The *d* of *daqä* is therefore a clear reflex of **ḍ* -- even clearer than the *ṣ* of Gafat *ṣaqä* which "strictly speaking provides evidence for an initial emphatic only."[10]

Based on the above evidence, Hetzron (1972:37) concluded, like Diakonoff (1965:22) before him, that the various words for "laugh" in the Semitic languages must go back to two PS originals:

> One of the interesting isoglosses is the distribution of the survival of two parallel Semitic roots for "to laugh." They are **ṣ́ḥq* and **ḍḥq* with an initial emphatic consonant. Both are attested in Hebrew. Other Semitic languages have only one of them. Arabic has the second one with some modification: **ḍḥk (q > k)*. NE [= North-Ethiopic] has *śḥq*. In the South, the TSE [= Transversal South-Ethiopic] group also has the same root, Amharic and East Gurage *saqä*, Argobba *sähaqa* and Harari *seḥaqa*. The OSE [= Outer South-Ethiopic] group has developments of the other root that starts with an emphatic consonant, Gafat *ṣaqä* and in the Gunnan-Gurage languages *daqä*, in which *d* comes from the deglottalization of *ḍ* in this context (see Hetzron - Habte Mariam 1966, p. 19, n. 6).

As we shall see at the end of this chapter, the PS origin of Hebrew *śḥq* is not as certain as Hetzron assumed; but even so, the PS origin of *Geez šḥq* can still be posited on the basis of the Aramaic evidence which we shall now consider.

Mandaic *ahk, ghk - shq*

To those who are unfamiliar with the strange peregrinations of etymological *ḍ* in Aramaic, these three Mandaic[11] roots will seem completely unrelated (genetically), even though they all mean "laugh" and even interchange in idiomatic expressions.[12] The consonants which fill the R_1 slot could not be more dissimilar phonetically: *ghk* has a voiced velar stop, *shq* has a voiceless dental fricative, and *ahk* has no consonant at all. Even R_3 is not identical in all three roots. Nevertheless, the common origin of these three roots is indisputable, and, in the case of *ahk* and *ghk*, was already recognized by Nöldeke (1875:73fn):

> Diese Wurzel [= ḍhk] findet sich im Mand. nicht bloss als *ghk*...sondern auch in regelmässiger Gestalt als *ʔhk* ...erscheint (das zu erwartende *ʕḥk* müsste ja zu *ʔḥk* werden) ... Eine Sprossform daraus ist erst *hyk* (wie aus [Syriac] *ʔʕf* = [Arabic] *ḍʕf* weiter *ʕāf*, *ʕff* wird). Eine andere aram. Nebenform ist endlich *dḥk*. Man sieht, auf wie verschiedene Weise man sich die unbequemen Laute umformte.

As Nöldeke points out, *ahk* (<*ʕḥk) is the expected outcome of *ḍḥk*, since ʕ (the regular Aramaic reflex of PS *ḍ*) is regularly dissimilated to ʔ or Ø in the vicinity of a second pharyngal (ʕ or ḥ) in the Late Aramaic[13] dialects. (The *unconditional* loss of ʕ in Mandaic (Malone 1971:407, 1973: 161) would seem to be a later development.)[14] Nevertheless, as Nöldeke also recognized (loc. cit.), the appearance of *g* for *ḍ* in *ghk* (or, in many other dialects, *gḥk*) is not entirely unparalleled. Thus, for example, the Arabic cognate of Syriac *gʕīṭā* "oppressed by grief" is *ḍaǧaṭa* "press, compress, oppress, suppress."

The fact that both *gḥk* (the ancestor of *ghk*) and *gʕṭ* contain a pharyngal points once again to dissimilation, but an earlier dissimilation than the one which had produced *ahk*. Our earliest Aramaic documents represent etymological *ḍ* with the sign for *q*, showing that it was a velar or uvular before it wound up as a pharyngal (merged with ʕ). It was presumably at this stage of its development that etymological *ḍ* dissimilated to *g* in the vicinity of pharyngals in Aramaic.

These two dissimilations point up an interesting fact about PS *ḍḥq*.[15] The history of this root is marked by a surprising number of dissimilations, no doubt because it contained two emphatics and a pharyngal -- an unusually high[16] concentration of dissimilation-prone consonants. In several of the daughter-languages we find either the first emphatic or the last emphatic replaced with its non-emphatic counterpart (yielding *śḥq* and *ḍḥk*, respectively).[17] In Aramaic, however, this was not enough, and in the course of time, the second emphatic was also dissimilated.

At the same time, another process was taking place, namely, the mysterious journey of the unmerged *ḍ* from one end of the vocal tract to the other. The various dissimilated reflexes of *ḍ* in Aramaic capture, as if with time-lapse photography, three (or possibly four)[18] stages of the journey:

	alveolar lateral		velar		pharyngal
emphatic	*ḍ*	⟶	q_2	⟶	ʕ
	↓		↓		↓
unemphatic	*ś* (› *s*)		*g*		ʔ(› Ø)

The great phonetic diversity of the reflexes of *ḍ* in the Mandaic roots for "laugh," which at first seemed so troublesome, is seen therefore to be only a reflection of the great phonetic diversity of the various realizations (through time) of *ḍ* itself.

In fact, far from being troublesome, this phonetic diversity now turns out to be of great value; for, whereas it is still within the realm of possibility that Hebrew *śḥq* developed from Hebrew *ṣḥq* rather than from **ḍḥq*, or that Gafat *ṣaq̈ä* developed from an older *saq̈ä*, and consequently that the formation of these doublets shows nothing about the relationship between *ḍ* and *ś*, the common origin of such phonetically dissimilar Mandaic roots as *ahk, ghk,* and *shq* can be demonstrated only by going back to an earlier period in which *ḍ* and *ś* were still unmerged and unshifted. Hetzron's Ethiopian material suggests that this earlier period may be the PS period.

Shahari *źḥk, źḥq*, Mehri *źḥk*,
Harsusi *źḥk, źḥq* - Botahari *śḥq*

One is tempted to claim that we have in these MSA forms (Thomas 1937:306-7) another demonstration of the surprising longevity of the PS doublet-pair reconstructed above. Before making such a claim, however, it is important to see these forms in the context of other MSA forms recorded by Thomas.

Thomas' transcriptions show a great deal of inter- and intra-dialectal fluctuation between *ś* and its (perhaps only partially) voiced counterpart, *ź*. It is probable that this fluctuation simply reflects Thomas' inability to distinguish the two MSA fricative-laterals (which, as Jahn (1905:5) remarked, "can easily be confused .. by the untrained ear"), for his transcriptions of the fricative-laterals are often contradicted by those of Jahn (1905) and, even more damagingly, Carter's native informant (1847), not to mention etymological expectations (to which the Viennese and native transcriptions consistently conform). But even if Thomas' transcriptions were accurate, the MSA forms for "laugh" cited above could hardly be considered evidence for a PS doublet-pair unless cogent reasons could be found for separating this pair of *ź-ś* doublets from the many others in Thomas' word-list whose origin is demonstrably late.[19]

The morphemic, geographical, literary-critical, and chronological distribution of *ṣḥq* vs. *śḥq* in the Bible

Many scholars have felt instinctively that the Biblical forms *ṣḥq* and *śḥq* could not have co-existed within one and the same dialect. This feeling, no doubt fostered by the perfect synonymity of the roots,[20] cannot be accepted uncritically. Perfectly synonymous doublets *do* exist in the better-known languages,[21] and their existence cannot always be attributed to dialect mixture. It is therefore necessary to examine the relative distributions of these forms in the sources before any judgment can be made. It will naturally be to our advantage to examine as many kinds of distribution as possible in our search for complementarity. As we have pointed out,[22] no trace of complementarity is exhibited by the morphemic distribution of the roots in the Bible. We may turn then to geographical distribution -- and the theory of Bauer and Leander ([1922] 1965:28):

> Wenn...in unseren Worterbüchern die Wurzeln *ṣḥq* und *śḥq* "lachen," *zʕq* und *ṣʕq* "schreien," *(ʕls)*, *ʕlz* und *ʕlṣ* "sich freuen" nebeneinanderstehen, so liegt es auf der Hand, dass die lebendige Sprache diese Formen nicht in Wirklichkeit nebeneinander gebraucht hat, sondern dass sie aus verschiedenen Gegenden stammen.

A certain degree of plausibility is lent to this theory by the observation that the very striking form *yiśḥåq* "Isaac" occurs twice (out of four times in the entire Bible) in the book of Amos (7:9,16; the ordinary form *yiṣḥåq* does not occur), and thus seems at first glance to be a northern dialectal form; for Amos, though a southerner from Tekoa, preached in the northern kingdom, probably had his words recorded in the northern kingdom, and, in one of the abovementioned verses (7:16) is quoting the ruler of the northern kingdom. If we look further, however, we find that *śḥq* is very common in southern books as well. The only thing which sets the book of *Amos* apart is that it uses the *śḥq*-variant for the proper noun Isaac -- and even this usage finds a parallel in two southern sources (Jeremiah 33:26 and Psalms 105:9).

Nor does the distribution of the two variants correspond in any way with the Pentateuchal sources isolated by literary critics, since *ṣḥq* occurs in passages assigned (Speiser 1964, Driver 1956) to P (Gen. 17:17), J (Gen. 18:13,15, Gen. 19:14, Gen. 26:8, Gen. 39:14), E (Gen. 21:6,9, Ex. 32:6) and, if we include the name Isaac, D, while *śḥq* occurs nowhere in the Pentateuch.

It is this latter observation, taken together with the

fact that *ṣḥq* is very rare outside of the Pentateuch (except in the name Isaac) which provides the real key to the distribution of the two doublets. As several scholars (Gesenius 1834 s.v. *śḥq*, Nyberg 1952:23, Bendavid 1967:15 and Moreshet 1968) have seen, the variable with respect to which the variants are in complentary distribution is not space but rather time. The passages in Genesis, Exodus, and Judges (Samson story)[23] where *ṣḥq* occurs are certainly among the oldest prose passages in the Bible -- apparently even older than the Samuel passages in which *śḥq* occurs. As for the one occurrence of *ṣḥq* in Ezekiel, it is of a piece with many other well-known linguistic and thematic similarities between Ezekiel and the Pentateuch,[24] and is probably due to borrowing on the part of Ezekiel. Bendavid (1967:15) and Moreshet (1968:128) have also pointed out that *śḥq* (and its regular post-Biblical outcome, *sḥq*) is the form which occurs in Tannaitic literature (cf. also the Syriac and Arabic form ʔIsḥāq "Isaac" with unemphatic *s* and Jewish Babylonian ʔIsāq < *ʔIsḥāq[25] likewise with unemphatic *s*, perhaps going back to a dialect of Post-Biblical Hebrew in which the name in question was likewise pronounced with an unemphatic *s*). Since the Hebrew of that literature is, in many respects, the direct heir of Late Biblical Hebrew, it would seem to partially corroborate the conclusions we drew from the relative distribution of the forms in the Bible itself (cf. Hurvitz 1972:43).

If it is true that *śḥq* must have been created out of **ḍḥq*[26] and in the Biblical period, it follows that, despite appearances (i.e. graphemic shape), the initial segment of < *ṣḥq* > was still phonetically and functionally different from the initial segment of < *ṣʕq* > in early Biblical times --a conclusion which will not surprise anyone who is familiar with the relatively high degree of polyphony which characterized so many ancient Semitic writing systems[27] including the Hebrew alphabet.[28] It also follows that the creation of *śḥq* in Hebrew was independent of the creation of Mandaic *shq* and Ethiopic *šḥq*. This is really not surprising either since the proto-root from which all of these forms must be derived -- **ḍḥq* -- is an unusually good candidate for dissimilation, containing as it does, an unusually high concentration of dissimilation-prone consonants. In such a case, our *a priori* prejudice against unnecessary assumption of parallel innovation must yield to the direct testimony of Biblical usage.

[1] In fact, these two roots appear to satisfy Lyons' definition (1968: 448) of "complete and total synonymy." Note that they apparently lack certain trivial characteristic environments (for the term, see Hoenigswald 1960: 15) which other root-morpheme doublets ordinarily have. Thus, for example,

we find that *zʕr* occurs with the vowel pattern *ĕ-e* (*zĕʕer*) but not with *å-i*, while *ṣʕr* is just the opposite (*ṣåʕir* but not **ṣĕʕer*). Similarly, we find a form *ʕalliz* in the Bible but no **ʕalliṣ*. In the case of *ṣḥq* and *śḥq*, however, there is no vocalic morpheme which occurs with one but not the other. Both roots occur in the *qal* and *piel* stems, in the verbal noun meaning "a laugh, laughter" (*ṣĕḥoq - śĕḥoq*) and, as we shall see, even in the name of the Patriarch Isaac. In *modern* Hebrew, the roots have, of course, become differentiated.

[2]E.g., Brockelmann 1908:239 and Kutscher 1961:105.

[3]The examples are well known: *ʕlṣ-ʕlz* "exult," *ṣʕq-zʕq* "cry out," and *ṣʕr-zʕr* "be small" (although *zʕr* could be an Aramaic loan as Wagner 1966:49 believes). Cf. also Hebrew *qpṣ* - Arabic *qfz* "jump," Hebrew *ṣeḏå*, Ugaritic *mṣd* - Arabic *zād*, Aramaic *zwādin* "provisions," Hebrew *ṣdq*, Arabic *ṣdq*, etc. - Syriac *zdq* "be right," and also the inner-Arabic doublets collected by Jahn (1905:8): *ṣʕq-zʕq* "cry out," *bṣq-bzq* "spit," *qrṣ-qrz* "pinch," *rqṣ-rqz* "leap, dance," *ṣrr-zrr* "tie together," *bxṣ-bxz* "pluck out an eye," *lṣq-lzq* "cling to." On the other hand, *ṣḥq-śḥq* are not the only *ṣ-ś* doublets in Biblical Hebrew. We also find *ṣpn-śpn-spn* "hide" and, according to several modern scholars (Greenfield 1959: 149-51, Morag 1963b:143 and cf. also Ginsberg 1967:72, Driver 1951:180, and Kopf 1959:276), *ṣmḥ* "grow" - *śmḥ* "rejoice; shine brightly" (cf. Syriac *ṣemḥā* "a sprout; radiance") as well. We shall return to these doublets in fn. 6.

[4]The changes *ṣ* › *ś* and *ṣ* › *z* may have been operative at different periods in the history of Hebrew or pre-Hebrew. Or one could claim that *ṣ* dissimilates to *z* in the vicinity of voiced consonants, but to *ś* in the vicinity of voiceless consonants.

[5]*ʕlṣ* "exult" corresponds to ESA *mʕlṣ* "joy," *ṣʕq* "cry out" corresponds to Arabic *ṣʕq* "cry out," and *ṣʕr* "small" corresponds to Arabic *ṣġr* "small."

[6]The other two examples of *ṣ-ś* in Hebrew (cf. fn. 3 above) are etymologically obscure. The root *ṣpn* "hide" seems to be related to Assyrian *pṣn* "cover, hide" (just as *spn* = Babylonian *psm* and *śpn* = Babylonian *pšn*). But Akkadian *ṣ* can be the reflex of PS *ṣ* or *ḍ*, so we are back where we started from. The correspondence between Hebrew *ṣmḥ* "grow" and Syriac *ṣemḥā* "a sprout, radiance" is not much more revealing, contrary to prevailing scholarly opinion, since,as we shall see (chapter xx), Aramaic *ṣ* is often a reflex of PS *ḍ* in the vicinity of liquids and nasals.

[7]Gesenius 1834 s.v. *śḥq*, BDB s.v. *ṣḥq*, Leslau 1958:151, Gordon 1965:473. *ṣḥq*, Leslau 1958:151, Gordon 1965:473.

[8]Private communication from Prof. Robert Hetzron, who also informs me that the Gafat form *ṣäma* "hear," reported by Leslau (1945:18) and derived by him from Ethiopian *smʕ* (through assimilation?), "is most certainly a mistake, not to be considered seriously."

[9]The reference is to the Chaha form *dəgər* "hair," where the *d* seems to result from the de-glottalization of *ṭ*; cf. Amharic *ṭəgur*.

[10]Personal communication from Prof. Robert Hetzron.

[11]At least some of these roots occur in other dialects as well (with *ḥ* instead of *h*). The root *gḥk*, for example, occurs in Syriac, Talmudic, and Galilean Aramaic, just to name a few. The root **śḥq* is not well attested outside of Mandaic, a fact which leads Prof. Daniel Boyarin (personal communication) to question its Aramaic *bona fides* and to theorize that it might be a borrowing from Hebrew (assuming that the Mandaeans originated in Palestine) or a dissimilated form of an earlier **ṣḥq* (presumably also borrowed from a Canaanite dialect). Prof. Boyarin may well be right (in which case it is obvious that we cannot adduce Mandaic *shq* as evidence for the existence of a PS *śḥq*), but the following points should be noted: a) the normal dissimilated reflex of **ṣḥq* in Mandaic would be **ṣhk* rather than *shq* since emphatic-dissimilation usually (perhaps always) affects *q* rather than *ṭ* or *ṣ* in that dialect; b) according to Ingholt (Rosenthal 1967:1/2,50), the root *śḥq* (orthographical ‹šḥq›) occurs in a Hatran inscription with the meaning "smile kindly" (cf. Caquot 1963:15 for a different rendering and ibid. 1952:102 for the original publication of the inscription).

[12]Cp. the expression *gahkin umitparpin* "they laugh and make merry" (Drower and Macuch 1963 s.v. *ghk*) with *libaihun sahiq umitparpa* "their heart rejoiceth and is merry" (ibid., s.v. *shq*).

[13]The term as used by Fitzmeyer and Kutscher (1970:347-8), refers to the Aramaic dialects which flourished around the middle of the first millenium CE: Syriac, Mandaic, Jewish Babylonian Aramaic, Samaritan Aramaic, Christian Palestinian Aramaic, and Galilean Aramaic. Other scholars use the term "Middle Aramaic" for these dialects.

[14]Possible attestations of this loss already in Official Aramaic (Kutscher 1970:373) do not alter the relative chronology, since they are matched by an isolated occurrence of the dissimilation in Old Aramaic (ibid., 353).

[15]This is the PS root posited by Hetzron (see above in this chapter) on the basis of Hebrew *ṣḥq*, Ugaritic *ṣḥq* (UT 75: *ẓḥq*), Gafat *ṣaq̈ä*, and Gurage *daq̈ä*. Barth (1893:34), Brockelmann (1908:238) and Kutscher (1961:104) posited a slightly different root -- **ḍḥk* -- on the basis of Arabic *ḍḥk* and Aramaic *ghk, *ʔḥk*. It is impossible to say which opinion is supported by Akkadian *ṣâḫu*, if it is really a cognate, as Landsberger (1931:298) intimates. In MSA, the difference between *ḍḥk* and *ḍḥq* would be expressed by glottalization (see the beginning of chapter ii, esp. fn. 3), and since neither Jahn nor Thomas seems to have been sensitive to this distinctive feature, their testimony cannot tip the scale in either direction. However, Hetzron's reconstruction seems slightly preferable because it enables us to account for the creation of both *ḍhk* and *ś́ḥq* using one explanation (i.e. dissimilation) and because it does not require us to assume that PS had *three* parallel roots.

[16]One other PS root -- *ṣʕq* "cry out" -- has a similarly high concentration of dissimilation-prone consonants. It is highly instructive to note that both Hebrew and Arabic have two reflexes of this root: *ṣʕq* and *zʕq*. Cf. also common Aramaic *zʕq*.

[17]We are leaving open here the question of when these dissimilations took place.

[18]There is certainly a fourth parallel root for "laugh" in Aramaic (Nöldeke 1875:73fn quoted above in this chapter; Kutscher 1961:106), namely *dḥk* (with an unemphatic *d*). The question is only whether the initial segment of this root really reflects a very early stage in the development of the proto-Aramaic *ḍ* when the latter was still in alveolar position. The appearance of this root in only one late dialect (Galilean Aramaic) would seem to suggest that we must answer this question in the negative. It seems more likely that *dḥk* is a dissimilated form of *gḥk*. In this case, the dissimilation has nothing to do with the emphatic feature but rather is connected with the incompatibility of *g* and *k* (due to identical place of articulation) in Semitic roots. Cf. Talmudic *dlosqĕmā* "case, chest" ‹ *glosqĕmā* ‹ Greek *glossokomon*.

[19]Shahari *iśeku, iźukuna* "those" is a good example. The fricative-laterals in these forms correspond to *l* in Harsusi *ilik* "those" and Botahari *ilak* "those." The voiced fricative-lateral was created by a conditioned sound-change peculiar to Shahari (see the section entitled "Shahari ɮ" in chapter iii) and is therefore late. Even this recently created fricative-lateral is not immune to the voiced-voiceless fluctuation in Thomas' word-lists.

[20]See fn. 1 above.

[21]E.g. the two different pronunciations of "economics" in English.

[22]See fn. 1 above.

[23]The Samson story also has one occurrence of *śḥq*. It is possible that we have here the kind of fluctuation of competing forms which is so common while sound-change is in progress.

[24]Cf. Redpath 1907:xxi, Cooke 1937:63, and the literature cited there.

[25]This etymology for the name ʔIsāq was suggested by Prof. Daniel Boyarin.

[26]See the beginning of this chapter.

[27]One need only think of the Arabic and Old Aramaic alphabets, and the various cuneiform syllabaries.

[28]I refer here of course to the polyphony of ש, ח, and ע during the Biblical period. It is true that the polyphony of the last two is a controversial question, but the recent study of the Greek transcriptions of ח by Wevers (1972) seems to be definitive, and occasional counter-examples cannot alter the over-all pattern of close correlation between transcription and etymology which Wevers has uncovered. The two counter-examples cited by Moscati (1964b:40) do not hold water. The ח of Hebrew *ʔăḇiḥayil* is quite properly rendered *kh* by the Septuagint since exactly the same name has been preserved in ESA with a *x* (KBHK s.v.). The existence of this ESA name obviates the need for any etymological analysis of the component parts of the Hebrew name. The rendering of Hebrew *ʕåp̄rå* by Greek *Gophera* is similarly correct from an etymological point of view. As BDB (s.v.) saw, this toponym is related not to Hebrew *ʕåp̄år* "dust" (= Arabic *ʕafar*) but to Hebrew *ʕop̄ɛr* "young hart" (=Arabic *ġufur*). This is clear both from the vocalization of the name and from the fact that many Biblical toponyms contain animal-names. Cf. Blau 1966:141 for a very similar discussion of Moscati's supposed counter-examples, which was discovered by the present writer after having written the above lines.

XV.

Evidence from a Phonological Correspondence that Pre-Hebrew Ḍ and Ś were Phonetically Similar: Semitic Words for "Press" in Old Arabic Dialects

We spoke in the previous chapter about the correspondence between Arabic *ḍġṭ* "press, oppress" and Syriac *gʿṭ* "oppress," discovered by Nöldeke (1875:73fn), and how Syriac *g*, in this case, represents PS *ḍ*, sidetracked by dissimilation at the (post-)velar stage of its shift to the pharynx. The Arabic root, in turn, has been matched with Hebrew *śḥṭ* "press out" (Jensen *apud* Gesenius and Buhl [1915] 1962 s.v.) as has Akkadian *ṣḫt* (Daiches 1903:92, CAD s.v.[1]).

At first glance, the matching of Arabic *ḍġṭ* with Hebrew *śḥṭ* may appear forced, in spite of the near-identity of meanings, since neither the first radicals nor the second correspond in the normal manner. However, in considering the second radicals we should keep in mind that one of the ancestors of Hebrew *ḥ* is **ḫ*, which differs from *ġ* only in the feature of voicing. And the fact that Hebrew R_2 is voiceless while Arabic R_2 is voiced fits nicely with the fact that Hebrew R_1 is voiceless and Arabic R_1 is voiced. Finally, the fact that Akkadian has *ḫ* in the R_2 position rather than *:*,[2] supports the suggestion made above that the *ḥ* of Hebrew *śḥṭ* goes back to **ḫ*.

The Akkadian form is valuable in another respect. It serves as a bridge between the Arabic and Syriac forms and the Hebrew form, by siding with Arabic and Syriac forms in one case (R_1) and Hebrew in the other (R_2). This strengthens the case for matching the Arabic form with the Hebrew, since any attempt to separate them would now entail separating one of them from the Akkadian form as well.

All of these correspondences are presumably well known since they appear in a standard dictionary of Hebrew (Gesenius and Buhl [1915] 1962 s.v. *śḥṭ*[3]). Nevertheless, as in the case of *ṣḥq* - *śḥq*, etc., scholars have not drawn the appropriate conclusion from the correspondence of Arabic *ḍ* with Hebrew *ś*.

Since three of the four forms point to *ḍ* as the original R_1, we may assume that Hebrew *ś* was the innovation, created out of an original **ḍ* by dissimilation. This means that pre-Biblical *ḍ* was the emphatic counterpart of *ś* -- a finding which corroborates our earlier conclusion based on *ṣḥq* - *śḥq*.

[1]It is curious that the CAD discussion of *ṣḫt*, while affirming the etymological link with Hebrew *śḥṭ*, at the same time re-defines the former in such a way as to remove much of the justification for that link:

> "The verb seems to refer to the whole process of obtaining oil from sesame [ŠE.GIŠ.Ì] and, in late texts, a type of wine from grapes. The specific translation 'to press' is to be abandoned, since sesame oil is obtained by boiling seeds and skimming off the oil and not by pressing the seeds. This meaning 'to press' is, moreover, excluded by the occurrences in the medical texts... where the object of the process *ṣaḫātu* is not the herb but the already obtained juice (*mû* lit. water)..."

However, this discussion is not as definitive as it sounds, since it is not certain that ŠE.GIŠ.Ì means "sesame" (Kraus 1968:112). Moreover, the second objection to the translation "press" is rather trivial. If the English verb "press" cannot take "juice" as its object and consequently is not an appropriate translation of *ṣḫt* when the latter governs *mû* then we shall have to translate "press out" in that context. But this restriction on the use of "press" can certainly tell us nothing substantive about the meaning of *ṣḫt*, for there is no reason to expect the latter to be similarly restricted. Accordingly, the whole problem is fictitious and would never have occurred to anyone had the traditional translation of *ṣḫt* been "squeeze."

[2]*:* is of course the symbol for vowel length and is the usual Akkadian reflex of PS *ḥ*.

[3]Strangely, the entry implies that Arabic *ḍġṭ* cannot be matched both with Syriac *gʿṭ* and Hebrew *śḥṭ*: "Jensen vergl. ar. *ḍġṭ* "drücken," das aber Nöld. MG 73.2 *gʿṭ* stellt." The reason for this either-or approach is not apparent.

XVI.
Evidence from *Balsamon* - *Bśm* for Lateral *Ś*

The Greek word *balsamon* is a loanword that most proponents of the lateral theory have overlooked. *Balsamon* is the Greek name of the Commiphora opobalsamum. The sap of this tree, used in perfumes and medicines, was treasured all over the ancient world.

It has long been recognized[1] that *balsamon*, like many other Greek plant-names, is a Semitic loanword, related directly or indirectly to Hebrew *bśm*, Punic *bšm*, Aramaic *bsmʔ*, ESA *bs*^{2}*m*, and Arabic *bšām*[2] but the standard explanations for the presence of *l* in this word leave much to be desired. In fact, to Masson (1967) the problem is so serious that she relegates *balsamon* to a chapter entitled, "Words whose Semitic origin is possible." In her opinion also, "attempts to explain this phenomenon have not been at all convincing" (pp. 77-8). Let us begin by reviewing some of these explanations.

Jastrow (1903:114) has a laconic note on the Jewish Palestinian form *blsm(wn)*: "*bsm* with inserted *l* = *r*." Jastrow has a well-known tendency to supply Semitic etymologies for Greek loanwords in Rabbinic literature and this note is a good example. Nevertheless, it contains an interesting insight, namely, that *balsam*, in spite of its four consonants, could theoretically be a Semitic form.

The Semitic languages have quadriliteral nouns and verbs of the form $C_1VC_2C_3VC_4(V)$ where C_2 is most often a liquid or nasal. In Aramaic C_2 is usually *r*; hence Jastrow's note "with inserted *l* = *r*," meaning: "with C_2 = *l* instead of the usual *r*." In Akkadian, on the other hand, *r* and *l* are about equally common. In fact, when C_3 is *s* (or most any other voiceless obstruent), only *l* -- never *r* -- occurs (Reiner 1966:73). So *balsam* would blend very nicely into the Akkadian lexicon were it attested in that language.

The fact is, however, that the form *balsam* occurs only in Hebrew and Jewish Palestinian Aramaic (*ʔpwblsmwn*, *ʔpwplsmwn*[3]), where it has a Greek prefix (*ʔpw-* = *opos* "sap"[4]) and a Greek suffix (*-wn* = *-on*),[5] and in Arabic (*balsam*), where it appears only in dictionaries dealing with the modern language. The classical Arabic word for "balsam" is *balasān* (with triliteral root!), but this is clearly a Semitized form of a Greek original rather than vice versa (Lewy 1895:41, Lagarde 1866:17, cf. also ibid. 1877:25). It may have come into Arabic from Palestinian Aramaic rather than directly from Greek (Kutscher 1969:43).

It seems, therefore, that *balsam* with an *l* is not attested as a native Semitic form. Why then does Greek have an *l* in this word? We could, of course, assume that such a form once existed and that the *l* later dropped out, as does Benfey (1842:65). Presumably this would have happened in Proto-Semitic since almost all the Semitic languages have *l*-less forms of this word. But then there would be no way of explaining how the form was borrowed by the Greeks in the first millennium BCE! Moreover, there are no other reconstructable examples of such a loss, as far as the present writer knows.

Mayer (1960:321), followed by KBHK (s.v. *bśm*), suggests that *balsamon* may have developed from an older Greek form **bansamon*. This could have come, she thinks, from an Aramaic form **bansam* or **banśam*, which in turn could have developed from **bassam* or **baśśam* in accordance with the well-known Aramaic sound-change *VC:* › *VnC*, or, according to some, *VC:* › *Ṽ̃C*.

While this explanation is better than its predecessors, its assumption of a whole series of unattested forms is hardly convincing. Moreover, the change **bansamon* › *balsamon*, presumably a dissimilation-at-a-distance, is unparalleled in Greek.[6]

Gumpertz[7] (1942:114fn) has proposed a much simpler explanation for the presence of *l* in this intriguing loanword, namely, that *ś* was realized in the lending language as a voiceless fricative-lateral (just as *ś* is realized today in MSA) which the Greeks heard and reproduced as *ls*.

Such a compound rendering of ɬ would not be at all unusual: combinations like *lś*,[8] *shl*,[9] *thl*,[10] and *lth*[11] have been used by European explorers to represent MSA ɬ, and Norman scribes in medieval England often rendered Welsh ɬ with *thl* and *lth* (Zeuss 1871:1063, Nettlau 1890:68-9). Trubetzkoy (1922:203) compared the acoustic impression made by [ɬ] (or rather [ɬ̄]) in Adygian and Avar to that of [x́l] (i.e. [çl]), and the sequences [xl], [θl], and [šl], are (or, at least, used to be) used by European speakers as an approximation of Zulu [ɬ] (Doke 1926:99).

The Norman rendering of Welsh ɬ is explained by Jones (1913:19) as follows:

> It conveys the effect of the hiss in the *th*, and gives the side effect in the *l*. But *ll*, of course, is a sim-

> ple sound, which may be described shortly as a unilateral hiss.

That Jones' interpretation is possible is shown by the use of digraphs to render such simple sounds as [ž] and [š] in Yiddish and Greek, respectively.[12] Additional parallels are given by Anttila (1972:158):

> In sound substitution, the borrowers apparently make a kind of distinctive feature analysis of the foreign sounds and assign them to the closest native bundle. In oldest Germanic loanwords, an *f-* is reflected by Baltic Finnic *p-*...Later *f* is rendered by *-hv-*, that is, [voiceless] = *h* and [labial, spirant] = *v*. Splitting a bundle of features into two segments like that is not infrequent. French [ü] was replaced by [u] in English, but [ṻ] gave a decomposite [iu] or [yū]. Similarly, Russian borrowings render Baltic Finnic [ü] by [u], or more often with *palatalization* + [u], *sysmä* → *s'uz'om* [or s-] 'thicket.' And Russian [ɯ] has a similar fate in Baltic Finnic as in *mylo* → Karelian *mui̯ła* 'soap.'

Jones' interpretation could be applied to all of the other transcriptions above except for that used by Hein (1909): *ls̀*.[13] An *l* is not needed here to "give the side effect" because *ś* by itself gives the side effect. All members of the Viennese Südarabische Expedition, including Hein, wrote the voiceless fricative-lateral with *ś*. Indeed, as Bittner (1910:81) points out, Hein writes one word -- the word for "milk" -- sometimes with a *ś* and sometimes with *lś*: *śhauf* (p. 140, line 22) and *śhôf* (p. 140, lines 13,15)[14] vs. *ilśhauf* (p. 22, line 16).[15]

Once we look more carefully, we find that Jones' interpretation does not fit Carter's *shl* either. His *shl* transcription is inadequate and must be interpreted in the light of his careful description:

> ش has a very peculiar sound in the Mahra dialect; it is formed by placing the tip of the tongue against the anterior part of the palate, and allowing the air to pass out of the mouth on one side or the other of it, in the manner of a lisp, following it with the sound of the letter *l* as in شبوط "fire" pronounced *shleeote* (p. 343).

Here we see clearly that what Carter meant by *šl* was [ɬl] -- not [ɬ] as in Jones' interpretation of *thl*. It seems very likely that Hulton's and Bent's *thl* and Greek *ls* (and perhaps even Norman *thl* and *lth*) have to be interpreted in the same way.[16] But why does this *l* behave in such an odd way -- sometimes appearing, sometimes not,[17] sometimes before ɬ, sometimes after?

In connection with the latter question, it should be noted that *l* precedes ɬ only when a vowel precedes ɬ and follows it only when a vowel follows it.[18] (This is true of the Welsh examples as well.)[19] Thus Hein hears an *l* in *ilśḫauf* where there is a prefixed *i* but none in *śḫauf*. Carter hears an *l* following ɬ in *shleeote* "fire"[20] but Hein hears an *l* preceding ɬ in a variant of the word with a prefixed *i*: *ilśiwuoḍ*.[21]

In view of this distribution, we are justified in seeing this *l* as a voiced on-glide or off-glide from the preceding or following vowel, respectively.[22] This glide is heard only if the speaker happens to leave his tongue in the ɬ position an instant too long (i.e. after voice-onset) or put it in the ɬ position an instant too soon.

In support of this interpretation let me mention that a voiced off-glide is reported for initial Icelandic ɬ (Kress 1937:121fn, Sveinbjörnsson 1933:64) and for initial Welsh ɬ.[23] It should also be noted in this connection that when the phoneme *l* occurs before MSA *ś* it is treated the same as the *l*-glide: it is optionally (or variably) deleted. Thus, Thomas (1937:296): Shahari *kulśi* "everything" (*kul* = every, *śi* = thing) but also *kośi*; Mehri *kalśayen* "everything" but also *kaśiyen* .[24] We are thus justified in speaking of a merger of /lś/ with /ś/ in MSA.

The origin of *balsamon*

The importance of this loanword as evidence for the lateral hypothesis will depend in large part upon what language it proves to have been borrowed from. If it turns out to be from South Arabic, it will show only that the MSA realization of *ś* as a voiceless fricative-lateral goes back to the fourth century BCE, when the word is first attested (Aristotle, *On Plants*, 820b). But if it turns out to be from a language other than South Arabic, it will enable us to project the lateral realization of *ś* much further back into the past. Accordingly, an attempt to trace the origin of the word (by tracing the origin of the plant) would not be idle.

Theophrastus' *Enquiry into Plants* (end of fourth century BCE) is our most important source, since it contains the earliest report about the location of the balsam groves. Unfortunately, it is also the vaguest. It tells us only that balsam "grows in the valley of Syria" and that "they say that there are only two parks in which it grows" (IX.vi.1). However, it is possible to interpret this statement in the light of information given by later authors.

Pliny, for example, reports in the first century CE that "the only country to which this plant has been vouchsafed is Judaea, where formerly it grew in only two gardens both belonging to the king" (Natural History XII.lix.111).[25] Since the two accounts agree concerning the number of balsam groves in the ancient world (two) and their general location (Greater Syria), it seems likely that they refer to the same groves and that Theophrastus' groves were located in the Judean part of Greater Syria. The expression *en tō aulōni tō peri Surian* "in the valley (literally: hollow) of Syria" (Theophrastus op. cit.) would then refer to the Syria Graben (of which the Jordan Valley is a part),[26] which Strabo (16.2.16) describes as a *pedion koilon* "hollow plain." This interpretation of Theophrastus' "valley" is supported by Diodorus (first century BCE) who also reports that the balsam trees are found "in a certain valley." The valley is in the region of the Dead Sea (19.98.1) and Petra (2.48.9) -- a description which fits the Jordan Valley perfectly.

The Greek and Roman sources, then, lead us to Palestine. But when we turn to Hebrew sources, we find that both the meaning of *bśm* (it denotes any perfume or pleasant-smelling substance) and its usual vocalization (*bośɛm*) do not match those of the Greek word *balsamon*. This problem is easily solved, however, by identifying the latter with the hapax *båśåm*, which, in context (Cant. 5:1 *ʔåriṯi mori ʕim bĕśåmi* "I plucked my myrrh with my *båśåm*"), seems to refer to a specific plant (*Encyclopedia Miqrait* s.v.).

Another possible Semitic source for the Greek word *balsamon* is suggested by the fact that the tree is indigenous not to Palestine but to South Arabia (Warburg 1921:282, Moldenke and Moldenke 1952:84, Grohmann 1922:155-6, M'lean 1899:466, Berendes 1902:49, Diodorus 3.46.2, Strabo 16.4.19). Nor should we forget the most obvious and perhaps most likely possibility of all (Movers [1856] 1967:226, 231-2): that it was neither a Jew nor a South Arabian but a Phoenician[27] sailor, who, standing long ago on a moonlit Aegean beach, held out a pottery jug and said:

- I brought something new for you this time.
- What is it?
- Smell it first.
- Mmm. What is it?
- Baɫam.
- Balsamon...

[1]See Masson (1967:77) for a list of references.

[2]I have purposely omitted Akkadian *bašmu*, adduced as a cognate by Thompson (1949:340) on the basis of EA 25, iv, 51, since Thompson's reading there has been shown to be incorrect (personal communication from Prof. Erle Leichty). The occurrences that remain are in lexical texts where *bašmu* is equated with various thorny plants (ibid.). Mayer (1960:321) cites an Akkadian **bašamu* "perfume" which, as Masson correctly notes, "does not seem exact." Masson herself cites Akkadian *buʔšanu* "evil-smelling plant" but this is from a completely different root.

[3]In printed editions, e.g., of *Genesis Rabba*, shorter forms (*blsmwn* and *plsmwn*) co-occur with the longer ones. But the best manuscript of *Genesis Rabba* available to the present writer (Codex Vatican 30) has only *ʔpwblsmwn* and *ʔpwplsmwn*, so these are the only forms which will be cited.

[4]The compound *opobalsamon* is frequently attested.

[5]The possibility that Hebrew *-wn* represents Arabic *tanwīn* or the ESA emphatic noun-state morpheme is ruled out, because of the Greek origin of *ʔpw-*.

[6]Personal communication from Prof. Henry Hoenigswald.

[7]The same idea occurred independently to the present writer.

[8]In *h-lś-m* (Hein 1909:1,2) *ilśȟauf* (ibid., 22), *ilśiwuoḍ* (ibid., 28); cf. Bittner 1910:81.

[9]In *shleeōt* (Carter 1847:351).

[10]In Curia Muria (= Shahari) *thluf* "hair" (Hulton 1840:195) cp. Shahari *śuf* "hair" (Thomas 1937:300); Mehri *thlef* "hair" (Bent 1900:440) cp. Mehri *śīf* "hair" (Thomas 1937:300); Socotri *thlaub* "leg" (Bent 1900:442) cp. Socotri *śab* "pied" (Leslau 1938:424); Mehri *thluf* "feather" (Bent 1900:446) cp. Harsusi *źif* "feathers" (Thomas 1937:297) and Mehri *śif* "hair," Shahari *śuf* "hair"; Socotri *thlab* "stream" (Bent 1900:447) cp. Socotri *śaʕab* "vallée, wadi" (Leslau 1938:431) and Shahari *śaʔab*, *śap* "valley" (Thomas 1937:324).

[11]In *hamilthtor* "buy" (Bent 1900:444) cp. Arabic *muštarī*.

[12]In Yiddish, [ž] is written *zš*, and *khs* is used in the Greek version of Lamentations to render Hebrew [š] (cf. the Hebrew letter-names *rekhs* and *khsen*).

[13]Cf. fn. 8 above.

[14]Cf. Jahn (1902:256) *śȟof* and Thomas (1937:308-9) *śokōf*, *śkōf*.

[15]Cf. Carter (1847:355) *ishakhof*.

[16]Thomas (1937:313) *aqalthar* "panther" in Harsusi (alongside *aqaiźar*) is counter-evidence because Thomas could have written *aqaltȟar*.

[17]Carter usually renders ɬ with *sh*, Hein with *ś*, and the Greeks with *s* e.g. Abasēnoi "Abyssinians" = ESA *ḥbs²* in Uranius apud Stephanus of Byzantium, and Ilasaros, the Sabaean king < ESA *ʔls²rḥ* (Strabo 16.4.24).

[18]I am indebted to Malcah Yaeger for suggesting that I investigate this possibility.

[19]Dynthlayn (Dinllaen), Thlanrethlon (Llanrillo), Thlanlibyon, Thlannor, Penthlyn (Penllyn) (Zeuss 1871:1093), Thlintegid, Thloyt (Lloyd), Thlewelyn, Thleen (Lleyn), Enthli, but also Cadewalthan (Cadwallawn) with preceding *l* (Nettlau 1890:68-9).

[20]Cf. Thomas (1937:296) *śiyot*.

[21]Cf. Thomas (1937:296) *śiwot*.

[22]Cf. also Johnstone 1973:98, published after this chapter was written: "*ś* is a voiceless lateral fricative and *ź* [Südarabische Expedition *ḏ̌*] its voiced correlate. These last have an *l* offglide."

[23]Personal communication from Malcah Yaeger; for the opposite view, cf. Rositzke 1939:8.

[24]*ay* and *i(y)* are free variants in Thomas' Mehri list, e.g., *ḥaiyōt*, *ḥiyūt* "life;" *khulai*, *khulī* "empty," *hair*, *hīr* "donkey," *khaimit*, *khīmit* "tent," *askair*, *askīr* "soldier," *raiś*, *rīśīt* "snake," *qalaid*, *qalīdīt* "key," *anbai*, *annabī* "prophet."

[25]Cf. also Strabo, who in the preceding century named Jericho as the site of "the palace and the balsam park" (16.2.41). Harrison (1962:344) interprets Strabo (16.2.16) as meaning that balsam "flourished beside the Sea of Galilee" as well as in Jericho and then proceeds to prove that Strabo was wrong. However, careful reading shows that Strabo says nothing about balsam flourishing beside the Sea of Galilee. What he says is that the hollow plain which contains the Jordan and a lake called Gennesarites, "*also* produces balsam." The balsam producing area is connected with the Sea of Galilee only in that they are both part of the same long plain. Furthermore, Strabo's description of Jericho -- "a plain surrounded by a kind of mountainous country" (16.2.41) -- is very similar to his description of the plain which produces balsam, which shows that Strabo did indeed consider Jericho part of the larger plain.

[26]This is also the interpretation of M'lean et. *al.* (1899:466): "Veslingius (Opobalsami Vindiciæ, 243) rightly remarks 'Vallem hic intelligendam esse Hierichuntis...persuademur.'"

[27]It has never been shown conclusively that the Phoenician use of one grapheme to represent both the reflex of PS ś and the reflex of PS š reflects a merger (cf. Blau 1970:25), let alone that the merger product was realized [š] rather than [ś]. And even if it could be demonstrated, the demonstration would apply only to the standard dialect reflected in the inscriptions.

XVII.
Evidence from ʕ*Arsĕlā* - ʕ*Arsā* for Lateral *Ś* in Aramaic

Scholars have long recognized that Jewish Aramaic ʕ*arsĕlā* "watchman's hammock" is historically related to common Aramaic ʕ*arsā* "bed" (< PS ʕ*arśum*)[1]. This recognition has generally gone hand in hand with the notion of a "diminutive *l*" (Fränkel 1878:49, 1886:138, Jastrow [1903] 1950:117, Epstein 1960:116), but the existence of such a morpheme must be considered unlikely, or, at least, unproven. The other parade example upon which this notion is based -- Hebrew ʕ*ărå̄p̱ɛl* "thick cloud, fog" (cf. Targumic ʕ*arpilā* "darkness" (used to render Hebrew *ḥošɛḵ* -- not Hebrew ʕ*ărå̄p̱ɛl*!), Syriac ʕ*arpelā* "dark fog, thick darkness," Mandaic *arpila*, Jewish Babylonian ʕ*urpilā* (*a* > *u* before bilabials) "drizzle," Ugaritic *ġrpl* "thick cloud") -- has an augmentative and frequently divine[2] connotation *vis à vis* Hebrew ʕ*å̄rip̱* rather than a diminutive one, and in any case has a different vowel before the *l* than ʕ*arsĕlā* (construct ʕ*arsal*) has. Moreover, the lack of agreement between the initial segments of Ugaritic ʕ*rpt* "clouds" and *ġrpl* "*thick cloud*" puts the relationship between Hebrew ʕ*ărå̄p̱ɛl* and ʕ*å̄rip̱* under a cloud of suspicion, even if the cloud is not exactly impenetrable.[3] The present writer believes that in the case of ʕ*arsĕlā* a phonological solution is called for -- a solution based on an "excrescent" or "parasitic" *l* rather than a diminutive one.[4]

Several solutions of this type suggest themselves, but, whichever one we choose, the fact remains that Aramaic *sĕl*, phonemically /sl/, is descended from, or at least corresponds to, PS *ś*. This correspondence is evidence that *ś* was a lateral in Aramaic or some northern dialect of Arabic, depending on which explanation we choose.

One possible explanation would be to take ʕ*arsĕlā* as a loan-word -- the result of an attempt by speakers of a ɬ-less Aramaic dialect to imitate the pronunciation of speakers of an Aramaic dialect which had not yet merged ɬ with *s* or an Arabic dialect which had not yet shifted ɬ to *š*.[5] As in the case of *balsamon* and the many parallels[6] cited in the previous chapter, the closest approximation was a combination of sibilant plus *l*, probably representing ɬ plus an *l*-glide (the *l*-glide is an off-glide in this case because the conditioning vowel follows ɬ). The *šĕwå* in ʕ*arsĕlā* resulted from the application of well-known Aramaic rules concerning consonant clusters. The full vowel which separates *s* from *l* in the construct form ʕ*arsal*[7] is just as automatic (ʕ*arsl* or ʕ*arsĕl* would have been impossible) except for the fact that any of the other full vowels which alternate with *šĕwå* would have served just as well.

A second, more interesting possibility is that ʕ*arsĕlā* developed from *ʕ*arɬā* within *one* dialect of Aramaic, in the following way:

1. */ʕarɬā/ developed a non-phonemic glide after ɬ, i.e. *[ʕarɬlā].
2. Speakers (e.g. children) began to analyze *[ʕarɬlā] as a quadriliteral (phonemic */ʕarɬlā/) instead of triliteral plus non-phonemic glide (phonemic */ʕarɬā/).
3. The overt sign of this metanalysis was the insertion of *šĕwå* between ɬ and *l*, i.e. [ʕarɬĕlā].
4. *[ʕarɬĕlā] › [ʕarsĕlā] by the normal Aramaic sound-change ɬ › *s*.

Step 4 is well known, and we have already discussed step 1 at great length. The only novel part of this explanation is the metanalysis in 2-3 (really one step). This kind of metanalysis seems to have parallels in the MSA languages. Mehri *afŝ́ail* "lunch" (Thomas 1937:306) seems to have developed from an older **afŝ́ai* ~ *afŝ́i*[8], cf. Harsusi *afŝ́ī* (Thomas 1937:307), Mehri *faŝ́i* (Thomas 1937:306), *fŝ́ê* (Jahn 1902:256), Shahari *ifŝ́o, faŝ́o* (Thomas 1937:306), *fŝ́o* (Bittner 1917:28), Soḳotri *fŝ́o* "repas du matin" (Leslau 1938:343).

Another possible example is Harsusi *fiḓ́halāt, fiẓ́alāt* "silver" (Thomas 1937:319) which seems to have developed from a form like Mehri *fiẓ́āt*, Shahari *fīẓ́at* (Thomas 1937:318) through an intermediate **fiẓ́lat*, with a frictionless *l*-glide after fricative ẓ́. Such a glide would be heard if, for some reason, friction was reduced in passing from ɮ to the following vowel, e.g. the side of the tongue might be lowered before the breaking of apical contact. It is also possible, however, that *fiẓ́alāt* developed from **fiẓ́ẓ́at* (cp. Arabic *fiḍḍa*) before MSA simplified geminated consonants, in which case metanalysis would be irrelevant here.

A final parallel is provided by North African Arabic *qašlef* "aufspringen (Haut)," which Kamil (1963:10) has equated with Egyptian *qaššafa* "rissig werden, aufspringen (Hände)." This example is of particular interest, since it provides additional evidence (cf. chapters x-xiii) that Arabic ش was once a fricative-lateral.

The evidence for the lateral theory adduced in this chapter obviously depends on the correctness of our original definition of the *ʕarsĕlā* as a type of bed. But there is considerable evidence suggesting that the word *ʕarsĕlā*, known only from Targum Yonāṯån (i.e. in this exact form -- with *s* rather than *z*, etc.), referred to a type of shelter.

The word in question is the Targumic equivalent of Hebrew *mĕlunå(h)*, which occurs only twice in the Bible -- once in Isaiah 1:8 and once in Isaiah 24:20. Since it is apparent from the poetic structure of the former passage that *mĕlunå(h)* is a synonym of *sukkå(h)* and since later Jewish exegetes pointed out this synonymy (David Qimḥi on Isaiah 1:8 and Rashi on Isaiah 24:20), it is likely that the author(s) of the Targum also understood *mĕlunå(h)* to refer to some type of shelter. There is no evidence here for the meaning "hammock."

The same may be said for Syriac *ʕarzōlō* (given here with West Syriac vocalization for reasons which will soon become apparent; note also *s* › *z* by assimilation[9]) which is the Peshiṭta's rendering[10] of *mĕlunå(h)* in the two Isaiah passages. For Arabic *ʕirzāl* -- a Syriac loanword (Fraenkel 1886:138; cf. Ibn Durayd's *Jamharat al-Luġa* s.v., where the word is characterized as Iraqi, and Maclean 1901:244, where the East Syriac vocalization of *ʕ-rz-l-* is given as *i-ā-ā*) used by Saadia Gaon and the Arabic Bible to render *mĕlunå(h)* in the second of the two passages[11] -- we have the explicit statement of the native lexicographers (Al-Azharī, Ibn Manẓūr s.v.) that an *ʕirzāl* is a watchman's shelter (*saqīfatu n-nāṭūr*).[12] Finally, there is the word *ʔarzĕlā*[13] which occurs once in the Babylonian Talmud (ʕErubin 25b). It too seems to refer to some type of shelter, rather than a bed, since it has a roof (ʕErubin 25a) and is contrasted with an *ʔaksadrā* -- a structure with three walls and a roof.

All of the above sources seem to agree on the meaning "watchman's shelter." What, then, is the source of the rendering "watchman's hammock"? This rendering is based on a traditional Jewish definition of Talmudic *ʔarzĕlā* found in the *Tosåpoṯ* (Sens, 13th century), the *ʕÅruḵ* (Rome, 11th century), and the commentary of Rabbenu Ḥananel (Kairouan, 11th century). Its occurrence in the last-named work means that it probably goes back to the Geonim (*ʕÅruḵ ha-Šålem* introd. xii, *Encyclopedia Judaica* s.v. Ḥananel ben Ḥushiʔel) -- whose glosses on the Talmud are no less a native source than the Talmud itself. The text of the definition is cited here from Kohut's edition of the *ʕÅruḵ* (s.v. *ʔarzĕlā*):

> *ʔarzĕlā. peruš ʕarsĕlā ... wĕ-hu(?) ḥăbålim mĕtuḥim me-ʔilån lĕ-ʔilån kĕ-min miṭṭå(h) liškaḇ ʕåleha haš-*

šomer bal-laylå(h) wĕ-lešeb̲ taḥat̲ ṣillåh bay-yom wĕ-taḥtɛhå påt̲uaḥ kullo.

ʔ*arzĕlā*. An ˁ*arsĕlā* ... that is, [a set of] ropes stretched from tree to tree as a kind of bed for the watchman to sleep on at night and sit under, in its shade, during the day -- the space below which is completely open [i.e. from all sides].

This definition, as it is traditionally interpreted (by Tosåpot̲, Kohut, Jastrow, and others) classifies the ʔ*arzĕlā* as a type of bed (cf. also Ibn Durayd, s.v. ˁ*irzāl: wa-kullu šayʔin jamaˁtahu wa-waṭṭaʔtahu li-tanāma ˁalayhi fa-huwa ˁirzāl*. "Anything which you gather and fix up for sleeping is an ˁ*irzāl*."); nevertheless, any contradiction between it and the sources considered above is immediately resolved by the revelation that this bed also serves as a shelter from the burning sun during the day.

It is striking, to say the least, that this secondary use of the watchman's bed is also mentioned in a nineteenth century description of the Syrian (?) watchman's hut by the Arabist Johann Wetzstein (Delitzsch 1882:74-5):

> The watchman's hut, for the protection of the vineyards and melon and maize fields against thieves, herds, or wild beasts, is now called either ˁ*arîshe* and *manṭara* if it is only slightly put together from branches of trees, or *chême* if it is built up high in order that the watcher may see a great distance. The *chême* is the more frequent; at harvest it stands in the midst of the threshing floors (*bejâdir*) of a district and it is constructed in the following manner: -- Four poles (ˁ*awâmîd*) are set up so as to form the corners of a square, the sides of which are about eight feet in length. Eight feet above the ground, four cross pieces of wood (ˁ*awâriḍ*) are tightly bound to these with cords, on which planks, if they are to be had, are laid. Here is the watcher's bed which consists of a litter. Six or seven feet above this, cross beams are again bound to the four poles, on which boughs, or reeds (*qaṣab*), or a mat (*ḥaṣîrah*) forms a roof (*saṭḥ*), from which the *chême* has its name; for the *Piel* forms שטח ,חים , ערש signify, "to be stretched over anything after the manner of a roof." Between the roof and the bed, three sides of the *chême* are hung round with a mat, or with reeds or straw (*qashsh*) bound together, in order to keep off the cold night-winds, and also to keep the thieves in ignorance as to the number of watchers. A small ladder, *sullem*, frequently leads to the bed-chamber. The

space between the ground and this chamber is closed only on the west side to keep off the hot afternoon sun, for through the day the watcher sits below with his dog, upon the ground. Here is also his place of reception, if any passers-by visit him; for, like the village shepherd, the fieldwatcher has the right of showing a humble hospitality to any acquaintances. When the fruits have been gathered in, the *chême* is removed. The field-watchman is now called *nâṭûr* and the verb is *naṭar* "to keep watch," instead of which the quadriliteral *nôṭar* (from the plur. *nawâṭîr* "the watchers"), has also been formed. In one part of Syria, all these forms are written with *ḍ* instead of *ṭ*, and pronounced accordingly.

It will be noted that this structure differs from the Talmudic *ʔarzĕlā* in having a roof over the bed. This seemingly minor detail is of crucial importance from a semantic point of view, since it means that the essential component which makes this structure a shelter is not the bed (in spite of the secondary use of the latter referred to above) but the roof above the bed -- as Wetzstein explicitly states. The same is true of the watchman's hut from Arabia (Tihāma) depicted in Niebuhr's *Description de l'Arabie* (1774: plate XV, figure F). It would be rash to assume that structures of this type did not go by the name of *ʕarsĕlā* (or the various phonetic variants thereof) in the ancient Near East, and it is unnecessary as well. The evidence for the lateral theory presented in this chapter will in no way be weakened if we assume that after the watchman's bed acquired a secondary function, the term *ʕarsĕlā* may have been broadened to include the kind of structure described by Wetzstein and depicted by Niebuhr.

Would our argument be weakened if it turns out that such structures were included among the *denotata* of *ʕarsĕlā* from the very beginning? It would, but not as much as one might suppose; for, though it was the meaning "watchman's hammock" which prompted scholars to connect *ʕarsĕlā* with *ʕarsā* in the first place, the meaning "watchman's hut" also leads us to *ʕarsā*, or at least to the South Semitic cognates of *ʕarsā*: Mehri *arś̌īt, areś̌ten* "hut (palm)," Harsusi *arś̌it arś̌ait, ariś̌ten* "hut (palm), tent" (Thomas 1937:302-3,323), Shahari *arś̌ait, arś̌et* "hut (palm)" (loc. cit.), *ʕarś̋it ʕarś̋et* "Rohrhütte" (Bittner 1917:18),[14] Arabic *ʕarīš* "hut (made of palm-leaf sticks or other materials)" (Al-Azharī s.v.),[15] Ethiopic *ʕäriš* "tabernaculum, umbraculum" (Dillman 1865 s.v.). Even Hebrew *ʕɛrɛś*, which ordinarily means "bed," may mean "bower" in the phrase *ʕarśenu raʕănånå(h)* (Song 1:16), for, according to Kutscher (1961:16), it is doubtful that the adjective *raʕănan* "fresh, luxuriant," used elsewhere of trees, can be used to describe a bed. Following Rabbenu ʕOḇaḏiah of Bertinoro (15th century CE), Kutscher compares *ʕεrεś* in the above verse with Mishnaic *ʕåris* "(structure made of) trellised vines." It follows that the derivation *ʕarsĕlā* < **ʕarś-* is relatively independent of the semantic problem we have been discussing, and that this bit of evidence for the lateral theory is solidly based.

[1]According to Fraenkel (1886:138), the relationship was already recognized by Buxtorf. Fraenkel is apparently referring to the fact that Buxtorf's *Lexicon Chaldaicum Talmudicum et Rabbinicum* (1640) renders *ʕarsā* with Latin *lectus* "couch" and *ʕarsĕlā* with the Latin diminutive of *lectus*, i.e., *lectulus* "small couch."

[2]Could *ʕaråpεl* be derived from an earlier **ʕrp ʔl* "cloud of God"? Cf. Hebrew *Båḇεl* "Babylon" < Akkadian *Bābili*, which meant, according to popular etymology, "gate of the gods" (*Encyclopedia Miqrait* s.v. *Båḇεl*). Cf. also Hebrew *Karmεl* "Carmel," which may have meant "vineyard of God," especially in light of its use in II Chronicles 26:10 (cited by *Encyclopedia Miqrait* s.v. *Karmεl* to prove that *karmεl* is also a common noun meaning "wine-producing area"). Finally cf. Hebrew *harăre ʔel* "mountains (worthy) of God" in Psalms 36:7.

[3]Fluctuation between ʕ and *ġ* in the vicinity of *r* (*ġ* and *r* are both trills and are actually merged in Jewish Baghdadi Arabic) was noted already by Brockelmann (1908:225,226) and, to judge from Brockelmann's reference, Nöldeke. Beeston (1962a:11) has a nice list of examples, but unfortunately he did not take the Ugaritic and Canaanite evidence into account in determining the direction of the change. Thus, he compares Arabic *mġrb* with ESA *mʕrb*, but does not mention *mʕrb* in Ugaritic (and MSA and the Arabic dialects of Datīna, Haḍramawt, and Ẓufār, for that matter). He also compares ESA *tʕrt* "sluices" with Arabic *ṯġr* "mouth; seaport," but leaves out Ugaritic *ṯġr* "gate" and hieroglyphic Canaanite *ša-ʕa-ru*. The latter form, *pace* Harris (1939:63), proves nothing about the existence of *ġ* in twelfth-century Canaanite.

[4]"Excrescent" and "parasitic" are the terms used by Anttila (1972:67ff) and Malmberg (1963:60), respectively, to describe consonants which are, as it were, spontaneously generated out of nothing in clearly defined phonetic environments.

[5]The latter may be more likely since there is a distinct possibility that the meaning "hut" for *ʕarś* is a South Semitic innovation, as the following chart shows:

	BED	HUT
1) East Semitic		
Akkadian *eršu*	X	
2) Northwest Semitic		
Hebrew *ʕεrεś*	X	?
Ugaritic *ʕrś*	X	
Aramaic *ʕarsā*	X	
3) South Semitic		
MSA *arɬīt, arɬet*		X
Ethiopic *ʕäriš*		X
Arabic *ʕarīš*		X

[6]The most striking parallel is (West) Mehri *Arzhlìt* "tent" reported by Bent (1900:443). It is clearly identical with (East) Mehri *arśīt* "hut" and Harsusi *arśit* "hut, tent" reported by Thomas (1937:302-3,323). The *zh* transcription in this word and in *Izhhè* "evening meal" (cp. Thomas 1937:294 *aiśi*,

aiŝai "dinner"; Jahn 1902:243 *iŝê* "Abendmahlzeit"; Arabic ˁašāʔ "dinner, supper") indicates a voiced allophone of /ɬ/ in West Mehri. This widening of the field of dispersion of /ɬ/ was made possible by the merger of /ɮ/ with /l/ in that dialect (see the section entitled "Landberg's ض and the ض-isogloss" in chapter ii).

[7]This is a back-formation since, historically, /ˁarsal/ must have developed from /ˁarslV/ (assuming that we are right about *l* representing an off-glide from an original ɬ) which is the reverse of the historically prevalent pattern /CVCCVC/ › /CVCCCV/. In our synchronic rules, of course, we will derive /ˁarslV/ from /ˁarsal/, following the historically prevalent pattern.

[8]See chapter xvi, fn. 24, for the free variation of ī and *ai* in Mehri.

[9]The form ˁ*rzl*ʔ is also found in some editions of the Targum including Lagarde's edition of Codex Reuchlinianus and a Yemenite manuscript from the 16th-17th century (Stenning 1949).

[10]For a discussion of the historical relationship between the Targum and the Syriac translation, cf. Rowlands 1959.

[11]Where the image is of shaking, but not in the first of the two passages (Isaiah 1:8) where the image is of desertion. For various reasons, ˁ*arāzil* were constructed on the tops of trees, where, no doubt, the slightest wind would set them shaking.

[12]Note that the word for a watchman, like the word for his shelter, (ˁ*irzāl*) is Aramaic, cf. Jewish Aramaic *nāṭōrā*.

[13]Our printed editions of the Talmud and even some manuscripts (e.g. Codex Munich) have ʔ*urzilā* (ʔ*wrzyl*ʔ), but this reading is apparently due to contamination with the word ʔ*urzilā* meaning "gazelle." Codex Oxford and some versions of Rashi's commentary have ʔ*rzl*ʔ (Rabbinovicz 1960:III,93), as do the ˁ*Åruḵ* (s.v.), Rabbenu Ḥananel's commentary, and the *Maggid Mišneh* and *Kesep̄ Mišneh*, both on Maimonides' *Mišneh Torah*, Hilkoṯ Šabbaṯ, XVI, 7.

[14]Cf. also the MSA words for "anchorage" reported by Thomas (1937:284-5): Shahari *arŝet*, Harsusi *eriŝait*, *eriẑ*, Mehri *marsai*.

[15]Several native Syriac-Arabic dictionaries actually give this Arabic word (along with ˁ*irzāl*) as a gloss of ˁ*arzālā* (Payne Smith 1901 s.v.). Examples of ˁ*arīš(a)* used of a watchman's hut come from Wetzstein, who states that "the watchman's hut, for the protection of the vineyards and melon and maize fields against thieves, herds, or wild beasts, is now called either ˁ*arîshe* [or] *manṭara*..." (Delitzsch 1882:74-5), and from Saadia, who renders *sukkå(h)* in Isaiah 1:8 (where the context points to a watchman's hut) with ˁ*arīš* (Derenbourg edition; cf. also *mĕlunå(h)* = *manẓūra* in the parallel hemistich) instead of *ẓalāl*, which is his rendering of *sukkå(h)* in most of the fourteen other places in the translation and in his dictionary (Allony 1969:365). We might also note in passing that, according to Al-Azharī, an ˁ*arīš* (like an ˁ*irzāl*) is a kind of *miẓalla*, and that *miẓalla* is the Arabic cognate of Aramaic *mĕṭallĕṯā*, which, as the Targumic equivalent of Hebrew *sukkå(h)*, occurs in synonymous parallelism with ˁ*arsĕlā* (more precisely, ˁ*arsal mĕḇāṯuṯā*) in the Targum of Isaiah 1:8. In other words: ˁ*arīš* : *miẓalla* :: ˁ*arsĕlā* : *mĕṭallĕṯā*.

XVIII.
Evidence from *Kaldu - Kaśdim* for Lateral *Ś* in Hebrew

Striking evidence for the lateral theory is contained in any Hebrew-English Bible: the equation *kaśdim* = Chaldaeans is evidence that Hebrew *ś* sounded like *l*. Of course the facts are far more complicated than this simple observation, but all of the facts and interpretations that follow cannot change the fundamental correspondence of Hebrew *ś* with *l* in the two variants of this name.

Let us first trace back English "Chaldaean" to its source. The earliest translation of the Bible, the Septuagint, has *khaldaioi* for Hebrew *kaśdim*, a term which Herodotus (I,81ff) used in c. 460 BCE to refer to the priests of Bel. This Greek form is no doubt a rendering of the Aramaic *kaldāy*[1] -- attested only later in Syriac, Jewish Babylonian, Mandaic, Christian Palestinian and Palmyrene[2] *kald(ā)y(ā)* "Chaldaean; astrologer, fortune-teller"[3] -- plus the Greek plural ending *oi*. The Aramaic name in turn probably derives from the Akkadian gentilic *kaldāy-* (*kal-da-a-a*; Strassmaier 1886:512, lines 7,9) which must come straight from the Chaldaeans themselves (since Akkadian was the language of Babylonia when the Chaldaeans arrived there). The name is first attested in an inscription of Ashurnasirpal II dated approximately 878 BCE: *māt Kaldu* "Chaldaea" (Brinkman 1968:260). The *l*-variant of the name[4] is obviously old and widespread. In fact, it appears at first glance to be the only variant attested in non-Jewish sources. Further investigation, however, reveals that there are some exceptions to this general rule -- and some highly interesting ones at that.

In medieval Iraq, for example, the Aramaic-speaking descendants of the ancient Babylonians were still calling themselves *al-kasdāniyyūn* (Brinkman 1968:265, Chwolson 1859:1ff) or rather some Aramaic version of this. We owe this information to Aḥmad ben ʕAlī ibn Waḥšiyya who, in the ninth or tenth century, translated some works of his people into Arabic from "the language of the *kasdāniyyūn*"[5] (loc. cit.). His gentilic epithet, al-Kasdānī,[6] is recorded both on the title pages[7] of these works (found by Chwolson in the Leiden University Library) and in the *Kitāb al-Fihrist* (I,311). The latter (loc. cit.) as Brinkman points out, uses al-Kaldānī and al-Kasdānī indiscriminately in referring to Ibn Waḥšiyya; and Ibn Waḥšiyya himself called one of his books *Maḏāhibu al-kaldāniyyīn fī al-aṣnām* "Chaldaean Teachings about Idols," no doubt referring to his own people.

This equation of *kasdānī* and *kaldānī* enables us to use the testimony of Al-Masʿūdī concerning the *kaldāniyyūn* in *Al-tanbīh wa-al-išrāf*. In this history-book, Al-Masʿūdī is primarily interested in the ancient Chaldaeans, but after one of his references[8] to the *kaldāniyyūn* he adds: "that is, the Babylonians whose remnants at present [967 CE] are in the swamps between Wāsiṭ and Baṣra in villages"[9] (p. 137). This note places the medieval *kasdāniyyūn* - *kaldāniyyūn* right smack in the middle of the old Chaldaean homeland.[10] It seems reasonable to infer that these people are the direct heirs of the ancient Chaldaeans, and that the form *kasd-* is a direct descendant of the original Chaldaean name, one of the few witnesses to that name which are independent of Akkadian.

Another possible sibilant-variant occurs in a royal inscription from al-ʿUqlah (Jamme 1963:44) which describes three legations that Ilʿaḏḏ Yaliṭ, King of Ḥaḍramawt (third century CE) received at his al-ʿŮqlah resort. One of the legations was composed of "Ḏu Matrân and Falaqat, the two Kašadites (*ks²dyyhn*)." Jamme believes that these *ks²dyyhn* were members of a local tribe but the only evidence he is able to adduce for the existence of such a clan is a small set of personal names and a place-name outside of South Arabia.

A different interpretation -- and, for our purposes, a more interesting one -- has been offered by Müller (1964:380) and accepted by Wissman (1964:457). Müller argues that *ks²dyyhn* means "the two Chaldaeans" since:

a) the members of the other two legations are described as *tḏmryyhn* "two Taḏmarites" and *hndyyhn* "two Hindites" -- terms which could easily refer to men of Palmyra and India. Legations from two such distant lands would be compatible with a legation of Chaldaeans.

b) none of the three supposedly South Arabian tribes is mentioned elsewhere.

c) *nisba*-adjectives like *ks²dy*, *tḏmry*, and *hndy* are used for foreign peoples rather than South Arabian tribes.

d) the phonemes of ks^2dy correspond perfectly to those of Hebrew *kaśdi(m)* and Biblical Aramaic *kaśday*.

Müller's argument is not convincing as it stands. It fails to provide a motive for a visit to Ḥaḍramawt by Indians and Chaldaeans or to explain why Chaldaeans would have South[11] Semitic names.[12]

Upon closer examination, however, the history of the kingdom of Ḥaḍramawt provides a perfect context for Müller's interpretation of the inscription. During the Greco-Roman period, Ḥaḍramawt was a far more important place than it is today. The reason for its importance can be summed up in one word: frankincense. In those days, Ḥaḍramawt included Ẓufār[13] -- one of the two regions in the world which produced frankincense (Van Beek 1964:103-4), a product for which there was a tremendous, worldwide demand. One of the biggest markets for this product was India. The anonymous *Periplus of the Erythraean Sea* describes in great detail the lucrative sea-trade between South Arabia and Barygaza, Muziris, and other ports on the west coast of India (Van Beek 1964:109).

Of particular interest is the fact that the *Periplus* names an Eleazos as the reigning king of Ḥaḍramawt, the king who presided over this booming trade with India. According to Wissman (1964:72 and Tafel IIIa) this Eleazos is none other than the Ilʿadd Yaliṭ of our inscription![14]

It is also interesting to note that Ilʿazz[15] Yaliṭ is mentioned repeatedly in the inscriptions found at Khor Rori in the frankincense region, whereas only one inscription from this region mentions any other king (Albright 1953: 39).[16] This suggests that Ilʿazz took a particularly active part in the frankincense trade.

Given the magnitude of the trade with India under Ilʿazz Yaliṭ and the extent of his power to grant preferential tariffs or any number of other concessions, it is reasonable to expect that he would receive visits from Indian merchants. If, however, Jamme were still to insist that the *hndyyhn* were local subjects of the Ḥaḍramī king, we might be able to accept that, for, according to the *Periplus*, there were Indian merchants living on the northern coast of Socotra (par. 30) and Socotra was also ruled by Eleazos (par. 31). These Indians would presumably satisfy both Müller and Jamme.

Visits by Palmyrene and Chaldaean merchants would make just as much sense. Palmyra owed its fame and fortune to its location along "the king's road" -- one of the routes by which Ḥaḍramī frankincense was brought north. A second northward route of great importance sheds unexpected light on the origin of the ks^2dyyhn. The following is Van Beek's (1958:145) description of that route:

> Strabo reports that a journery from Gerrha to Hadhramaut required forty days (16.4.4). This suggests the existence of an overland route across the middle of the Arabian peninsula, since a course skirting the sands would require more time. Presumably, this route was primarily used for the transport of Dhofâr frankincense to the north. From Gerrha, frankincense was distributed to Mesopotamia and to Palestine, according to Strabo (16.4.18; 16.3.3) and Diodorus Siculus (III.42.5). The relationship between Gerrha and South Arabia is gradually being brought into sharp focus. *It will be remembered that Gerrha was inhabited by Chaldaean exiles from Babylon* [my italics] according to Strabo (16.3.3). While his source -- probably Eratosthenes in this instance -- goes back only to the third century B.C., Gerrha must have been a Chaldaean stronghold for some centuries earlier. W.F. Albright has shown that the probable source of the Chaldaean script is Southeast Arabia. Since Hadhramaut was generally oriented toward its eastern neighbors, including the Mahra country and Dhofar, in the first century A.D.[17] (*Periplus* para. 27) and possibly throughout its entire history, the existence of a route connecting Gerrha and Hadhramaut is not at all surprising.

Van Beek apparently overlooked the fact that this route is actually drawn on the map of Ptolemy Claudius' *Geography* (c. 150-160 CE). It began at Sabbatha (=ESA s^2bwt, capital of Ḥaḍramawt) and passed through Nagara metropolis (=ESA ngrn, Arabic Najrān), ending at Gerrha polis (Wissman and Hofner 1952:12).

In view of the fact that the Chaldaean colony of Gerrha was one of Ḥaḍramawt's oldest and biggest trading partners, it is difficult to avoid the conclusion that the *ks²dyyhn* who accompanied the Ḥaḍramī king from *S²abwat* to his resort in al-ʕUqlah were Chaldaeans from that town -- not Chaldaens in the broad sense of "Babylonians" but Chaldaeans in the narrow, ethnic sense, descendants of the southern wing of the Bit Yakin tribe whose territory extended along the Persian Gulf as far south as Dilmun (Dougherty 1932:153, *Encyclopedia Miqrait* s.v. *kaśdim*), the region of modern Baḥrain and of ancient Gerrha.[18] These southern Chaldaeans, far away from the glitter of Babylonian civilization, must have succeeded a good deal better than their northern cousins in preserving their South Semitic (Moritz 1926:206, Albright 1952, Biggs 1965 and cf. Mitchell 1969:114; but cf. Ephʕal 1974 for a different view) language and culture. It follows that we ought not be surprised to find Chaldaeans with South Semitic names instead of the East Semitic names (Albright 1952:44, Brinkman 1968:265) borne by the Chaldaeans mentioned in our cuneiform sources.

Let us return now to the subject of our chapter: the correspondence between Akkadian *l* (*kaldu*) and Hebrew *ś* (*kaśdim*). In order to evaluate this correspondence as evidence for the lateral hypothesis, we must first determine the origin of the corresponding forms. We have already pointed out that the Akkadian form is probably a direct rendering of the original Chaldaean name as pronounced by the Chaldaeans themselves. But what about the Hebrew form? What can we deduce about *its* origin?

We can immediately rule out an Aramaic borrowing, since all of the Aramaic dialects, except for some of the Jewish ones, have an *l* in the word for "Chaldaean." A first millennium borrowing from Akkadian is, *pace* Kaufman (1974:141)[19], excluded for the same reason.[20] However, it *is* possible, and in fact widely believed, that Akkadian *kaldu* developed from an earlier **kašdu* (in accordance with the well-known Akkadian sound law discussed in the next chapter) and that Hebrew *kaśdim* is a rendering of this very early[21] form.

It must be admitted that this theory weakens the effectiveness of the *kaldu* - *kaśdim* correspondence as evidence for lateral *ś* in Hebrew (although some evidence can be squeezed out of the putative fact that precisely the allophone of Akkadian /š/ which was later to split off and merge with /l/ was heard by the Hebrews as being closer to *ś* than to *š*). But the theory is far from proven. It is flawed by the fact that the crucial form **kašdu* has never been found, or, according to proponents of the theory, "has not yet been found" (*Encyclopedia Miqrait* s.v. *kaśdim*). It was probably this problem which motivated A.L. Oppenheim's judgment (1962:556) that "no linguistically satisfactory explanation of this difference [between the Hebrew and Akkadian forms of the name] is known."

One last possibility exists: that Hebrew *kaśdim*, like Akkadian *kaldu* and the Aramaic prototype of *kasdānī*, is a direct and independent rendering of the original name as it was heard from the mouths of the Chaldaeans themselves. In that case, we have Hebrew *ś* and Akkadian *l* rendering the same Chaldaean phone, suggesting that Hebrew *ś* had some feature in common with Akkadian *l*.

Naturally, this cannot be confirmed at the present time given the state of our knowledge about the Chaldaeans; but if it turns out that the Chaldaeans spoke an eastern dialect of ESA, as the present evidence linking them to Ẓufār (Albright 1952:44, Biggs 1965, but cf. Ephʿal 1974:113 for a different view) suggests, and if the ESA word for "Chaldaean" really was *ks²dy*, it will follow that the original Chaldaean name probably contained a voiceless fricative-lateral,[22] a phone which could easily have given rise to the two renderings (Akkadian *l* and Hebrew *ś*) which we have been discussing.

[1]It is unlikely that the Greek form comes directly from Akkadian *kaldāy-* since it is almost inconceivable that the Greeks could have heard of the Chaldaeans before the reign of Nabopolassar (626-605), the first king of the Chaldaean dynasty. Even by this time, Akkadian was on the wane, if not actually extinct.

[2]Of course the vocalization of this name is attested for only some of the dialects named.

[3]"Astrologer" is the usual meaning of Biblical Aramaic *kaśdāy* as well.

[4]Henceforth, simply the "*l-* variant" as opposed to the various "sibilant-variants."

[5]*lisānu l-kasdāniyyīna,* not *lisān al-kasdānī* as Brinkman reports (1968:265), cf. also *luġatu l-kasdāniyyīna* in *Kitāb al-Fihrist* I, 358.

[6]It is interesting to note that Kasdan occurs as a Jewish family-name today, e.g. Sara Kasdan, the author of *Love and Knishes*.

[7]Or possibily one of the prefaces. Chwolson is not specific on this point.

[8]Not in his chapter on "The Seven Nations of Antiquity" which contains his major discussion of the Chaldaeans, but in the chapter on "The Kings of Byzantium from the Hijra to 345 [967 CE]" -- as an after-thought.

[9]*Wa-humu l-bābiliyyūna l-ladīna baqiyyatuhum fī hādā l-waqti bi-l-baṭā?ihi bayna Wāsiṭ wa-l-Baṣra fī quran hunāk*.

[10]The swamp-lands belonged to the territory of Bit Yakin, the most powerful of the Chaldaean tribes (*Encyclopedia Miqrait* s.v. *kaśdim*).

[11]An examination of the names in Harding 1971 reveals that the particle *dū* is almost always associated with ESA names, but the Safaitic parallels to these names adduced by Jamme (1963:44) (cf. also Harding 1971:471) show that a North Arabic origin is not excluded.

[12]On the other hand, Jamme himself admits (1963:45) that the names of the two Hindites, *dhrdh* and *mndh* "may be of Indian origin." The sequence *dh* which occurs three times in these two names was used during the Islamic period to represent Indian "aspirated" d^h. It may be objected that this was an orthographic practice used by the Indians themselves to distinguish aspirated d^h from unaspirated *d*, and that it is not at all certain that a South Arabian in the pre-Islamic period would hear Indian d^h as *dh*. But this difficulty disappears once we learn that "the king's guests and servants wrote their own texts" (Jamme 1963:10). There is no difficulty in assuming that the Indian guests wrote their own texts or at least spelled their names for the engraver, since, as merchants (see immediately below), they would have to be able, at the very least, to sign their names in South Arabic script -- particularly if they were members of the Indian community on Socotra, for the latter was a dependency, of Ḥadramawt (see immediately below).

[13]Today Ẓufār is dependency of Oman.

[14]This is a reversal of Wissman's earlier position (Wissman and Hofner 1952:332). In 1952, he was working with a first century CE date for the *Periplus;* in 1964, he switched, with other scholars, to a third century date. As a result, Ilʕazz I, II, and III became one man.

[15]For the Ilʕadd - Ilʕazz fluctuation, cf. Beeston 1962:13.

[16]Albright calls him Ilʕazz Yaliṭ I, but see fn. 14, above.

[17]Or whenever the *Periplus* was written; see fn. 14, above.

[18]For the location of Gerrha, cf. James 1969.

[19]Kaufman's position that the *l* of *kaldu* "was heard as *śin* by the West Semites (but as *l* by the Greeks)" is, in addition to being factually incorrect (cf. the Aramaic renderings of *kaldu* listed at the beginning of this

chapter) and historically implausible (cf. fn. 1, above), linguistically improbable, if it is to be interpreted as meaning that the *l* of *kaldu*, being derived from older *š*, was phonetically different from etymological *l*. Although it is theoretically possible that the large-scale replacement of ‹š› by ‹l› in Middle Babylonian and Assyrian texts is a "false report of merger" *à la* Labov, Yaeger, and Steiner (1972:229-57), the burden of proof clearly rests on the proponent of such a theory.

[20]Unless Lehmann (1892:158) and Brockelmann (1900:396) were correct in their belief that Akkadian *l* was voiceless, but cf. the next chapter for objections to this theory. Moreover, even if it was voiceless, would it not have had a voiced allophone before the *d* of *kaldu*, as Lehmann himself (loc. cit.) suggested?

[21]Cf. Grintz 1962:190fn10:

> "Akkadian grammar ... is clear on this point, that beginning with Middle Babylonian (1500 B.C.) the consonantal group *šd* had changed into *ld*. And this is borne out by the very name of the Chaldaeans, which from the first appear in the inscriptions as *Kaldu*. This is also the name given them in non-Biblical Aramaic (*kldyʾ*) and in Greek (*khaldaioi*). Thus, the combined Hebrew name *ʾUr-Kaśdim*, which as an exception evinces a form prior to the fifteenth century B.C., must necessarily be an old designation which had come down from the Patriarchal epoch just in this form. Apparently it is because of this combination, long established in Hebrew tradition that, when the Chaldaeans appear later on the historical scene, the old form *Kaśdim* was applied to them in spite of the universally accepted more modern form *Kaldu*."

[22]For evidence that ESA s^2 was already a fricative-lateral in the fourth century BCE, see chapter xvi.

XIX.
Evidence for Lateral *Š* in Akkadian

The Akkadian merger of *š* with *l* before apical stops (e.g. *ildu* < *išdu* "foundation" homonymous with *ildu* < *ildu* "offspring," *ilti* < *išti* "with" hononymous with *ilti* < *ilti* "goddess (gen.)," *qiḻtu* < *qištu*[1] "forest; gift" hononymous with *qiltu* < **qiltu*[2] "alkali," *baltu* < *baštu*[3] "shame; vital power" hononymous with *baltu* < *baltu* "a thorny plant") and apical spirants (e.g. *ulziz* < *ušziz* "he placed," *ilsi* < *išsi* "he called") is one of the most famous sound-changes in all of the Semitic languages, and certainly one of the best documented. Hundreds of tablets allow us to follow its progress from sporadic beginnings in Old Babylonian (Reiner 1973: 35, von Soden 1969:5) to full-blown maturity in Middle Babylonian and Assyrian (Böhl 1909:23, Aro 1955:38, Jucquois 1966:272,275). Nevertheless, in spite of this wealth of data, few Semitists would claim to understand this sound-change fully. In the words of Moscati (1964b:35), "The causes of this phenomenon are still not clear."

The problem, of course, is to explain the sudden jump from *š* to *l*, from a voiceless palatal central fricative to a voiced alveolar lateral approximant. This is not an insuperable problem since intermediate stages (one of which would almost certainly be a voiceless fricative-lateral) can easily be imagined. This is the explanation offered by Bouda (1947:52-3) for similar shifts in Iranian and Ostyak. Another approach might be to re-examine the conventional descriptions, given above, of the Akkadian phonemes conventionally designated *š* and *l*, in an attempt to bring these two end-points closer together. Lehmann's claim (1892:158, cf. also Brockelmann 1900), in connection with our sound-change, that Akkadian *l* was voiceless is a good example of this approach applied to one of the end-points. Gumpertz's[4] suggestion (1942:114fn), in the same connection, that Akkadian *š* was a voiceless fricative-lateral exemplifies the same approach applied to the second end-point.

Of the three possibilities, the second is the least likely. It is difficult to believe that one phoneme spontaneously underwent unconditional de-voicing in Akkadian while all of the others were unaffected, especially when the phoneme in question happens to be /l/. We have already seen[5] that it is extremely unusual to find a language which has a voiceless lateral phoneme with no voiced counterpart. Thus, Lehmann's proposal entails the assumption of a change from a typologically normal to a typologically aberrant system, and should therefore be rejected in favor of the other proposals.

The first of the three possibilities has the great advantage of not requiring any dislocation of established views, but it is uneconomical, for, in positing a ɬ secondarily developed from š, it fails to exploit the MSA evidence suggesting that Akkadian š may have inherited a lateral realization from one of its PS ancestors (proto-phonemes). In fact, the Socotri ɬ undergoes a merger with *l* before *s* and *š*[6] (Leslau 1938:32) which is the closest thing to an exact replica of the Akkadian sound-change that we can reasonably hope to find. Surely, when we find, in two cognate languages, two phonemes which are descended from the same proto-phoneme and undergo the same distinctive sound-change, we have a right to assume that they are phonetically similar or even identical.[7] If so, it follows that Akkadian š was a lateral, as Gumpertz suggested.

Since the merger seems to have begun with *št* rather than *šd* (von Soden 1969:5), it seems fair to make the further assumption (reminiscent of, but quite different from, Lehmann's) that /l/ had a voiceless allophone before /t/.[8] If so, the original change was [ɬ] › [l̥]/_[t], i.e. a simple loss of friction. The slightly later change [ɬ] › [l]/_[d] involved in addition the acquisition of voicing through assimilation.

In arguing for Gumpertz's solution, we are not unmindful of the difficulties it entails. The conventional transliteration š is firmly based on the agreement between etymology (the phoneme in question is the reflex not only of PS *ś* but also of PS š) and the rendering of the phoneme in Akkadian loanwords in Hebrew, Aramaic, and Persian (Delitzsch 1889:106). On the other hand, it should be remembered that these loanwords were borrowed in the Neo-Babylonian period, a thousand years after the sound-change we are investigating. By that time, Akkadian /š/ could have shifted (without undergoing any new merger) from [ɬ] to [š], just as Arabic ش did centuries later. Moreover, the evidence of the Jerusalem Amarna letters (14th century -- almost contemporary with the sound-change), though extremely fragmentary, seems to give a picture of Akkadian š which is entirely different from the conventional one (Harris 1939:34, Nitzan 1973:43):

ša-te-e = *śådε(h)* "field"
še-e-ri = *śeʕir* "Seir"
u-ru-sa-lim = *yĕrušålem (kĕṯiḇ)* "Jerusalem"
la-ki-si = *låḵiš* "Lachish"
bit sa-a-ni = *beṯ šĕʔån* "Beisan"

The rendering of Canaanite *ś* with Akkadian *š*[9] (although it should be noted that Canaanite *ṯ* is also rendered with Akkadian *š* in *ša-ak-mi* = *šĕḵεm* "Shechem"[10]) and Canaanite *š* with Akkadian *s* gives support to Gumpertz's proposal and suggests that the realization [š] (of Akkadian /š/) may have been an innovation of the post-Amarna period.

Further support for this proposal comes from the variant spellings of a non-Assyrian name in the Old Assyrian texts (c. 1950-1750 BCE) from Kültepe: *I-la-li-el-kà* = *E-lá-li-iš-kà* (Hecker 1968:53).

The most likely explanation for these variants seems to be that the name was phonemically /Ilalilka/ but that it was, at least on occasion, realized [Ilal̥ilka], with partial assimilation of *l* to voiceless *k*. This explanation -- or rather, the simple fact that Old Assyrian *š* and *l* could be used to render the same foreign phone(me) -- suggests that Old Assyrian *š* may have been a lateral.

It is interesting to note that even according to the conventional view, Akkadian had a phoneme with the same phonetic value as PS *ś* until the end of the Old Akkadian period. This phoneme represented the product of a merger of PS *ś* and PS *š* in which the latter, not the former, gave up its phonetic identity. It was only at the end of this period that Akkadian is said to have lost its *ś* by merging it with *š*, the phonetically altered reflex of PS *ṯ*. Thus, the only change in the conventional view entailed by Gumpertz's proposal concerns this second merger, specifically its direction. If this proposal is correct we must write: Old Akkadian *š* › *ś* rather than *ś* › *š*.

One possible objection to this theory is that we usually expect the uncommon phone -- in this case, the lateral phone -- to give up its identity in a merger (i.e. we expect the "marked" feature to be lost), and in fact this was the usual fate of *ś* in its various mergers in the various Semitic languages and of the ض in its independent (Blau 1969:42) mergers with ظ in the various Arabic dialects. Nevertheless, there are exceptions to this rule. In Ẓufār and Daṯīna, for example, central ظ merged with lateral ض rather than vice versa.[11] The merger of *š* with *ś* in Pre-Old Akkadian is another example, assuming that the conventional view is correct.

Moreover, it is possible to remedy the abovementioned defect by assuming that the direction of the Old Akkadian merger was š › ś in some environments (including /_apical), but ś › š in others.[12] This would mean that the Old Babylonian /š/ phoneme had two allophones -- [š] and [ś] -- each continuing an originally independent Proto-Semitic phoneme.

[1]Many Assyriologists write the word for "gift" with a long vowel (*qīštu*), but this practice may be "only etymologically and morphophonemically correct" (Reiner 1966:121).

[2]This word is not attested in the period before the merger, but its original form (with etymological *l*) can be reconstructed from its Semitic cognates, e.g. Syriac *qelyā* "alkali," Arabic *qily* "alkali"; cf. Thompson 1949:35.

[3]Many Assyriologists write the word for "shame" with a long vowel (*bāltu*), but this practice may be "only etymologically and morphophonemically correct" (Reiner 1966:121).

[4]The same idea occurred independently to Diakonoff (1965:22), Pia (1974), Hetzron (personal communication), and the present writer.

[5]See chapter i.

[6]See chapter x.

[7]It is true that other Akkadian sibilants not descended from PS *ś* (namely, *ṣ*, *s*, and *z*) also alternate with *l* in a few instances, but this does not weaken our argument, for Held (1959) has shown that in such cases, the *l*-allomorph goes back to an earlier *š*-allomorph. Thus, for example, we find that *marultu* "evil, sick," the feminine counterpart of *marṣu*, goes back to an earlier *maruštu* (ibid., 173). We might add that in one case (*mazzaztum* › *mazzaštum* › *manzaltu* "station") the *š*-allomorph is attested already in Old Akkadian (Gelb 1957 s.v.).

[8]This assumption, when coupled with the further assumption that the voiceless allophone came to be produced with friction (presumably for the sake of audibility, cf. Dieth 1950:149) in Neo-Assyrian (when /š/ was no longer realized as a voiceless fricative-lateral and the way was thus cleared for /l/ to acquire that realization before /t/), makes the Neo-Assyrian merger of /lt/(including both /lt/ ‹ /št/ and etymological /lt/) with /ss/ look very much like the Neo-Assyrian merger of /št/ with /ss/ identified by Kaufman (1974:141). On the other hand, sporadic examples of *tt* › *ss* in Neo-Assyrian (*maʔattu* › *maʔassu* "much" (von Soden 1952:29), *ašarettu* › *šaressu* (ibid 1969:5), *ambatte* › *ambassi* (Gelb 1955:103)) suggest that the explanation for *lt* › *ss* is to be sought in the phonetic nature of *t* rather than *l*. Akkadian *t* -- if we may judge from Greek transcriptions (Pinches 1902 and Schileico 1928) which consistently render it with *th* rather than *t* (the latter *is* used however to render Akkadian *ṭ*) --was an aspirate, and, as the history of many European languages shows, aspirates have a tendency to turn into spirants. In the Germanic Sound Shift, for example, PIE *th* and *t* were shifted to [θ] while *tt* was shifted to [ss]. It is not unreasonable to suppose that something similar took place in Neo-Assyrian, although it was naturally only the phonemic merger with /ss/, not the sub-phonemic shift to [θ], which succeeded in finding expression in the cuneiform orthography.

[9]Goetze (1941:128fns15&19), followed by Moran ([1961] 1965:66 and 1975:152), dismissed these renderings as a matter of orthography rather than phonetics, but cf. Moran 1975:163fn51 for the telling admission that "all the problematic cases [cited by Goetze as evidence for his theory] concerned place names and possibily one or two Canaanite words; there is no confusion of the sibilants in the writing of Akkadian."

[10]The fact that early Egyptian transcriptions also render Canaanite *ṯ* and *ś* with one phoneme (viz. *s*) is an interesting parallel, which may turn

out, upon further research, to be more significant than it appears to be at present.

[11]See chapter ii.

[12]This type of merger, or "reorganization" is not uncommon; cf. for example, the merger of Old French *oe* (< Latin ŏ) and ø (< Latin ō) into a phoneme realized [ø] in final position and [oe] in non-final position (Fox and Wood 1968:35,36). A similar sound-change took place in Gothic where *e* (orthographical *ai*) and *i* merged into *i*, except before *h* and *r*, where the merger product was *e* (lecture by Prof. Henry Hoenigswald). In Semitic, we have the Gurage merger reported by Polotsky (1938:141-2) in which *n*, *r* and *l* appear as *n* in some environments and as *r* in others.

XX.
Evidence for Lateral *Ḍ* in Pre-Aramaic

Interesting evidence for the lateral theory comes from a set of Aramaic words in which PS *ḍ* is represented by *ṣ* instead of the usual ʕ. These puzzling exceptions have continued to defy explanation since their discovery by Nöldeke (1878:406) and Lagarde (1878:27) a century ago. Even Yushmanov, a brilliant Semitist who made important contributions to our understanding of the phonetic nature of *ḍ*, was stymied by this problem (1926:44):

> Beaucoup plus difficile est la question sur les cas, où l'araméen a le ص *S'adhe* pour le ض *D'ad* arabe, etc. Nous espérons trouver les traces de cette nuance problématique en dehors de ces cas d'une seule langue.

A good collection of examples, based in part on Nöldeke 1878 and Lagarde 1878, is found in Brockelmann 1908 (pp. 135, 236):

ṣmad̲ "bind up (a broken limb)"[1] = Arabic *ḍamada* "bandage a wound"
ʕmaṣ, *ʕammeṣ* "shut(the eyes)" = Arabic *ġammaḍa* "shut (the eyes)"
ḥmaṣ (also *ḥmaʕ*) "be sour" = Arabic *ḥamuḍa* "be sour"
ṣrik̲ "in need of" = Arabic *ḍaruka* "be in need of"
ʕraṣ "befall" = Jewish Aramaic *ʕraʕ* "befall, meet"[2] = Behistun inscription *ʕrq* "meet"
ṣerʕā "breast" = Arabic *ḍarʕ* "udder, teat"

Brockelmann 1908 is a remarkable work, but it suffers from a lack of organization. The above list, for example, is presented piecemeal (on pages 135 and 236), obscuring the remarkable fact that all of these roots have *m* or *r* immediately preceding or following *ṣ*. As a result, Brockelmann winds up naming four conditioning phones (*ġ*, *ḥ*, *r*, *d*) for a sound-change (PS *ḍ* › Aramaic *ṣ*) known from only six words.

An environment consisting of *m* and *r* also suffices to describe the new examples of **ḍ*›*ṣ* discovered in Aramaic inscriptions after Brockelmann's time. One such example is *ṣr* "enemy" in the Hadad inscription (line 30) instead of the usual *ʕr*, corresponding to Hebrew *ṣar* "enemy," Ugaritic *ṣrt* "enemy," Akkadian *ṣerru* "enemy," ESA *ḍr* "war, enemy,"[3] Ethiopic *ḍärr* "enemy," and *ḍr* "war" in the Arabic inscriptions from Taymāʔ (Winnett and Reed 1970:192). The only Late Aramaic reflex of this Old Aramaic form seems to be Mandaic *ṣara* "enemy" (Drower and Macuch 1970:192). This is not likely to have been a borrowing of Akkadian *ṣerru* since Akkadian *e* appears in Mandaic as *i*:[4] *Ilul* "name of month" < Akkadian *Elūlu* (ibid., 351), *Bil* "name of deity" < Akkadian *Bēl* (ibid., 60), *ikura* "a pagan temple" < Akkadian *ē-kūr* (ibid., 349), *Nirba* "place-name" < Akkadian *Nēribu* (ibid., 299). We should also point out that the word in question -- *ṣr* -- is a particularly revealing example of PS *ḍ* > Aramaic *ṣ*, since it leaves no doubt as to the identity of the conditioning phone.

Another example is the much-debated *ḥṣr* "grass, verdure" of the vassal treaties found at Sefire:

> IA 28 wʔl ypq ḥṣr wlytḥzh yrq
> Let not grass come out; let not greenery appear.

It is generally agreed that the *ṣ* of *ḥṣr* corresponds to the *ḍ* of Arabic *xaḍir* "verdure, greenery" (or *xaḍar*, *xuḍar*, etc.), but there is no agreement about the origin of this correspondence. Kutscher (1967:171) dismisses *ḥṣr* as a Canaanism.[5] Degen (1969:37) is not happy with this solution, but is unable to offer a substitute. Only Blau, viewing *ḥṣr* from the perspective of Brockelmann's discussion, realizes that this form may be another product of "the well known 'weak' sound change" (1971:8fn, 1970:61).

Blau (1970:61-2) also considers a number of Syriac and Jewish Aramaic examples which Brockelmann seems to have overlooked. If we eliminate those which he suspects may be Hebrew loans or considers doubtful on other grounds, we are left with two good examples:

> Syriac *raṣ* "bruise, crush" alongside *raʕ* "beat, break to pieces" = Arabic *raḍḍa* "bruise, crush"
> Syriac *np̱aṣ* "shake off (esp. dust)" = Arabic *nafaḍa* "shake off (esp. dust)"

The first of these has the by-now-expected *r*. In fact, as in the case of *ṣr*, no other consonant is present in the root aside from *ṣ*. We note with satisfaction that we now have an Aramaic *ṣ* in the two roots where the influence of *r* on **ḍ* is, so to speak, unadulterated by the influence of other consonants, and should therefore be at its strongest: **ḍarra* and **raḍḍa*. One could think of these as test cases.[6]

The second example requires a revision of our original rule -- a welcome revision as it turns out, since the rule **ḍ>ṣ/ central resonant* is more general[7] than the rule **ḍ>ṣ/ r, m*.

We might also mention a third Syriac example considered by Blau:

> *ṣarwā* "balm" = Arabic *ḍirw* "a kind of fragrant tree whose leaves are used in the manufacture of perfume" (Našwān 1916 s.v.) = ESA *ḍrw* "genus arboris odoriferae" = Hebrew *ṣŏri* "balm" = Amarna 48 (Ugarit) *ṣurwa* "aromatic plant"

Blau asserts that this is a loanword but gives no evidence for his assertion. We may therefore be permitted to note that if *ṣarwā* does turn out to be a genuine Aramaic form, our rule will be able to accommodate it.[8]

One last example has been reported (Leslau 1938:187) of an Aramaic *ṣ* which corresponds to *ḍ* -- not the *ḍ* of Arabic but the *ḍ* of Socotri: *maḥṣaltā* "mat" = Socotri *hadhel* "rug." Leslau assumed that the *ḍ* in this Socotri word is secondary (ibid., 29-30), but the examples he gives of *ṣ>ḍ* in Socotri are not very convincing. It is possible, therefore, that we have here an example of **ḍ>ṣ* in Aramaic. That would produce the most general rule of all: **ḍ>ṣ/ resonant*.

This conditioned sound-change takes on great significance when viewed in the light of a strikingly similar sound-change described by Leslau (1938:31) involving the Socotri fricative-lateral *ḍ*. Leslau assembled from the texts of the Südarabische Expedition a list of Socotri words in which *z* (once *ž*) occurs as a free variant of *ḍ*. He did not notice that every root on the list has a liquid or nasal immediately preceding or following *ḍ/z*:

> *maʕrizoh, maʕriḍoh* "tablier"
> *šizeher, šiḍeher* "vert"
> *enzof, enḍof* "étendre"
> *šizre, šiḍre* "s'étonner, admirer"
> *zanḥ, ḍanḥ* "giron"
> *ḥazhel, ḥaḍhel* "tapis"
> *ʕežanoh* "elle a aimé," *ʕeḍan* "il a aimé"[9]

The similarity between the behavior of Socotri *ḍ* in the vicinity of liquids and nasals and the behavior of Pre-Aramaic *ḍ* in the same environment is obvious.[10] Since it is unlikely that the alternations go back to Proto-West Semitic (the Socotri alternation gives the impression of being productive and therefore recent), the similarity of treatment would seem to indicate that the Pre-Aramaic ḍ was phonetically similar to its etymological counterpart in Socotri.

An interesting by-product of our theory is that it enables us to provide a phonetic rationale for the Aramaic sound-change -- to explain why it was the liquids and nasals which caused the Pre-Aramaic ḍ to merge with ṣ. Liquids and nasals are, as a class, best known to historical linguists for their strange, dissimilatory effects upon each other. These effects are well-known in European languages (Malmberg 1963:62) and in the Semitic languages as well (e.g. Cantineau [1941] 1960:51,53). When two members of this class occur in the same word, it often happens that one of them is replaced by a third member of the class. Thus, in the Arabic dialects, *l* is often replaced by *r* or *n*[11] in the vicinity of *l*,*r*,*n* or *m* (loc. cit.). The Socotri examples show that an *l* made with friction can also be affected by the presence of liquids and nasals, but, unlike the frictionless lateral which dissimilates to *n* or *r*, the Socotri fricative-lateral dissimilates to *z*. This is because ɮ and *l* are acoustically very different[12]: the former sounds much like ž[13] or *z*,[14] while the latter is closest acoustically to frictionless continuants like *n* and (one type of) *r*. We might also note that Socotri ḍ dissimilates to an unemphatic *z*, because it itself, like MSA ḍ in general, is unemphatic (Johnstone 1973:98fn).

It is interesting to note that similar sound-changes have been reported for *voiceless* fricative-laterals in Welsh and Socotri. The Socotri change is described by Beeston (1951:8) as follows:

> As Leslau has pointed out, there is a series of forms in sq which exhibits š where mh and šḫ have ŝ, and in these instances the sq form must be regarded as a secondary development. To this remark I would only add the comment that out of a total of sixteen instances of this, twelve are roots containing *m*, *n*, or *r*; one may therefore conjecture that this phenomenon is to a large extent due to the influence of a liquid or nasal in the root.

The Welsh change, reported by Nettlau (1890:69) is not quite as well documented:

> *Th* is said to be a dialectal (Gwentian) pronunciation of *ll*; in the examples which I am going to quote, *r*, *l*, or *ll* occur in the neighboring syllables; hence I am unable to say whether dissimilation took place or whether a real change of sounds must be stated. cf. Schuchardt in *Keltische Briefe, Allg. Zeitung* 1876, p. 2323b: *ll* be-

> comes *th* in Monmouthshire from Penmarc and Llandunod until Gwentlwg (these boundaries are given in the Camb. Journ. IV p.207); he quotes *arath*; cf. in a text from Ebbw Vale, Monmouthshire, pl. *erish* and *erith = erill*, sing. *arall* ...*cylleth* for *cyllell* is more generally spread ...

These reports, especially the first, tend to confirm our interpretation of the Socotri alternation between *ḍ* and *z* and add plausibility to our reconstruction of a fricative-lateral *ḍ* for Pre-Aramaic.

[1]Brockelmann uses the meaning *anschirren* "to harness," but, as the dictionaries I consulted do not give this meaning for Arabic *ḍamada*, I have used a second meaning. There is, however, a noun *miḍma*, denoting a type of yoke, cf. Akkadian *naṣmadu* "yoke" < **maṣmadu* (the feminine form *naṣmattu*, which might correspond more exactly to *miḍma*, means "bandage").

[2]Brockelmann compares Arabic *ġrḍ* instead, but this root does not seem to have the required meaning cf. *ʔaġraḍa* "to attain the goal," *taġarraḍa* "to take sides," and, besides, it is clear enough from the inner-Aramaic correspondence alone that the *ṣ* of Syriac *ʕraṣ* is a reflex of PS *ḍ*.

[3]Actually, *ṣr* occurs in a context in the Hadad inscription (*ʔnšy ṣry*) which makes the translation "war" just as possible as "enemy," cf. II Samuel 8:10 *ʔiš milḥămoṯ toʕi* "Toi's enemy," but literally, "the man of (the) wars of Toi," and, even better, Isaiah 41:11-12 *ʔanše riḇɛkå // ʔanše maṣṣuṯɛkå// ʔanše milḥamtɛkå* "your enemies." Incidentally, the last of these can also mean "your men of war;" I hope to deal with the transformational derivations of this phrase at some time in the future.

[4]I would like to thank Prof. Joseph Malone for correcting an earlier version of this chapter by pointing out to me that this *i̱* is a grapheme which is "moot with respect to *i* vs. *e*"(Malone 1971:401fn).

[5]"Wir hatten jedoch im Altaramäischen entweder **ḥqr* oder *ḥʕr* und wahrscheinlicher *ḥʔr* erwartet, siehe arabisch خضر, genau wie bei der wurzel *mhḍ* (arabisch مخض) die schon in der ZKR-Inschrift als *mḥʔ* erscheint. Tätsächlich kennt nun Syrisch *ḥʔr* = 'Papyrus'... Demnach ist ein aramäisches *ḥṣr* höchst problematisch und in Sefire eher kanaanismus anzunehmen." For the correspondence *ḥʔrʔ - xḍr* see Schulthess (1905-6:127). Of course, the existence of this word in Syriac does not strengthen Kutscher's argument very much, since we find interdialectal doublets like *ʕrṣ/ʕrʕ* and *ṣr/ʕr* and even intradialectal doublets, e.g. Syriac *ḥmṣ/ḥmʕ* and *rṣ/rʕ*.

[6]Other conceivable test cases -- *ḍamma* and *maḍḍa* -- do not seem to have any Aramaic cognates.

[7]For a discussion of generality of rules, cf. Harms 1968:7.

[8]The problematic Jewish Palestinian cognate *ṭrw* (Kutscher 1969:18) **ḏrw* may be the product of a sound change similar to the one being discussed.

[9]The feminine form *ʕeḏanoh* by chance does not occur in the texts from which Leslau gathered his material.

[10]There are even two pairs of cognates on the lists: *šiḍeher* "green" = *ḥṣr* "grass, verdure," *ḥaḍhel* "rug" = *maḥṣaltā* "mat."

[11]Before a labial, of course, this *n* becomes *m*.

[12]Cf. Fresnel (1938:540) on the voiced fricative-lateral which alternates with *l* in Shahari:

> "...une espèce de *z* ou de ذ *dhal* qui, pour mes oreilles, n'a aucun rapport avec l'*l* [in spite of the fact that the former replaces the latter

for euphony]... comme le rapport acoustique qui doit exister entre ces deux articulations échappe complètement à nos sens, je n'ai pas voulu représenter la nouvelle articulation par un ل avec addition d'un point, de peur qu'on ne s'imaginât que le son de l'une a quelque ressemblance avec celui de l'autre."

[13] Johnstone compares it to the sibilant in "pleasure" (personal communication) and writes it ǯ (1968:517).

[14] Thomas (1937) writes the MSA voiced fricative-lateral as ź, read: lateralized z.

Conclusions

The case for fricative-laterals in Proto-Semitic presented above is, in the opinion of the present writer, quite substantial. Lateral ś-- once the stepchild of the lateral hypothesis (cf. Moscati 1954:38) -- is now attested in every branch of the Semitic family. Ironically, it is now the case for lateral ḍ which looks weak by comparison. The lone piece of evidence for lateral ḍ from outside of South Semitic (chapter xx) is rather indirect. That is why we need chapters xiv and xv. Strictly speaking, the doublets presented in those chapters show only that ḍ was the emphatic counterpart of ś in Proto-Semitic and in pre-Biblical Hebrew, but it is hard to imagine how a central (i.e. non-lateral) ḍ could have been the emphatic counterpart of a lateral ś.

Another, more pragmatic, argument in favor of the lateral hypothesis is that it has no serious competitor. The conventional wisdom of fifty years ago -- that [ḏ̣] and [ç] were the original phonetic values of PS ḍ and ś -- was based more on guesswork than on any solid evidence. Such evidence as was presented in support of this position came from Arabic, which we now recognize to be one of the strongest bastions of the lateral hypothesis. In view of the strong likelihood that ḍ and ś were fricative-laterals in Proto-South Semitic, it is a priori unlikely that Arabic could supply any evidence for non-lateral ḍ or ś in Proto-Semitic.

What else can we say about PS ḍ and ś aside from the fact that they were probably fricative-laterals? Judging from their reflexes in the various Semitic languages, the former was emphatic while the latter was unemphatic and voiceless. Here we come up against one of the perennial problems of Semitic linguistics: were the PS emphatics velarized or glottalized? The present writer has new evidence for the latter alternative which he hopes to present in the near future (cf. also chapter ii, fn. 5), but for the purposes of this monograph it is not necessary to take sides on this issue. We may simply say that if PS ḍ was velarized, it was probably voiced as in Arabic and MSA, i.e. [ɮ̴], and if it was glottalized, it was necessarily voiceless and possibly also an affricate, i.e. [tɬ'] (Martinet 1953: 71, Cantineau [1951-2] 1960:284), rather than a simple fricative, since the audibility of fricatives produced with a glottalic air-stream tends to be rather low (Malmberg 1963:29). It is also possible that both [ɬ'] and [tɬ'] existed in the language as social variants, a possibility suggested to the present writer by the status of [ɬ'] and [tɬ'] in Ubykh (Dumézil and Namitok 1954:163).

Was there in Proto-Semitic a complete lateral triad? If so, where is the third (i.e. voiced unemphatic) member? Cantineau ([1951-2] 1960:287) considered the possibility that *l* was that third member, but rejected it on the grounds that "en arabe les groupements *ḍl* et *lḍ*, *šl* et *lš* sont bien attestés au début comme en fin de racine," whereas members of the same triad would ordinarily be incompatible. However, now that we have shown that *l is* in fact incompatible with *š* and *ḍ* in Arabic (cf. chapter xiii), this counter-argument is invalid.

Another problem, hinted at by Cantineau (loc. cit.), is the phonetic difference between [l] (a lateral approximant or liquid) and [ɬ] (according to Cantineau, a "lateralized" fricative). Cantineau's peculiar conception of [ɬ] (cf. chapter iv), led him to exaggerate the importance of this difference and to believe that it would be necessary to posit a sound change to account for it: "[*l*] pourrait être une sonore latéralisée ayant perdu son articulation antérieure..." Actually, as we have shown (chapter i), the phonological pairing of frictionless [l] with fricative [ɬ] is attested in several languages and is easily explainable on acoustic grounds.

Add, to the above, considerations of symmetry and the possibility that Hebrew *lˁg* is related to *śḥq* and **ḍḥq* (cf. chapter xiv), and the scales begin to tip in favor of a lateral triad, most probably of the form:

l ɬ ɬ' = l ś ḍ

Directions for Further Research

The first draft of this monograph was three chapters longer than the present version. The chapters in question were deleted because they were plagued with problems which could not be easily explained away. It is, nevertheless, possible that further research will solve some of these problems and thus pave the way for the rehabilitation of these chapters.

One chapter raised the possibility that the Aramaic cognate of Hebrew *śěrok̲* "shoe-strap" (= Arabic *širāk* "shoe-strap") is the word used by Targum Onqelos, the Peshiṭta, and the Genesis Apocryphon to render *śěrok̲* (Genesis 14:23), namely, *ʕarqat-* (TO), *ʕeraqtā* (P), *ʕrqʔ* (GA). Such a correspondence would presuppose a sound-change *ś*>*ḏ̣* in pre-Aramaic, and thus provide further evidence for the phonological pairing of *ḏ̣* and *ś* outside of South Semitic (cf. chapters xiv-xv).

One problem with this equation is that the vowels do not correspond. Neither the vowel pattern of *ʕarqat-* nor the vowel pattern of *ʕeraqtā* can go back to **i - ā*. (Nor should one be misled into thinking that *e - a* of *ʕeraqtā* is a reflex of **i - a*, for the latter sequence would have yielded *e - Ø*, as we see from *ʕenb̲t̲ā* "cluster of grapes" < **ʕinabatā*. Forms like *ʔenaqtā* "groan" < **ʔanaqatā* and *zedeqtā* "alms" < **zadaqatā* prove that the *e* of *ʕeraqtā* need have no relationship to an older **i*.) Secondly, it is difficult to explain what caused this entire root to become emphatic in pre-Aramaic, although the presence of *r* mitigates somewhat the seriousness of this problem (cf. Kutscher 1970: 373).

In another chapter, the order of the Ugaritic alphabet--specifically the fact that *š* comes right before *l* -- was adduced as evidence that Ug. *š* may have been a lateral. The problem with this argument is that the order of the Ugaritic alphabet shows no trace of a phonetic principle. The only way to save this argument would be to show that the alphabet developed piece-meal and that the sequence *š*, *l* was not created at the same time as, e.g., *m*, *n*, *s* (where the order seems to be related to the names of the letters: *mem* "water," *nun* "fish," *såmɛk̲* "fish").

The third chapter dealt with the alternation of ṣ with *l* before apical stops in Akkadian, beginning with the observation that in all of the examples of this alternation collected by Held (1959:173), ṣ is the reflex of PS ḍ (rather than PS ṣ or ḏ):

> *emṣu* "sour (masc.)" ~ *emiltu* "sour (fem.)"; cf. Arabic *ḥāmiḍ* "sour," Aramaic *ḥamiʕā* "sour."
> *marṣu* "sick (masc.)"~ *marultu* "sick (fem.)"; cf. Arabic *marīḍ* "sick," ESA *mrḍ* "sick," Shahari *marīẑ́* "sick," Harsusi *mirīẑ́* "sick," Botahari *mereẑ* "sick," Socotri *meroḍ* "he healed," Aramaic *mraʕ* "sick."
> *miḫṣu* "blow" ~ *miḫiltu* "blow, wound"; cf. ESA *mḫḍ* "strike," Aramaic *maḥā* "blow, wound."
> *riḫṣu* "inundation" ~ *riḫiltu* "inundation"; cf. Arabic *raḥaḍa* "wash," Mehri, Harsusi, Shahari *raḥaẑ* "wash," Socotri *raḥaḍ* "wash," Geez *rəḥəḍa* "sweat," Egyptian Aramaic *rḥʕ* "wash."

The special treatment accorded to etymological ḍ would seem to indicate that ḍ was still a distinct phoneme at the beginning of the Middle Babylonian period. The fact that the special treatment consists of alternation with *l* would seem to indicate that MB ḍ was a lateral, especially since, as we have seen (chapter x), lateral ḍ alternates with *l* in Arabic (before apical stops!) and in Socotri. In fact, two of the three Socotri examples reported by Leslau (**lirḥaḍ ~ lirḥal-s, *imeroḍ ~ imerol-s*) have the same root as two of the four Akkadian examples reported by Held (*riḫṣu ~ riḫiltu, marṣu ~ marultu*), although little significance can be attached to this fact, since it is virtually certain that the alternations in the two languages do not go back to a common source. (The Akkadian alternation was created by a two-stage shift, *ṣt › št › lt* (loc. cit.), the second stage of which did not take place until the end of the OB period.)

At first, this argument seemed to be quite convincing, but closer examination revealed that it is based on incomplete data. A fifth example of the Akkadian alternation, already noted by Delitzsch (1889:119) but overlooked by Held, seems to involve etymological ṣ:

> *eṣēdu* "to harvest" ~ *eldu* "harvested"; cf. Arabic *ḥaṣada* "harvest," Aramaic *ḥṣad* "harvest."

Furthermore, it is possible to reconstruct further examples of this alternation from examples of ṣ ~ š given by Held, and one of these also seems to involve etymological ṣ:

karṣī akālu "slander" (lit. "eat bits of") ~**karriltu* "slanderous" (unattested but cf. *karrištu*); cf. Aramaic *ʔmr krṣy* (OA), *ʔkl qarṣe* (BA) "slander," Arabic *qaraṣa* "pinch, scratch, sting,"

This is not an insurmountable problem. For one thing, it is possible that the etymologies given above for *eṣēdu* and *karāṣu* are incorrect. The Aramaic cognate of *karṣī akālu* is probably a borrowing, and if so, there is no reason why the Arabic cognate should not be given as *qaraḍa* "gnaw, nibble, bite" instead of *qaraṣa;* and *eṣēdu* may be connected with Arabic *ʕaḍada* "lop trees with a reaping hook (*miʕḍad*)" and Ethiopic *miʕḍäd* "sickle" as Gordon has suggested (1965:460) rather than with Arabic *ḥaṣada* and Aramaic *ḥṣad*. If all else failed, we could admit that etymological *ṣ* and *ḍ* were merged in MB, but argue that the merger product preserved the phonetic value of the latter rather than the former.

A far more serious criticism of our argument is that it conveniently but arbitrarily overlooks the fact that *all* of the Akkadian sibilants -- not just the reflexes of PS *ś* and *ḍ* -- alternate with *l* before *t* in at least a few roots. This fact seriously dilutes the strength of the Akkadian evidence for lateral *ḍ* in Proto-Semitic. Further research is needed to determine whether there is any justification for distinguishing between *ṣ* ~ *l* on the one hand and *s* ~ *l*, *z* ~ *l* on the other.

Another area for further research is the question of the pre-PS history of *ś* and *ḍ*, or the narrower question of extra-Semitic evidence for fricative-laterals in Proto-Semitic. One scholar has suggested that PS *ḍ* corresponds to various clusters of consonant plus *l* in Indo-European (Brunner 1969:100-3). This is certainly an interesting suggestion, but the cognates adduced as proof are not convincing.

The possibility that Proto-Chadic ɬ (cf. Kraft 1971) and PS *ḍ* go back to a common source is more promising. Possible cognates are PC *bɬ* "egg" (Kraft 1971:276) = PS *byḍ-t* "egg" and PC *ʔɬ* "ground" (loc. cit.) = PS *ʔrḍ* "earth, ground." On the other hand, there are also cognates in which PC ɬ corresponds to PS *š*: PC *ɬm* "name" (Newman and Ma 1966:237) = PS *šm* "name" and PC *ɬn* "tooth" (ibid., 240) = PS *šn* "tooth." Moreover, the very existence of a PC ɬ is the subject of a controversy, which centers around the fact that most of the languages of the Plateau-Sahel branch of Chadic have *s* in words where languages of the Biu-Mandara branch have ɬ. Newman and Ma (1966:226) reconstruct *s* from this correspondence (the present writer has replaced their *s* with ɬ in the PC forms cited above in their name), while Kraft (1971:276) feels that the ɬ may well be original. According to the former view, the ɨ = *s* correspondence between Biu-Mandara and Plateau-Sahel is in complementary distribution with an *s* = *s* correspondence, and cannot, therefore, be considered the reflex of an autonomous PC phoneme. The fact that PS š corresponds to Plateau-Sahel *s* regardless of whether Biu-Mandara has ɨ (as in the examples above) or *s* (as in the reflexes of PC *(w)sn* "sleep" = PS *(w)šn* "sleep"; Newman and Ma 1966:239) lends support to this view.

List of References

Abercrombie, David. 1967. *Elements of General Phonetics.* Chicago: Aldine.

Abraham, R. C. 1962a. *Somali-English Dictionary.* London: University of London Press.

______. 1962b. *Dictionary of the Hausa Language.* 2nd ed. London: University of London Press.

Abun-Nasr, Jamil M. 1971. *A History of the Maghrib.* Cambridge: University Press.

AHw. *Akkadisches Handwörterbuch.* 1959-. Unter Benutzung des lexikalischen Nachlasses von Bruno Meissner (1868-1947) bearbeitet von Wolfram von Soden. Wiesbaden: Otto Harrassowitz.

Alarcón, Maximiliano A. 1925. "Precedentes islamicos de la fonetica moderna," *Homenaje ofrecido a Menéndez Pidal,* 3, 281-308. Madrid: Hernando.

Al-Azharī, Muḥammad ibn Aḥmad. 1964. *Tahḏīb al-luġa.* ʕAbd al-Salām Muḥammad Hārūn,ed.). Cairo: al-Dār al-Miṣriyya li-l-Taʔlīf wa-l-Tarjama.

Albright, William F. 1952. "The Chaldaean Inscriptions in Proto-Arabic Script," *Bulletin of the American Schools of Oriental Research,* 128, 38-45.

______. 1953. "Review of *L'institution monarchique en Arabie Méridionale avant l'Islam,*" by Jacques Ryckmans, *Journal of the American Oriental Society,* 73, 36-40.

Alcalá, Pedro de. 1505. *Vocabulista arauigo en letra castellano.* (Reprinted 1928 with *Arte para ligeramẽte saber la lẽgua arauiga* by the Hispanic Society, New York.)

Al-Jazarī, Muḥammad. 1908. *Kitāb al-tamhīd fī ʕilm al-tajwīd.* N.p.

Allony, Neḥemya. 1969. See Saadia ben Yosef al-Fayyūmī.

Al-Masʕūdī, ʕAlī ibn al-Ḥusayn. 1938. *Al-tanbīh wa-al-išrāf* (ʕAbd Allāh Ismāʕīl al-Ṣāwī, ed.). Baghdad.

Al-Murtada al-Zabīdī, Muḥammad ibn Muḥammad. 1967-70. *Tāj al-ʕarūs.* Kuwait: Ḥukūma al-Kuwait.

Al-Suyūṭī. n.d. *Kitāb al-muzhir.* n.p.

Al-Xalīl ibn Aḥmad al-Farāhīdī. 1967. *Kitāb al-ʕayn* (ʕAbd Allāh Darwīš, ed.). Baghdad: al-ʕAnī.

Anttila, Raimo. 1972. *An Introduction to Historical and Comparative Linguistics*. New York: Macmillan.

Aristotle. 1936. "On Plants," *Aristotle's Minor Works* (trans. by W.S. Hett). Cambridge, Mass.: Harvard University Press.

Aro, Jussi. 1955. *Studien zur Mittelbabylonischen Grammatik* (*Studia Orientalia*, 20). Helsinki: Societas orientalis Fennica.

______. 1959. "Die semitischen Zischlaute (ṯ), š, ś und s und ihre Vertretung im Akkadischen, Orientalia NS, 28, 321-335.

ʕÅruk̲ (ha-šalem). See Natan ben Yeḥiel.

Asín Palacios, Miguel. 1944. *Contribución a la toponimia árabe de España*. 2nd ed. Madrid: Las Escuelas de Estudios Arabes de Madrid y Granada.

Bargery, G.P. 1934. *A Hausa-English and English-Hausa Dictionary*. London: Oxford University Press.

Barth, Jakob. 1893. *Etymologische Studien*. Leipzig: J.C. Hinrich.

______. 1902. *Wurzeluntersuchungen zum hebräischen und aramäischen Lexicon*. Leipzig: J.C. Hinrich.

Basset, René. 1906. "Les mots arabes passés en berbère," *Orientalische Studien Theodor Nöldeke zum siebzigsten Geburtstag (2 März 1906) gewidmet* (Carl Bezold, ed.). 2 vols. 439-443. Gieszen: Alfred Töpelman.

______. 1909. *Mission au Sénégal* (Publications de l'École des Lettres d'Alger, Bulletin de Correspondance Africaine, 39). Paris.

Batlle y Prats, Luis. 1954. "'Alcalde'--difusión de un arabismo en catalán," *Homenaje a Millás-Vallicrosa*, 1, 67-92. Barcelona: Consejo Superior de Investigaciones Científicas.

Bauer, Hans, and Pontus Leander. 1922. *Historische Grammatik der hebräischen Sprache des Alten Testamentes*. Halle. (Reprinted 1965 by Georg Olms,Hildesheim.)

Baumstark. 1899. "Chaldaioi," *Paulys Realencyclopädie der Classischen Altertumswissenschaft* (Georg Wissowa, ed.). Stuttgart: J. B. Metzler.

BDB. Brown, Francis, S.R. Driver,and Charles A. Briggs. 1907. *A Hebrew and English Lexicon of the Old Testament, based on the lexicon of William Gesenius*. Oxford: Clarendon Press. (Reprinted 1972 by Oxford University Press.)

Beeston, A. F. L. 1951. "Phonology of the Epigraphic South Arabian Unvoiced Sibilants," *Transactions of the Philological Society*, 1-26.

______. 1962a. *A Descriptive Grammar of Epigraphic South Arabian*. London: Luzac.

______. 1962b. "Arabian Sibilants," *Journal of Semitic Studies*, 7, 222-33.

Bendavid, Abba. 1967. *Lešon miqra u-lešon ḥaxamim*. 2 vols. Tel Aviv: Dvir.

Benfey, Theodor. 1842. *Griechisches Wurzellexicon*, 2. Berlin: G. Reimer.

Ben-Ḥayyim, Zeev. 1959. *Torat ha-hege* (Rachel Rosenberg, ed.). Jerusalem: Mifʕal Ha-Šixpul.

______. 1961. *ʕIvrit wa-ʔaramit nosaḥ šomron*, 3/1. Jerusalem: Ha-Akademia la-Lašon ha-ʕIvrit.

Bent, Theodore, and Mrs. Theodore Bent. 1900. *Southern Arabia*. London: Smith, Elder.

Berendes, J. (ed.and transl.). 1902. *Des Pedanios Dioskurides aus Anazarbos Arzneimittellehre in fünf Büchern*. Stuttgart: Ferdinande Enke.

Bergsträsser, Gotthelf. 1918. *Hebräische Grammatik*. Leipzig: F.C.W. Vogel.

______. 1928. *Einführung in die semitischen Sprachen*. Munich: Max Hueber. (Reprinted 1963 by Max Hueber, Munich.)

Bezold, Carl. 1926. *Babylonisch-Assyrisches Glossar*. Heidelberg: Carl Winter.

Biggs, Robert D. 1965. "A Chaldean Inscription from Nippur," *Bulletin of the American Schools of Oriental Research*, 179, 36-38.

Birkeland, Harris. 1940. *Altarabische Pausalformen*. Oslo: Det Norske Videnskaps-Akademi i Oslo.

Bittner, Maximilian. 1910. "Neues Mehri-Materiale aus dem Nachlasse des Dr. Wilhelm Hein," *Wiener Zeitschrift für die Kunde des Morgenlandes*, 24, 70-93.

______. 1917. *Studien zur Šḫauri-Sprache in den Bergen von Ḍofâr am Persischen Meerbusen*, 4 (*Sitzungsberichte der Kaiserl. Akademie der Wissenschaften in Wien, Philosophisch-historische Klasse*, 183/5). Vienna: Alfred Holder.

Blanc, Haim. 1967a. "The 'Sonorous' vs. 'Muffled' Distinction in Old Arabic Phonology," *To Honor Roman Jakobson*, 295-308. The Hague: Mouton.

______. 1967b. "Sefer ḥadaš ʕal ha-ʕaravit ha-yehudit šel yeme ha-benayim," *Tarbiz*, 36, 406-411.

______. 1969. "The Fronting of Semitic *g* and the *qāl-gāl* Dialect Split," *Proceedings of the International Conference on Semitic Studies held in Jerusalem, 19-23 July 1965*, 7-37. Jerusalem: The Israel Academy of Sciences and Humanities.

______. 1971. "Arabic," *Current Trends in Linguistics*, 7, 501-509. The Hague: Mouton.

Blau, Joshua. 1961a. *Diqduq ha-ʕaravit ha-yehudit šel yeme ha-benayim*. Jerusalem: Magnes.

______. 1961b. "The Importance of Middle Arabic Dialects for the History of Arabic," *Studies in Islamic History and*

Civilization (Scripta Hierosolymitana, 10). Jerusalem: Hebrew University.

______. 1966. "Diqduq mašwe ḥadaš šel ha-lešonot ha-šemiyyot," *Lešonenu*, 30,136-156.

______. 1968. "On Problems of Polyphony and Archaism in Ugaritic Spelling," *Journal of the American Oriental Society*, 88, 523-526.

______. 1969. "Some Problems of the Formation of the Old Semitic Languages in the Light of Arabic Dialects," *Proceedings of the International Conference on Semitic Studies held in Jerusalem, 19-23 July 1965*, 38-44. Jerusalem: The Israel Academy of Sciences and Humanities.

______. 1970. *On Pseudo-Corrections in Some Semitic Languages*. Jerusalem: The Israel Academy of Sciences and Humanities.

______. 1971. "Marginalia Semitica I," *Israel Oriental Studies I*, 1-35. Tel-Aviv: Tel Aviv University.

Böhl, Franz. 1909. *Die Sprache der Amarnabriefe mit besonderer Berücksichtigung der Kanaanismen* (*Leipziger Semitische Studien*, 5/2). Leipzig: J.C. Hinrich.

Borger, Riekele. 1956. *Die Inschriften Asarhaddons, Königs von Assyrien* (*Archiv für Orientforschung*, Beiheft 9). Graz: Ernst Weidner.

______. 1957. "Assyriologische und altarabische Miszellen," *Orientalia NS*, 26, 1-11.

Bosworth, C.E. 1974. "A Mamlūk Text on the Orthographic Distinction of Ḍād and Ẓā?," *Orientalia Hispanica Sive Studia F.M. Pareja Octogenario Dictata* (J.M. Barral, ed.), 1/1 (*Arabica et Islamica*), 135-149. Leiden: E.J. Brill.

Bouda, Karl. 1947. "Lateral und Sibilant," *Zeitschrift für Phonetik und Allgemeine Sprachwissenschaft*, 1, 48-53.

Bouvat, L. 1913. "Un essai de cheikh Sidia sur la proposition rituelle du ض dâd et du ظ dhâ," *Revue du Monde Musulman*, 23, 305-314.

Bowrey, Thomas. 1701. *A Dictionary, English and Malayo, Malayo and English*. London.

Bravmann, Max. 1934. *Materialen und Untersuchungen zu den phonetischen Lehren der Araber*. Göttingen: Dieterichsche Universitäts - Buchdruckerei.

Brinkman, J. A. 1968. *A Political History of Post-Cassite Babylonia* (*Analecta Orientalia*, 43). Rome: Pontificum Institutum Biblicum.

Brockelmann, Carl. 1900. "Das Assyrische *l*," *Zeitschrift für Assyriologie*, 5, 395-396.

______. 1908. *Grundriss der vergleichenden Grammatik der semitischen Sprachen*, 1. Berlin: Reuther & Reichard.

______. 1928. *Lexicon Syriacum*. 2nd ed. Halis Saxonum: Max Niemayer.

Brunner, Linus. 1969. *Die gemeinsamen Wurzeln des semitischen und indogermanischen Wortschatzes.* Bern: Francke.

Buck, Carl D. 1933. *Comparative Grammar of Greek and Latin.* Chicago: University of Chicago Press.

Buxtorf, Johann. 1640. *Lexicon Chaldaicum Talmudicum et Rabbinicum.* Basileae.

CAD. *The Assyrian Dictionary of the Oriental Institute of the University of Chicago.* 1956-. Chicago and Glückstadt: J. J. Augustin.

Cameron, Charles R. 1917. *Sulu Writing: An Explanation of the Sulu-Arabic Script as Employed in Writing the Sulu Language of the Southern Philippines.* Zamboanga, Philippine Islands: The Sulu Press.

Cantineau, Jean. 1930. *Le Nabatéen.* 2 vols. Paris: Ernest Leroux.

______. 1935-1945. "La 'mutation des sifflantes' en sudarabique," *Mélanges Gaudefroy-Demombynes*, 313-323. Cairo: Institut Français d'Archéologie Orientale.

______. 1941. *Cours de phonétique arabe.* Alger. (Reprinted in Cantineau 1960, 1-125.)

______. 1946. "Esquisse d'une phonologie de l'arabe classique," *Bulletin de la Société Linguistique de Paris*, 43, 93-140. (Reprinted in Cantineau 1960, 165-204.)

______. 1951-1952. "Le consonantisme du sémitique," *Semitica*, 4, 79-94. (Reprinted in Cantineau 1960, 279-294.)

______. 1960. *Études de linguistique arabe.* Paris: Klincksieck.

Canu, Gaston. 1968. "Remarques sur quelques emprunts lexicaux en Mo:re," *The Journal of West African Languages*, 5, 25-34.

Caquot, André. 1952. "Nouvelles inscriptions araméennes de Hatra," *Syria*, 29, 89-118.

______. 1963. "Nouvelles inscriptions araméennes de Hatra," *Syria*, 40, 1-16.

Carter, H. J. 1847. "Notes on the Mahra Tribe of Southern Arabia, with a Vocabulary of their Language, to which are appended additional observations on the Gara Tribe," *Journal of the Bombay Branch of The Royal Asiatic Society*, 2, 339-370. (Reprinted 1969 by Kraus-Thompson, Nendeln/Lichtenstein.)

Caskell, W. 1960. "Asad," *Encyclopedia of Islam*. new ed. Leiden: E. J. Brill.

Cerulli, Enricho. 1924. "Somaliland," *Encyclopedia of Islam*. Leiden: E. J. Brill.

Chantraine, Pierre. 1968. *Dictionnaire étymologique de la langue grecque.* Paris: Klincksieck.

Chen, Matthew Y., and William S-Y. Wang. 1975. "Sound Change: Actuation and Implementation," *Language*, 51, 255-281.

Cheneb, Mohammed, Ben. 1927. "Al-Kisā?ī," *The Encyclopedia of Islam*. Leiden: E. J. Brill.

Christian, V. 1944. *Die Stellung des Mehri innerhalb der semitischen Sprachen (Sitzungsberichte der Kaiserl. Akademie der Wissenschaften in Wien, Philosophisch-historische Klasse*, 222/3). Brunn: Rudolf M. Rohrer.

Chwolson, Daniel. 1856. *Die Ssabier und der Ssabismus*. 2 vols. St. Petersburg: Kaiserlichen Akademie der Wissenschaften.

______. 1859. *Über die Überreste der altbabylonischen Literatur in Arabischen Übersetzungen*. St. Petersburg: Kaiserlichen Akademie der Wissenschaften.

Cohen, David. 1963. *Le dialect arabe ḥassānīya de Mauritanie*. Paris: C. Klincksieck.

Cohen, Marcel. 1927. "Review of *Kurzgefasste Grammatik der biblisch-aramäischen Sprache* by Karl Marti," *Bulletin de la Société de Linguistique de Paris, 27, 172-173*.

Colin, Georges S. 1930a. "Notes de dialectologie arabe," *Hespéris*, 10, 91-120.

______. 1930b. "Mauritanica," *Hespéris*, 11, 131-143.

Collinder, Björn. 1960. *Comparative Grammar of the Uralic Languages*. Stockholm: Almqvist & Wiksell.

Conti Rossini, C. 1931. *Chrestomathia Arabica Meridionalis Epigraphica*. Rome: Istituto per l'Oriente.

Cooke, G. A. 1937. *A Critical and Exegetical Commentary on the Book of Ezekiel*. Edinburgh: T. & T. Clark.

Copland, B. D. 1938. "Notes on the Phonetics of Sandawe," *Le Maître Phonétique*, 64, 60-64.

Corominas, Juan. 1967. *Breve diccionario etimologico de la lengue castellana*. 2nd ed. Madrid: Editorial Gredos.

Crawford, John. 1852. *A Grammar and Dictionary of the Malay Language*. 2 vols. London: Smith, Elder.

Daiches, S. 1903. "Lexicalisches," *Zeitschrift für Assyriologie*, 17, 91-93.

Degen, Rainer. 1969. *Altaramäische Grammatik* (*Abhandlungen für die Kunde des Morgenlandes*, 38). Wiesbaden: F. Steiner.

Delafosse, Maurice. 1955. *La langue Mandingue et ses dialectes (Malinke, Bambara, Dioula)*. 2 vols. Paris: Imprimerie Nationale.

Delitzsch, Franz J. 1882. *Biblical Commentary on the Book of Job* (transl. by Francis Bolton). 2nd ed. Edinburgh: T. & T. Clark.

______. 1891. *Commentary on the Song of Songs and Ecclesiastes* (transl. by M. G. Easton). Edinburgh: T. & T. Clark.

Delitzsch, Friedrich. 1889. *Assyrische Grammatik*. Berlin: H. Reuther.

Destaing, E. 1914. *Dictionnaire français-berbère Dialecte des Beni-Snous*). Paris: Ernest Leroux.

Diakonoff, Igor M. 1965. *Semito-Hamitic Languages: An Essay in Classification*. Moscow: Nauka, Central Department of Oriental Literature.

______. 1970. "Problems of Root Structure in Proto-Semitic," *Archiv Orientální*, 38, 453-480.

Dianoux, Hugues Jean de. 1962-1963. "Les mots d'emprunt d'origine arabe dans la langue songhay," *Proceedings of the 25th International Congress of Orientalists, Moscow 1960*, 5, 603-610. Moscow.

Dieth, Eugen. 1950. *Vademekum der Phonetik*. Bern: A. Francke.

Diettrich, Gustav (ed.). 1905. *Ein Apparatus criticus zur Pešitto zum Propheten Jesaia* (*Beihefte zur Zeitschrift für die alttestamentliche Wissenschaft*, 8). Giessen: Alfred Töpelman.

Dillmann, August. 1865. *Lexicon Linguae Aethiopicae*. Leipzig: T. O. Weigel.

Diodorus. 1933-1967. *Diodorus of Sicily* (transl. by C. H. Oldfather). 12 vols. London: William Heinemann.

Doke, Clement M. 1926. *The Phonetics of the Zulu Language*. Johannesburg: University of the Witwatersrand Press.

______. 1954. *The Southern Bantu Languages*. London: Oxford University Press.

Dougherty, Raymond P. 1932. *The Sealand of Ancient Arabia* (*Yale Oriental Series, Researches*, 19). New Haven: Yale University Press.

Dozy, Reinhart, and Willem Herman Engelmann. 1869. *Glossaire des mots espagnols et portugais dérivés de l'arabe*. 2nd ed. Leiden: E. J. Brill.

______. 1967. *Supplément aux dictionnaires arabes*. 3rd ed. Leiden: E. J. Brill.

Drewes, G. W. J. 1955. *Een 16de Eeuwse Maleise Vertaling van de Burda van al-Būsīrī* (*Arabische Lofdicht op Mohammed*) (*Verhandelingen van het Koninklijk Instituut voor Taal-, Land- en Volkenkunde*, 18). The Hague: Martinus Nyhoff.

Driver, Godfrey R. 1951. "Problems in the Hebrew Text of Proverbs," *Biblica*, 32, 173-197.

______. 1956. *Canaanite Myths and Legends from Ugarit*. Edinburgh: T. & T. Clark.

Driver, Samuel R. 1956. *An Introduction to the Literature of the Old Testament*. Cleveland: World Publishing.

Drower, Ethel S., and R. Macuch. 1963. *A Mandaic Dictionary*. Oxford: University Press.

Dumézil, G. 1952. "Langues caucasiennes," *Les langues du monde* (A. Meillet and Marcel Cohen, eds.), 228-254. Paris: H. Champion.

Dumézil, G., and A. Namitok. 1954. "Le système des sons de l'oubykh," *Bulletin de la Société Linguistique de Paris*, 50, 162-189.

Dunstan, Elizabeth. 1969. *Twelve Nigerian Languages.* New York: Africana.

Dupont-Sommer, A. 1944-1945. "L'Ostracon araméen d'Assour," *Syria*, 24, 24-61.

Dussaud, René. 1903. *Mission dans les régions desertiques de la Syrie Moyenne.* Paris: Imprimerie Nationale.

Ebers, Georg. 1887. *Richard Lepsius* (transl. by Zoe D. Underhill). New York: William S. Gottsberger.

Edzard, Dietz O. 1967. "Die semitohamitischen Sprachen in neuer Sicht," *Revue d'Assyriologie*, 61, 137-149.

Eguilaz Y Yanguas, Leopoldo de. 1886. *Glosario Etimologico de las Palabras Españolas...de Orígen Oriental...* Granada: La Lealtad.

Elcock, W. D. 1960. *The Romance Languages.* New York: Macmillan.

Encyclopedia Miqrait. 1972-. Jerusalem: Mosad Bialik.

Entwistle, William. 1936. *The Spanish Language.* London: Faber & Faber.

Ephʕal, Israel. 1974. "'Arabs' in Babylonia in the 8th Century B.C.," *Journal of the American Oriental Society*, 94, 108-115.

Epstein, J. N. 1960. *Diqduq ʔaramit bavlit.* (Ezra Z. Melamed, ed.). Jerusalem: Magnes.

Ewald, G. H. A. von. 1846. "Ueber die Himjarische Sprache," *Zeitschrift für die Wissenschaft der Sprache*, 1, 295-315.

Fabricius, B. (ed.). 1883. *Der Periplus des Erythräischen Meeres.* Leipzig: Veit.

Fage, J. D. 1969. *A History of West Africa.* 4th ed. Cambridge: University Press.

Faidherbe, Louis Léon. 1887. *Langues sénégalaises.* Paris: Ernest Leroux.

Feliks, Jehuda. 1968. *ʕOlam ha-ṣemaḥ ha-miqraʔi.* Ramat Gan: Masada.

Ferguson, Charles A. 1966. "Assumptions about Nasals: A Sample Study in Phonological Universals," *Universals of Language* (Joseph H. Greenberg, ed.), 2nd ed., 53-60. Cambridge, Mass.: M.I.T. Press.

Ferrand, Gabriel. 1925. "Review of *The Book of the Himyarites* by Axel Moberg (ed.)," *Journal Asiatique*, 26, 305-310.

Fischer, Wolfdietrich. 1968. "Die Position von ض im Phonemsystem des Gemeinsemitischen," *Studia Orientalia in*

Memoriam Caroli Brockelmann (*Wissenschaftliche Zeitschrift der Martin-Luther-Universität Halle-Wittenberg Gesellschafts-und sprachwissenschaftliche* *Reihe*, 17/2 -3), 55-63.

Fitzmeyer, Joseph. 1971. *The Genesis Apocryphon of Qumran Cave I*. 2nd ed. Rome: Biblical Institute Press.

Fleisch, Henri. 1965. "Ḍād," *The Encyclopaedia of Islam*. new ed. Leiden: E. J. Brill.

______. 1968. *L'Arabe classique: Esquisse d'une structure linguistique*. Beirut: Dar el-Machreq.

Fox, John, and Robin Wood. 1968. *A Concise History of the French Language*. Oxford: Basil Blackwell.

Fraenkel, Siegmund. 1886. *Die aramäischen Fremdwörter im Arabischen*. Leiden: E. J. Brill.

______. 1878. *Beiträge zur Erklärung der mehrlautigen Bildungen im Arabischen*. Leiden: E. J. Brill.

Fresnel, Fulgence. 1838a. "Quatrième Lettre sur l'Histoire des Arabes avant l'Islamisme," *Journal Asiatique*, 5 (ser. 3), 497-544.

______. 1838b. "Cinquième Lettre sur l'Histoire des Arabes avant l'Islamisme," *Journal Asiatique*, 6 (ser. 3), 529-70.

Fück, Johann. 1955. *ʿArabīya: Recherches sur l'histoire de la langue et du style arabe* (transl. by Claude Denizeau). Paris: Marcel Didier.

Garbell, Irene. 1954. "Quelques observations sur les phonèmes de l'hébreu biblique et traditionnel," *Bulletin de la Société de Linguistique de Paris*, 50, 162-189.

______. 1965. *The Jewish Neo-Aramaic Dialect of Persian Azerbaijan* (*Janua Linguarum, Series Practica*, 3). The Hague: Mouton.

Garbini, Giovanni. 1960. *Il Semitico di Nord-ovest*. Naples: Istituto Universitario Orientale di Napoli.

______. 1971. "The Phonetic Shift of Sibilants in Northwestern Semitic in the First Millennium B.C.," *Journal of Northwest Semitic Languages*, 1, 32-38.

Gaudefroy-Demombynes, M. and R. Blachère. 1952. *Grammaire de l'arabe classique*. Paris: G. P. Maisonneuve.

Gelb, Ignace J. 1955. "Notes on von Soden's Grammar of Akkadian," *Bibliotheca Orientalis*, 12, 93-111.

______. 1957. *Glossary of Old Akkadian*. Chicago: University of Chicago Press.

Genesis Rabba. 1970. *Midrash Bereshit Rabba, ms. vat. Ebr. 30*. (Michael Sokoloff, ed.). Jerusalem: Makor.

Gerteiny, Alfred G. 1967. *Mauritania*. New York: Frederick Praeger.

Gesenius, Wilhelm. 1841. "Himjaritische Sprache und Schrift und Entzifferung der letzteren," *Allgemeine Literatur-Zeitung*, 2, 370-399.

______. 1834. *Hebräisches und chaldäisches Handwörterbuch über das Alte Testament.* 4th ed. Leipzig: F. C. W. Vogel.

Gesenius, Wilhelm and Frants Buhl. 1915. *Hebräisches und aramäisches Handwörterbuch über das Alte Testament.* 17th ed. (Reprinted 1962 by Springer, Berlin.)

Ginsberg, Harold Louis. 1967. "Lexicographical Notes," *Hebräische Wortforschung, Festschrift zum 80. Geburtstag von Walter Baumgartner (Supplements to Vetus Testamentum,* 16), 71-82. Leiden: E. J. Brill.

______. 1970. "The Northwest Semitic Languages," *The World History of the Jewish People,* 2 (*Patriarchs*), 102-124. Israel: Jewish History Publications.

Ginzberg, Louis (ed.). 1909. *Yerushalmi Fragments from the Genizah,* 1. New York: J. T. S.

Glaser, Eduard. 1895. *Die Abbessinier in Arabien und Afrika.* Munich: Hermann Lukaschik.

Goetze, Albrecht. 1941. "Is Ugaritic a Canaanite Dialect?" *Language,* 17, 127-138.

______. 1958. "The Sibilants of Old Babylonian," *Revue d'Assyriologie,* 52, 137-149.

Gordon, Cyrus H. 1949. *Ugaritic Literature.* Rome: Pontificium Institutum Biblicum.

______. 1965. *Ugaritic Textbook* (*Analecta Orientalia,* 38). Rome: Pontificium Institutum Biblicum.

Goshen-Gottstein, M. H. 1963. "The Rise of the Tiberian Bible Text," *Biblical and Other Studies* (A. Altmann, ed.), 79-122.

Gouilly, Alphonse. 1952. *L'islam dans l'Afrique occidentale français.* Paris: Larose.

Greenberg, Joseph H. 1947. "Arabic Loan-Words in Hausa," *Word,* 3, 85-97.

______. 1950. "The Patterning of Root Morphemes in Semitic," *Word,* 6, 162-181.

______. 1955. *Studies in African Linguistic Classification.* New Haven: Compass.

______. 1960. "Linguistic Evidence for the Influence of the Kanuri on the Hausa," *Journal of African History,* 1, 205-212.

______. 1969. "Some Methods of Dynamic Comparison in Linguistics," *Substance and Structure of Language* (Jaan Puhvel, ed.), 147-203. Berkeley and Los Angeles: University of California Press.

Greenfield, Jonas. 1959. "Lexicographical Notes II," *Hebrew Union College Annual,* 30, 141-151.

Griffin, David A. 1961. *Los Mozarabismos del "Vocabulista" atribuido a Ramon Marti.* Madrid: Imprenta y Editorial Maestre.

Grintz, Jehoshua. 1962. "On the Original Home of the Semites," *Journal of Near Eastern Studies*, 21, 186-206.

Grohmann, Adolf. 1922. *Südarabien als Wirtschaftsgebiet (Osten und Orient*, 4, Ser. 1). 2 vols. Vienna: Forschungsinstitut für Osten und Orient.

______. 1927. "Khawlan," *Encyclopaedia of Islam*. Leiden: E. J. Brill.

______. 1933a. "Al-Yaman," *Encyclopaedia of Islam*. Leiden: E. J. Brill.

______. 1933b. "Zailaʕ," *Encyclopaedia of Islam*. Leiden: E. J. Brill.

Gudava, T. E. 1964. *Konsonantizm andiiskix jazykov*. Tiflis: Akademiya Nauk Gruzinskoi SSR, Institut Jazykoznaniya.

Guerre, Ministère de la. 1844. *Dictionnaire français-berbère (dialecte écrit et parlé par les Kabaïles de la division d'Alger)*. Paris: Imprimerie Royale.

Guest, R. 1935. "Ẓufâr in the Middle Ages," *Islamic Culture*, 9, 402-410.

Gumpertz, Yeḥiel G. 1942. "Ha-šin, ṭilṭuleha we-gilguleha," *Tarbiz*, 13, 107-115.

Guthrie, Malcom. 1971. *Comparative Bantu*, 2. Hants, England: Gregg International.

Haex, David. 1961. *Dictionarium Malaico-Latinum & Latino-Malaicum*. Rome.

Hale, Kenneth. 1965. "Some Preliminary Observations on Papago Morphophonemics," *International Journal of American Linguistics*, 31, 295-305.

Harding, G. Lankester. 1971. *An Index and Concordance of Pre-Islamic Arabian Names and Inscriptions*. Toronto: University of Toronto Press.

Harms, Robert T. 1968. *Introduction to Phonological Theory*. Englewood Cliffs, New Jersey: Prentice Hall.

Harris, Zellig S. 1936. *A Grammar of the Phoenician Language* (American Oriental Series, 8). New Haven: American Oriental Society.

______. 1939. *Development of the Canaanite Dialects. (American Oriental Series*, 16). New Haven: American. Oriental Society.

Harrison, R. K. 1962. "Balm," *The Interpreters' Dictionary of the Bible*. New York: Abingdon Press.

Haupt, Paul. 1909. "Die Posaunen von Jericho," *Wiener Zeitschrift für die Kunde des Morgenlandes*, 23, 355-365.

Hecker, Karl. 1968. *Grammatik der Kültepe-Texte*. Rome: Pontificium Institutum Biblicum.

Heffner, R. M. S. 1964. *General Phonetics*. Madison: University of Wisconsin Press.

Hein, Wilhelm. 1909. *Mehri- und Hadrami-Texte (Kaiserliche Akademie der Wissenschaften, Südarabische Expedition*, 9). Vienna: Alfred Hölder.

Held, Moshe. 1959. "*mḫṣ/*mḫš* in Ugaritic and other Semitic languages (A Study in Comparative Lexicography)," *Journal of the American Oriental Society*, 79, 169-176.

Hendershot, Vernon, and W. G. Shellabear. 1945. *A Dictionary of Standard Malay*. Mountain View, California: Pacific Press.

Henderson, Eugénie J. A. 1970. "Acoustic Features of Certain Consonant Clusters in Kabardian," *Bulletin of the School of Oriental and African Studies*, 33, 92-106.

Herodotus. 1966. (transl. by A. L. Godley). 4 vols. Cambridge: Harvard University Press.

Hetzron, Robert. 1972. *Ethiopian Semitic: Studies in Classification* (*Journal of Semitic Studies Monographs*, 2). Manchester: Manchester University Press.

Hetzron, Robert and Habte Mariam Marcos. 1966. "Des traits pertinents superposés ennemor," *Journal of Ethiopian Studies*, 4, 17-30.

Hexham, Henry. 1648. *A Copious English and Netherduytch Dictionarie Composed out of our best English Authours*. Rotterdam: Aernovt Leers.

Hirth, Friedrich, and W. W. Rockhill. 1911. *Chau Ju-Kua: His Work on the Chinese and Arab Trade in the Twelfth and Thirteenth Centuries, entitled chu-fan-chi*. St. Petersburg: Imperial Academy of Sciences.

Hiskett, M. 1965. "The Historical Background to the Naturalization of Arabic Loan-words in Hausa," *African Language Studies*, 6, 18-26.

Hoenigswald, Henry M. 1965. *Language Change and Linguistic Reconstruction*. Chicago: University of Chicago Press.

Hoffman, Carl. 1963. *A Grammar of the Margi Language*. London: Oxford University Press.

Höfner, Maria. 1943. *Altsüdarabische Grammatik*. Leipzig: Otto Harrassowitz.

Hoijer, Harry. 1946. "Chiricahua Apache," *Linguistic Structures of Native America* (Cornelius Osgood, ed.), 55-84. New York: Viking Fund.

Hommel, Fritz. 1897. "Vorläufige Mittheilungen über die inschriftliche Ergebnisse der vierten Reise Eduard Glaser's," *Actes du dixième congrès international des Orientalistes, session de Genève, 1894*, part 3, section 2, 105-117. Leiden: E. J. Brill.

Hourani, George F. 1951. *Arab Seafaring in the Indian Ocean in Ancient and Early Medieval Times*. Princeton: Princeton University Press.

Houtman, Frederik de. 1680. *Dictionarium ofte Woord en Spraeck-boeck in de Duytsche en Maleysche Tale*. Amsterdam: Paulus Matthysz.

Howison, James. 1801. *Dictionary of the Malay Tongue as Spoken in the Peninsula of Malacca, the Islands of*

Sumatra, Java, Borneo, Pulo, Pinang, & c. & c. London: Arabic and Persian Press.

Hulton, J.G. 1840. "Notice on the Curia Muria Islands," *Transactions of the Bombay Geographical Society*, 3, 183-197.

Hurvitz, Avi. 1972. *Ben lašon le-lašon*. Jerusalem: Mosad Bialik.

Hyman, Larry. 1972. *A Phonological Study of Feʔfeʔ-Bamileke* (*Studies in African Linguistics*, supplement 4). Los Angeles: University of California.

Ibn al-Jazarī, Muḥammad ibn Muḥammad. n.d. (196?). *Kitāb al-našr fī al-qirāʔāt al-ʕašr* (ʕAlī Muḥammad al-Ḍabbāʕ, ed.). 2 vols. Egypt: Muṣṭafā Muḥammad.

Ibn Durayd, Muḥammad ibn al-Ḥasan. 1925-1932. *Jamharat al-luġa*. Hyderabad: Dāʔira al-Maʕārif.

Ibn Isḥāq, Muḥammad. 1871. *Kitâb al-fihrist* (Gustav Flügel, ed.). 2 vols. Leipzig: F. C. W. Vogel.

Ibn Janāḥ, Yonah. 1929. *Sefer ha-riqmah* (Michael Wilensky, ed.). Berlin: Ha-Akademia. (Reprinted 1964 by Ha-Akademia la-Lašon ha-ʕIvrit, Jerusalem.)

Ibn Jinnī, ʕUṯmān ibn ʕAbd Allāh. 1954. *Sirr ṣināʕat al-iʕrāb* (Muṣṭafā al-Saqqā, *et. al.*, eds.). Cairo: Wizārat al-Maʕārif al-ʕUmūmiyya.

Ibn Manẓūr, Muḥammad ibn Mukarram. 1955-6. *Lisān al-ʕarab*. Beirut: Dār Ṣādir.

Ingholt, Harald. 1934. "Palmyrene Sculptures in Beirut," *Berytus*, 1, 32-43.

Jacobsen, William H. 1969. "Origin of the Nootka Pharyngals," *International Journal of American Linguistics*, 35, 25-53.

Jahn, Alfred. 1900. "Zur Erklärung des Wortes 'Ḥadhramût' (Südarabien)," *Dr. A. Petermanns Mitteilungen aus Justus Perthes' Geographischer Anstalt*, 46, 215-216.

______. 1905. *Grammatik der Mehri-Sprache in Südarabien* (*Sitzungsberichte der Kaiserl. Akademie der Wissenschaften in Wien, Philosophisch-Historische Klasse*, 150). Vienna: Alfred Hölder.

Jahn, G. 1900. *Sîbawaihi's Buch über die Grammatik*. 2 vols. Berlin: Reuther & Reichard.

James, W. E. 1969. "On the Location of Gerra," *Die Araber in der Alten Welt* (Franz Altheim, and Ruth Stiehl, eds.), 36-57. Berlin: Walter de Gruyter.

Jamme, Albert. 1962. *Sabaean Inscriptions from Maḥram Bilqîs (Mârib)*. Baltimore: John's Hopkins Press.

______. 1963. *The Al-ʕUqlah Texts* (*Documentation Sud-Arabe*, 3). Washington: The Catholic University of America Press.

______. 1972. "Review of *Ancient Records from North Arabia* by F. V. Winnett and W. L. Reed," *Journal of the American Oriental Society*, 92, 519-529.

Jastrow, Marcus. 1903. *A Dictionary of the Targumim, the Talmud Babli and Yerushalmi and the Midrashic Literature*. London: Luzac.

Jean, Charles F., and Jacob Hoftijzer. 1963. *Dictionnaire des inscriptions sémitiques de l'ouest*. Leiden: E. J. Brill.

Jóhannesson, Alexander. 1956. *Isländisches etymologisches Wörterbuch*. Bern: Francke.

Johnstone, T. M. 1968. "The Non-Occurrence of a t-prefix in Certain Socotri Verbal Forms," *Bulletin of the School of Oriental and African Studies*, 31, 515-525.

______. 1970a. "A Definite Article in the Modern South Arabian Languages," *Bulletin of the School of Oriental and African Studies*, 33, 295-307.

______. 1970b. "Dual Forms in Mehri and Harsusi," *Bulletin of the School of Oriental and African Studies*, 33, 501-512.

______. 1972. "The Language of Poetry in Dhofar," *Bulletin of the School of Oriental and African Studies*, 35, 1-17.

______. 1973. "Diminutive Patterns in the Modern South Arabian Languages," *Journal of Semitic Studies*, 18, 98-107.

______. 1975a. "Contrasting Articulations in the Modern South Arabian Languages," *Hamito-Semitica* (James and Theodora Bynon, eds.)(*Janua Linguarum, Series Practica*, 200), 155-159. The Hague: Mouton.

______. 1975b. "The Modern South Arabian Languages," *Afroasiatic Linguistics*, 1/5, 93-121.

Jones, J. M. 1913. *A Welsh Grammar*. Oxford: Oxford University Press.

______. 1930. *A Welsh Grammar, Historical and Comparative*. Oxford: Clarendon Press.

Josephus. 1927. *The Jewish War* (transl. by H. St. J. Thackeray). 8 vols. London: William Heinemann.

______. 1963. *Jewish Antiquities* (transl. by Ralph Marcus). 9 vols. Cambridge: Harvard University Press.

Juanmarti, Jacinto. 1893. *Diccionario de la lingua de Maguindanao*. Manila: Amigos del País.

Jucquois, Guy. 1966. *Phonétique comparée des dialectes moyen-babyloniens du nord et de l'ouest* (*Bibliothèque du Muséon*, 53). Louvain: Université de Louvain, Institut Orientaliste.

Julien, Ch.-André. 1952. *Histoire de l'Afrique du Nord* (revised and updated by Roger Le Tourneau). 2nd ed. Paris: Payot.

Kalimov, A. 1965. "O fonetičeskoi modifikacii arabskix zaimstvovanii v dunganskom jazyke," *Semitskie jazyki, Materialy pervoi konferencii po semitskim jazykam*, 2, 610-616. Moscow: Akademiia Nauk.

Kamffmeyer, Georg. 1899. "Materialen zum Studium der arabischen Beduinen - dialekte Innerafrikas," *Mittheilungen des Seminars für Orientalische Sprachen*, 2, 143-221.

Kamil, Murad. 1963. *Beiträge zur Entstehung der vierradikaligen Verben in den gesprochenen semitischen Sprachen.* Cairo: Institut français d'archéologie orientale.

Kaufman, Stephen A. 1974. *The Akkadian Influences on Aramaic* (*Assyriological Studies*, 19). Chicago and London: The University of Chicago Press.

KBHK. Koehler, Ludwig, Walter Baumgartner, Benedikt Hartmann and Eduard Y. Kutscher. 1967-. *Hebräisches und aramäisches Lexicon zum Alten Testament.* 3rd ed. Leiden: E. J. Brill.

Koehler, Ludwig. 1953. *Lexicon in Veteris Testamenti Libros.* Leiden: E. J. Brill.

Koelle, Sigismund W. 1854. *Polyglotta Africana.* London: Church Missionary House.

Kofler, Hans. 1940. "Reste arabischer Dialekte," *Wiener Zeitschrift für die Kunde des Morgenlandes*, 47, 61-130.

König, Eduard. 1877. *Neue Studien über Schrift, Aussprache, und allgemeine Formenlehre des Aethiopischen.* Leipzig: J. C. Hinrich

Kopf, Lothar. 1954. "Ha-millon ha-ʕaravi ke-ʔemṣaʕi ʕezer le-valšanut ha-ʕivrit," *Lešonenu, qoveṣ meyuḥad*, 72-82.

______. 1959. "Arabische Etymologien und Parallelen zum Bibelwörterbuch," *Vetus Testamentum*, 9, 247-287.

Koskinen, Kalevi. 1964. "Kompatibilität in den dreikonsonantigen hebräischen Wurzeln," *Zeitschrift der Deutschen Morgenländischen Gesellschaft*, 114, 16-58.

Kraft, Charles. 1971. "A Note on Lateral Fricatives in Chadic," *Studies in African Linguistics*, 2, 271-7.

Kraus, F. R. 1968. "Sesam im Alten Mesopotamien," *Journal of the American Oriental Society*, 88, 112-9.

Krause, G. A. 1884. *Mittheilungen der Riebeck'schen Niger - Expedition I. Ein Beitrag zur Kenntniss der Fulischen Sprache in Afrika.* Leipzig: F. A. Brockhaus.

Kress, Bruno. 1937. *Die Laute des modernen Isländischen.* Berlin: Institut für Lautforschung an der Universität Berlin.

Krumm, Bernhard. 1932. *Wörter und Wortformen orientalischen Ursprungs im Suaheli.* Hamburg: Friederichsen, De Gruyter.

Kuipers, Aert H. 1955. "The North-west Caucasian Languages," *Analecta Slavica*, 195-206. Amsterdam: De Bezige Bij.

______. 1960. *Phoneme and Morpheme in Kabardian.* The Hague: Mouton.

Kurylowicz, Jerzy. 1973. *Studies in Semitic Grammar and Metrics* (*Prace Językoznawcze*, 67). London: Curzon Press.

Kutscher, Eduard Yechezkel. 1959. *Ha-lašon we-ha-reqaʕ ha-lešoni šel megillat yešaʕyahu ha-šelemah mi-megillot yam ha-melaḥ*. Jerusalem: Magnes.

______. 1961. *Millim we-toldotehen*. Jerusalem: Kiryath Sepher.

______. 1965. "Contemporary Studies in North-Western Semitic," *Journal of Semitic Studies*, 10, 21-51.

______. 1967. "Mittelhebräisch und Jüdisch-Aramäisch im neuen Köhler-Baumgartner," *Hebräische Wortforschung, Festschrift zum 80. Geburtstag von Walter Baumgartner* (*Supplements to Vetus Testamentum*, 16), 158-175. Leiden: E.J. Brill.

______. 1969. *Meḥqarim ba-ʔaramit ha-gelilit*. Jerusalem: Academon.

______. 1970. "Aramaic," *Current Trends in Linguistics* (Thomas A. Sebeok, ed.), 6, 347-412. The Hague: Mouton.

Labouret, Henri. 1952. *La langue des peuls ou foulbé*. Dakar: IFAN.

______. 1955. *La langue des peuls ou foulbé; lexique français-peul*. Dakar: IFAN.

Labov, William, Malcah Yaeger, and Richard Steiner. 1972. *A Quantitative Study of Sound Change in Progress*. 2 vols. Philadelphia: U.S. Regional Survey.

Lacroix, P. F. 1967. "Remarques préliminaires à une étude des emprunts arabes en peul," *Africa*, 37, 188-202.

Ladefoged, Peter. 1968. *A Phonetic Study of West African Languages*. 2nd edition. Cambridge: University Press.

______. 1971. *Preliminaries to Linguistic Phonetics*. Chicago: University of Chicago Press.

Lagarde, Paul de. 1866. *Gesammelte Abhandlungen*. Leipzig: F. A. Brockhaus.

______. 1877. *Armenische Studien*. Göttingen: Dieterich.

______. 1878. *Semitica*. Göttingen: Dieterich.

Landberg, Carlo von. 1898. *Critica Arabica*, 5. Leiden: E. J. Brill.

______. 1901. *Études sur les dialectes de l'Arabie mériodionale*. 2 vols. Leiden: E.J. Brill.

______. 1920-42. *Glossaire Datînois*. 3 vols. Leiden: E. J. Brill.

Landsberger, Benno. 1931. "Lexicalisches Archiv," *Zeitschrift für Assyriologie*, 40, 295-298.

Lane, Edward. 1874. *An Arabic English Lexicon*. London: Williams and Norgate. (Reprinted 1968 by Librairie du Liban, Beirut.)

Laroui, Abdallah. 1970. *L'histoire du Maghreb.* Paris: Maspero.

LaSor, William S. 1957. "The Sibilants in Old South Arabic," *Jewish Quarterly Review*, 48, 161-173.

Leander, Pontus. 1925. "Några Anteckningar till Geʕez-Språkets Historia," *Studier Tilegnede Professor, Dr. Phil. & Theol. Frants Buhl i Anledning af Hans 75 Aars Fødelsedag den 6 September 1925 af Fagfæller og Elever* (Johannes Jacobsen, ed.), 91-97. Copenhagen: V. Pios Boghandel-Povl Branner.

Leemans, W. F. 1945-1948. "Marduk-Apal-Iddina II, Zijn Tijd en Zijn Geslacht," *Jaarbericht van het Vooraziatisch-Egyptisch Genootschap Ex Oriente Lux*, 10, 432-455.

Lehmann, C. F. 1892. *Šamaššumukîn, König von Babylonien.* Leipzig: J. C. Hinrich.

Lepsius, Richard. 1861. *Über die Arabischen Sprachlaute und deren Umschrift.* Berlin: Königl. Akademie der Wissenschaften.

Leslau, Wolf. 1937. "Der š-Laut in den Modernen Südarabischen Sprachen," *Wiener Zeitschrift für die Kunde des Morgenlandes*, 44, 211-218.

______. 1938. *Lexique Soqoṭri.* Paris: C. Klincksieck.

______. 1945. *Gafat Documents.* (*American Oriental Series*, 28). New Haven.

______. 1946. "Modern South Arabic Languages; A Bibliography." *Bulletin of the New York Public Library*, 50, 607-633.

______. 1947a. "Four Modern South Arabic Languages," *Word*, 3, 180-203.

______. 1947b. "The Position of Curia Muria in Modern South Arabic," *Bulletin of the School of Oriental and African Studies*, 12, 3-19.

______. 1956a. "The Arabic Loanwords in Gurage (Southern Ethiopia)," *Arabica*, 3, 266-284.

______. 1956b. "Arabic Loanwords in Harari," *Studi Orientalistici in Onore di Giorgio Levi della Vida*, 2, 14-35. Rome: Istituto per L'Oriente.

______. 1956c. "Arabic Loan-words in Tigré," *Word*, 12, 125-141.

______. 1956d. *Étude descriptive et comparative du gafat (éthiopien méridional).* Paris: C. Klincksieck.

______. 1957. "The Semitic Phonetic System," *Manual of Phonetics* (L. Kaiser, ed.), 325-329. Amsterdam: North Holland.

______. 1958a. "Arabic Loan-words in Geez," *Journal of Semitic Studies*, 3, 146-168.

______. 1958b. *Ethiopic and South Arabic Contributions to the Hebrew Lexicon (University of California Publications in Semitic Philology*, 20). Berkeley: University of California Press.

______. 1970. "Ethiopic and South Arabian," *Current Trends in Linguistics* (Thomas A. Sebeok, ed.), 6, 467-527. The Hague: Mouton.

Lethem, G. J. 1920. *Colloquial Arabic Shuwa Dialect of Bornu, Nigeria, and of the Region of Lake Chad*. London: Crown Agents for the Colonies.

Levi Della Vida, Giorgio. 1933. "Murād," *Encyclopedia of Islam*. Leiden: E. J. Brill.

Levias, Caspar. 1900. *A Grammar of the Aramaic Idiom contained in the Babylonian Talmud*. Cincinnati: Bloch.

Lévi-Provençal, E. 1944. *Histoire de l'Espagne musulmane*. Cairo: Institut Français d'Archéologie Oriental du Caire.

Lewis, I. M. 1960. "The Somali Conquest of the Horn of Africa," *Journal of African History*, 1, 213-229.

Lewy, Heinrich. 1895. *Die semitischen Fremdwörter im Griechischen*. Berlin: R. Gaertner.

Li Fang-Kuei. 1946. "Chipewyan," *Linguistic Structures of Native America* (Cornelius Osgood, ed.), 398-423. New York: Viking Fund.

Lisān al-ʕarab. See Ibn Manẓūr, Muḥammad ibn Mukarram.

Löw, Immanuel. 1928. *Die Flora der Juden*. 4 vols. Vienna. (Reprinted 1967 by Georg Olms, Hildesheim.)

Lukas, Johannes. 1931. *Die Sprache der Káidi - Kanembu in Kanem*. (*Dreizehntes Beiheft zur Zeitschrift für Eingeborenen-Sprachen*). Berlin: Dietrich Reimer.

______. 1937. *A Study of the Kanuri Language*. London: Oxford University Press.

Lyons, John. 1968. *Introduction to Theoretical Linguistics*. Cambridge: Cambridge University Press.

MacLean, Arthur J. 1901. *A Dictionary of the Dialects of Vernacular Syriac as Spoken by the Eastern Syrians of Kurdistan, North-West Persia, and the Plain of Moṣul*. Oxford: Clarendon Press.

Magee, Walter L. 1950. "The Pronunciation of Prelingual Mutes in Classical Arabic," *Word*, 6, 74-77.

Malagòli, Giuseppe. 1939. *Vocabolario pisano*. Florence: Accademia della Crusca.

Malkiel, Yakov. 1950. "La derivación de *rebelde, rebeldía* y las fuentes del grupo de consonantes *-LD-* en iberorrománico," *Estudios dedicatos a Menéndez Pidal*, 91-124. Madrid: Consejo Superior de Investigaciones Cientificas.

Malmberg, Bertil. 1963. *Phonetics*. New York: Dover.

Malone, Joseph P. 1971. "Systematic Metathesis in Mandaic," *Language*, 47, 394-415.

______. 1973. "Heʕarot ʕal dimyon balšani ben ha-ʔaramit šel 'halaxot pesuqot' u-ven ha-mandaʔit," *Lešonenu*, 37, 161-164.

Maltzan, Heinrich von. 1871. "Ueber den Dialekt von Mahra, genannt Mehri, in Südarabien," *Zeitschrift der Deutschen Morgenländischen Gesellschaft*, 25, 196-214.

______. 1873a. "Dialektische Studien über das Mehri im Vergleich mit verwandten Mundarten," *Zeitschrift der Deutschen Morgenländischen Gesellschaft*, 27, 225-231.

______. 1873b. "Arabische Vulgärdialecte," *Zeitschrift der Deutschen Morgenländischen Gesellschaft*, 27, 232-294.

Marco Polo. 1926. *The Book of Ser Marco Polo* (Henry Yule, ed.). 3rd ed. 2 vols. London: John Murray.

______. 1938. *The Description of the World* (A. C. Moule and Paul Pelliot, eds.). 2 vols. London: George Routledge.

Marrison, G. E. 1951. "A Malay Poem in Old Sumatran Characters," *Journal of the Malayan Branch of the Royal Asiatic Society*, 24, 162-165.

Marsden, William. 1812. *A Grammar of the Malayan Language*. London.

______. 1812. *A Dictionary of the Malayan Language*. London.

Martinet, André. 1953. "Remarques sur le consonantisme sémitique," *Bulletin de la Société de Linguistique de Paris*, 49, 67-78.

Masson, Emilia. 1967. *Recherches sur les plus anciens emprunts sémitiques en grec*. Paris: C. Klincksieck.

Matthews, Charles D. 1957. "Non-Arabic Place Names in Central South Arabia," *Akten des Vierundzwanzigsten Internationalen Orientalisten-Kongresses München 1957*, 259-262. Wiesbaden: Deutsche Morgenländische Gesellschaft.

______. 1969. "Modern South Arabian Determination -- a Clue thereto from Shahari," *Journal of the American Oriental Society*, 89, 22-27.

Mayer, Maria L. 1960. "Gli imprestiti semitici in greco," *Rendiconti. Classe di Lettere e Scienze Morali e Storiche. Istituto Lombardo di Scienze e Lettere*, 94, 311-351.

Meijer, Adolf Bernhard. 1872. *Ein Beitrag zu der Kenntniss der Sprachen auf Mindanao, Solog und Sian, der Papuas der Astrolobe - Bayauf Neu-Guinea, der Negritos der Philippinen, und einige Bemerkungen über Herrn Riedel's Uebersetzungen ins Tagalische und Visayasche*.

Menaḥem. 1854. *Maḥberet Menaḥem*. [London] and Edinburgh: Meʕorere Yešenim.

Menendez Pidal, Ramon. 1956. *Origiñes del español*. 4th ed. Madrid: Espasa-Calpe.

Meulen, D. van der, and H. von Wissman. 1932. *Ḥaḍramaut: Some of its Mysteries Unveiled*. Leiden. (Reprinted 1964 by E. J. Brill, Leiden.)

Midrash Rabba. 1962. Jerusalem: Lewin-Epstein Brothers.

Mitchell, T. C. 1969. "A South Arabian Tripod Offering Saucer Said to be from Ur," *Iraq*, 31, 112-114.

M'Lean, Norman, William T. Thiselton-Dyer, and T. K. Cheyne. 1899. "Balsam," *Encyclopaedia Biblica*. New York: Macmillan.

Moldenke, Harold N., and Alma L. Moldenke. 1952. *Plants of the Bible*. Waltham, Mass: Chronica Botanica.

Monteil, Vincent. 1951. *Contribution à l'étude de la faune du Sahara occidental*. Paris: Larose.

______. 1963. "Sur l'arabisation des langues négro-africaines," *Genève-Afrique*, 2, 12-18.

______. 1964. *L'Islam noir*. Paris: Editions du Seuil.

Moraes Farias, Paul Fernando de. 1967. "The Almoravids: Some Questions Concerning the Character of the Movement During its Periods of Closest Contact with the Western Sudan," *Bulletin de l'Institut Fondamental d'Afrique Noire*, 29B, 794-878.

Morag, Shelomo. 1960. "Ha-ʔaramit ha-bavlit be-masortam šel yehude teman," *Tarbiz*, 30, 120-9.

______. 1963a. *Ha-ʕivrit še-be-fi yehude teman*. Jerusalem: Ha-Akademia la-Lašon ha-ʕIvrit.

______. 1963b. "ʔOr zaruaʕ," *Tarbiz*, 33, 140-148.

______. 1969. "Oral Traditions and Dialects," *Proceedings of the International Conference on Semitic Studies held in Jerusalem, 19-23 July 1965*, 180-189. Jerusalem: The Israel Academy of Sciences.

______. 1972. "Pronunciations of Hebrew," *Encyclopaedia Judaica*, 13, 1120-1145.

Moran, William L. 1961. "The Hebrew Language in its Northwest Semitic Background," *The Bible and the Ancient Near East: Essays in Honor of William Foxwell Albright* (G. Ernest Wright, ed.). Garden City, New York: Doubleday. (Reprinted 1965 in paperback edition of the above, 59-84, by Anchor Books, Garden City, New York.

______. 1975. "The Syrian Scribe of the Jerusalem Amarna Letters," *Unity and Diversity: Essays in the History, Literature and Religion of the Ancient Near East* (Hans Goedicke and Jimmy J. Roberts, eds.). Baltimore: Johns Hopkins University Press.

Moreshet, Menachem. 1968. "Ṣaḥaq-śaḥaq; yiṣḥaq-yiśḥaq," *Beth Mikra, Bulletin of the Israel Society for Biblical Research*, 35, 127-130.

Moritz, Bernhard. 1926. "Die Nationalität der Arumu-Stämme in Südost-Babylonien," *Oriental Studies Published in Commemoration of the Fortieth Anniversary of Paul Haupt as Director of the Oriental Seminary of the Johns Hopkins University* (Cyrus Adler and Aaron Ember, eds.), 184-211. Baltimore: Johns Hopkins Press.

Moscati, Sabatino. 1954. *Il sistema consonantico delle lingue semitiche*. Rome: Pontificio Istituto Biblico.

______. 1964a. *Lezioni di linguistica semitica*. Rome: Centro di Studi Semitici.

Moscati, Sabatino (ed.), Anton Spitaler, Edward Ullendorf and Wolfram von Soden. 1964b. *An Introduction to the Comparative Grammar of the Semitic Languages*. Wiesbaden: Otto Harrassowitz.

Mouradian, Jacques. 1940. "Note sur quelques emprunts de la langue wolof à l'arabe," *Bulletin de l'institut français d'Afrique noire*, 2, 269-284.

Movers, Franz K. 1856. *Die Phönizier*, 2/3. Berlin. (Reprinted 1967 by Scientia Verlag, Aalen.)

Mtouggui, Lhaoussine. n.d. *Vue générale de l'histoire berbère*. Paris: Larose.

Müller, Walter. 1964. "Review of *The Al-ʕUqlah Texts* by A. Jamme," *Bibliotheca Orientalis*, 21, 379-380.

Murtonen, A. 1966. "The Semitic Sibilants," *Journal of Semitic Studies*, 11, 135-150.

______. 1967. *Early Semitic: A Diachronical Inquiry into the Relationship of Ethiopic to the other so-called South-east Semitic Languages*. Leiden: E. J. Brill.

Našwān, ibn Saʕīd al-Ḥimyarī. 1916. *Die auf Südarabien bezüglichen Angaben Našwān's im Šams al ʕUlūm* (ʕAzīmuddīn Aḥmad, ed.). Leiden: E. J. Brill.

Natan ben Yeḥiel. 1955. *ʕÅruḵ ha-šalem* (Alexander Kohut, ed.). New York: Pardes.

Neck, Jacob Corneliszoon van. 1601. *Le second livre, Iovrnal ov comptcir, contenant le vray discovrs et narration historique, dv voiage faiĉt par les huiĉt Navires d'Amſterdam, au mois de Mars l'An 1598*. Amsterdam.

Nettlau, Max. 1890. "Notes on Welsh Consonants," *Revue Celtique*, 11, 68-79.

______. 1891. "Notes on Welsh Consonants," *Revue Celtique*, 12, 142-152.

Neuvonen, Eero K. 1941. *Los Arabismos del español en el siglo XII*. Helsinki: Society of Finnish Literature.

Newman, Paul. 1965. "A Brief Note on the Maha Language," *The Journal of West African Languages*, 2, 57-8.

Newman, Paul and Roxana Ma. 1966. "Comparative Chadic: Phonology and Lexicon," *Journal of African Languages*, 5, 218-251.

Nichols, Johanna. 1971. "Diminutive Consonant Symbolism in Western North America," *Language*, 47, 826-848.

Nicholas, Francis. 1953. *La langue berbère de Mauritanie*. Dakar: IFAN.

Niebuhr, Carsten. 1774. *Description de l'Arabie*. Amsterdam: S. J. Baalde.

Nitzan, Shemuel. 1973. "The Jerusalem Letters from the el-ʿAmārna Archive: Linguistic Aspects." Master's thesis, Tel-Aviv University.

Nöldeke, Theodor. 1826. "Review of *Lehrbuch der hebräischen Sprache* by Justus Olshausen," *Orient and Occident*, 1, 755-764.

______. 1875. *Mandäische Grammatik*. Halle: Buchhandlung des Waisenhauses.

______. 1878. "Review of *Semitica* by Paul de Lagarde," *Zeitschrift der Deutschen Morgenländischen Gesellschaft*, 32, 401-410.

Norris, H. T. 1971. "New Evidence on the Life of Abdullāh b. Yāsīn and the Origins of the Almoravid Movement," *Journal of African History*, 12, 255-268.

Nyberg, Henrik S. 1952. *Hebreisk Grammatik*. Uppsala: Almqvist & Wiksell.

Oppenheim, A. L. 1962. "Chaldea," *The Interpreters Dictionary of the Bible*, 1, 549-550. New York: Abingdon Press.

Orlinsky, Harry. 1960. "The Origin of the *Kethib-Qere* System: A New Approach," *Supplements to Vetus Testamentum*, 7, 184-92.

Patai, Raphael. 1971. *Society, Culture and Change in the Middle East*. 3rd ed. Philadelphia: University of Pennsylvania Press.

Paterson, H. S. 1924. "An Early Malay Inscription from Trengganu," *Journal of the Malayan Branch of the Royal Asiatic Society*, 2, 252-258.

______. 1901. *Thesaurus Syriacus*. Oxford: Clarendon Press.

Payne Smith, Robert. 1901. *Thesaurus Syriacus*. Oxford: Clarendon Press.

______. 1903. *A Compendious Syriac Dictionary* (Jessie Payne Smith Margoliouth, ed.). Oxford: Clarendon Press.

Pelliot, Paul. 1963. *Notes on Marco Polo*. 2 vols. Paris: Imprimerie Nationale.

Periplus (of the Erythraean Sea). See Fabricius, B. (ed.).

Phillips, Wendell. 1955. *Qataban and Sheba*. New York: Harcourt, Brace.

______. 1966. *Unknown Oman*. London: Longmans, Green.

Pia, J. Joseph. 1974. "The Strange Sibilant Surfeit of Ancient Semitic." Unpublished paper, Syracuse University.

Pigeaud, Theodore. 1963. *Java in the Fourteenth Century*. 5 vols. The Hague: Martinus Nijhoff.

Pinches, T. G. 1902. "Greek Transcriptions of Babylonian Tablets," *Proceedings of the Society of Biblical Archeology*, 24, 108-119.

Pliny. 1945. Natural History (transl. by H. Rackham). 10 vols. Cambridge: Harvard University Press.

Poerwadarminta, W. J. S. and A. Teeuw. 1952. *Indonesisch-Nederlands Woordenboek*. Djakarta: J. B. Wolters.

Polotsky, H. J. 1938. "Études de grammaire gouragué," *Bulletin de la Société de Linguistique de Paris*, 39, 137-175.

Porter, R. S. 1903. *A Primer and Vocabulary of the Moro Dialect (Magindanau)*. Washington: Government Printing Office.

Praetorius, Franz. 1871. *Grammatik der Tigriñasprache in Abessinien*. Halle: Buchhandlung des Waisenhauses.

Pritchard, James B. (ed). 1969. *Ancient Near Eastern Texts*. 3rd ed. Princeton: Princeton University Press.

Qimḥi, David. 1926. *The Commentary of David Kimhi on Isaiah* (Louis Finkelstein, ed.). New York: Columbia University Press.

Rabbinovicz, Raphael. 1960. *Diqduqe soferim*. Jerusalem: Meʕen ha-ḥoxmah.

Rabin, Chaim. 1951. *Ancient West-Arabian*. London: Taylor's Foreign Press.

______. 1965. *Yesodot ha-diqduq ha-mašwe šel ha-lašon ha-ha-ʕivrit* (A. Hurvitz, ed.). 2nd ed. Jerusalem: Academon.

______. 1970. *Torat ha-hege šel ha-ʕivrit ha-miqraʔit*. Jerusalem: Academon.

______. 1971. "Semitic Languages," *Encyclopaedia Judaica*. Jerusalem: Keter.

Ramstedt, G. H. 1906. "Mogholica: Beiträge zur Kenntnis der mogholsprache in Afghanistan," *Journal de la Société Finno-Ougrienne*, 23, 1-64.

Rauf, M. A. 1964. *A Brief History of Islam*. Kuala Lumpur: Oxford University Press.

Redpath, Henry A. 1907. *The Book of the Prophet Ezekiel*. New York: Edwin Gorham.

Reiner, Erica. 1966. *A Linguistic Analysis of Akkadian* (*Janua Linguarum, Series Practica*, 21). The Hague: Mouton.

______. 1973. "New Cases of Morphophonemic Spellings," *Approaches to the Study of the Ancient Near East: A Volume of Studies Offered to Ignace Jay Gelb on the Occasion of his 65th Birthday October 14, 1972* (Giorgio Buccellati, ed.) (*Orientalia*, 42/1-2), 35-38. Rome: Biblical Institute Press.

Reinisch, Leo. 1903. *Die Somali-Sprache*. 3 vols. (*Kaiserliche Akademie der Wissenschaften, Südarabische Expedition*, 1, 2, 5/1). Vienna: Alfred Hölder.

Revell, Ernest J. 1970. *Hebrew Texts with Palestinian Vocalization*. Toronto: University of Toronto Press.

Rhodokanakis, Nikolaus. 1911. *Der Vulgärarabische Dialekt im Ḏofâr (Ẓfâr)*, 2 (*Kaiserliche Akademie der Wissenschaften, Südarabische Expedition*, 10). Vienna: Alfred Hölder.

______. 1932. "Altsabäische Texte II," *Wiener Zeitschrift fur die Kunde des Morgenlandes*, 39, 173-226.

Rin, Svi. 1968. *ʕAlilot ha-ʔelim* (with collaboration of Shifra Rin). Jerusalem: Israel Society for Biblical Research.

Roberts, Bleddyn. 1951. *The Old Testament Text and Versions*. Cardiff: University of Wales Press.

Robinson, Charles H. 1899. *Dictionary of the Hausa Language* (assisted by W. H. Brooks). Cambridge: University Press.

Rödiger, E. 1840. "Fresnel über die Himjaritische Sprache," *Zeitschrift für die Kunde des Morgenlandes*, 3, 288-293.

Ronkel, Ph. S. van. 1904. "Over de herkomst von enkele Arabische bastaardwoorden in het Maleisch," *Tijdschrift voor Indische Taal-, Land- en Volkenkunde. Bataviaasch Genootschap van Kunsten en Wetenschappen*, 47, 189-194.

Rosenthal, Franz. 1936. *Die Sprache der palmyrenischen Inschriften* (*Mitteilungen der Vorderasiatisch-Aegyptischen Gesellschaft*, 41/1). Leipzig: J. C. Hinrich.

Rosenthal, Franz, (ed.). 1967. *An Aramaic Handbook*. (*Porta Linguarum Orientalum, Neue Serie*, 10). 2 vols. Wiesbaden: Otto Harrassowitz.

Rositzke, Harry A. 1939. "A further note on Welsh *ll* and Icelandic *hl*," *Le Maître Phonétique*, 65, 7-8.

Rössler, Otto. 1966. "Das ältere ägyptische Umschreibungssystem für Fremdnamen und seine sprachwissenschaftlichen Lehren," *Neue Afrikanistische Studien* (J. Lukas, ed.), 218-229. Hamburg.

Rowlands, E. R. 1959. "The Targum and the Peshiṭta Version of the Book of Isaiah," *Vetus Testamentum*, 9, 178-191.

Rubinchik, Y. A. 1965. "O xaraktere fonetičeskix izmenenii arabskix zaimstvovanii v persidskom jazyke," *Semitskie jazyki, Materialy pervoi konferencii po semitskim jazykam*, 2, 585-597. Moscow: Akademiia Nauk.

Růžička, Karel F. 1953. "Lehnwörter im Swahili," *Archiv Orientální*, 21, 582-603. Prague: Czechoslovak Academy of Sciences.

Růžička, Rudolf. 1909. *Konsonantische Dissimilation in den semitischen Sprachen* (*Beiträge zur Assyriologie und semitischen Sprachwissenschaft*, 6). Leipzig: J. C. Hinrich.

Ryckmans, Jacques. 1956. "Aspects nouveaux du problème thamoudéen," *Studia Islamica*, 5, 5-17. Paris: Larose.

______. 1964. *La chronologie des rois de Saba et Ḏū-Raydān*. Istanbul: Nederlands Historisch-Archaeologisch Instituut in het Nabije Oosten.

Saadia ben Yosef al-Fayyūmī. 1896. *Oeuvres complètes de Saadia ben Iosef al-Fayyoûmî*, 3, *version arabe d'Isaïe* (transl. and annotated by Joseph Derenbourg and Hartwig Derenbourg). Paris: Ernest Leroux.

______. 1969. *Ha-ʔegron; Kitāb ʔuṣūl al-šiʕr al-ʕibrānī* (Heb.). (Neḥemya Allony, ed.). Jerusalem: The Academy of the Hebrew Language.

Sacy, Silvestre de. 1813. "Traité de la Prononciation des lettres Arabes, extrait du Manuscrit Arabe, n.° 260, de la Bibliothèque impériale," *Notices et Extraits des manuscrits de la Bibliothèque Impériale*, 9, 1-75.

Sapir, Edward, and Morris Swadesh. 1939. *Nootka Texts.* Philadelphia: Linguistic Society of America.

Schaade, A. 1911. *Sībawaihi's Lautlehre.* Leiden: E. J. Brill.

Schileico, Woldemar G. 1928. "Ein babylonischer Weihtext in griechischer Schrift," *Archiv für Orientforschung*, 5, 11-13.

Schramm, Gene M. 1964. *The Graphemes of Tiberian Hebrew.* Berkeley: University of California Press.

Schulthess, Friedrich. 1903. *Lexicon Syropalaestinum.* Berlin: Georg Reimer.

______. 1905-1906. "Aramäisches," *Zeitschrift für Assyriologie*, 19, 126-34.

Semaan, Khalil I. 1968. *Linguistics in the Middle Ages: Phonetic Studies in Early Islam.* Leiden: E. J. Brill.

Sībawaihi. 1889. *Le livre de Sîbawaihi.* (H. Derenbourg, ed.). 2 vols. Paris: Imprimerie Nationale.

Sievers, Eduard. 1901. *Grundzüge der Phonetik.* 5th ed. Leipzig: Breitkopf & Härtel.

Smalley, William. 1962-1964. *Manual of Articulatory Phonetics.* Tarreytown, New York: Practical Anthropology.

Snoxall, R. A. 1938. "Word Importation into Bantu Language with Particular Reference to Ganda," *Uganda Journal*, 5, 267-283.

Soden, Wolfram von. 1952. *Grundriss der Akkadischen Grammatik* (*Analecta Orientalia*, 33). Rome: Pontificium Institutum Biblicum.

______. 1969. *Ergänzungsheft zum Grundriss der Akkadischen Grammatik* (*Analecta Orientalia*, 47). Rome: Pontificium Institutum Biblicum.

Sommerfelt, Alf. 1947. "Études comparatives sur le caucasique du nord-est," *Norsk Tidsskrift for Sprogvidenskap*, 14, 141-155.

Speiser, Ephraim Avigdor. 1964. *The Anchor Bible Genesis.* Garden City, New York: Doubleday.

Spencer, John. 1966. "S.W. Koelle and the Problem of Notation for African Languages, 1847-1855," *Sierre Leone Language Review*, 5, 83-105.

Sperber, Alexander. 1937-1938. "Hebrew Based Upon Greek and Latin Transliterations," *Hebrew Union College Annual*, 12-13, 103-274.

Sperber, Alexander (ed.). 1959-1962. *The Bible in Aramaic*. vols. 1-3. Leiden: E. J. Brill.

Spurrel, William. 1870. *A Grammar of the Welsh Language*. 3rd ed. Camarthen: William Spurrel.

Stehle, Dorothy. 1941. *Sibilants and Emphatics in South Arabic*. Philadelphia. (Reprinted from the *Journal of the American Oriental Society*, 1940, 60, 507-543.)

Steiger, Arnald. 1932. *Contribución a la fonética del hispano-arabe y de los arabismos en el ibero-románico y el siciliano*. Madrid: Imprenta de la Librería y Casa Editorial Hernando.

Stenning, J. F. (ed. & transl.). 1949. *The Targum of Isaiah*. Oxford: Clarendon Press.

Strabo. 1966. *The Geography of Strabo* (transl. by Horace L. Jones). 8 vols. Cambridge, Mass.: Harvard University Press.

Strack, Hermann L. 1969. *Introduction to the Talmud and Midrash*. New York: Atheneum.

Strassmaier, J. N. 1886. *Alphabetisches Verzeichniss der assyrischen und akkadischen Wörter*. Leipzig: J. C. Hinrich.

Stutterheim, W. F. 1936. "A Malay *Shaʔir* in Old Sumatran Characters, 1380 A. D.," *Acta Orientalia*, 14, 268-279.

Sveinbjörnsson, Sveinbjörn. 1933. "Icelandic Phonetics," *Aarsskrift for Universitetsundervisningen i Jylland*, 5 Supplement, 1-96.

Tāj al-ʕArūs. See Al-Murtada al-Zabīdī, Muḥammad ibn Muḥammad.

Talmud Yerušalmi. 1960. Jerusalem: Mifʕal Yerušalmi.

Taylor, F. W. 1932. *A Fulani-English Dictionary*. Oxford: Oxford University Press.

Teloni, B. 1889. "Aus einem Briefe des Herrn Prof. B. Teloni," *Zeitschrift für Assyriologie*, 4, 396.

Theophrastus. 1916. *Enquiry into Plants* (transl. by Arthur Holt). 2 vols. London: William Heinemann.

Thomas, Bertram. 1937. "Four Strange Tongues from South Arabia," *Proceedings of the British Academy*, 23, 231-331.

Thompson, R. Campbell. 1949. *A Dictionary of Assyrian Botany*. London: The British Academy.

Thompson, Richard N. 1953. *Survey Study of the Languages of the Philippine Islands*. Pampanga Province, Philippine Republic: Community Press.

Trimingham, Spencer J. 1962. *A History of Islam in West Africa*. London: Oxford University Press.

Trubetzkoy, N. S. 1922. "Les consonnes latérales des langues caucasiques-septentrionales," *Bulletin de la Société de Linguistique de Paris*, 23, 184-204.

______. 1930. "Nordkaukasische Wortgleichungen," *Wiener Zeitschrift für die Kunde des Morgenlandes*," 37, 76-92.

Tucker, A.N., and M.A. Bryan. 1966. *Linguistic Analyses: The Non-Bantu Languages of North-Eastern Africa*. London: Oxford University Press.

Tugault, Alfred. 1898. *Dictionnaire malais-français*. Paris: n.p.

Ullendorff, Edward. 1955. *The Semitic Languages of Ethiopia*. London: Taylor's Foreign Press.

Van Beek, Gus W. 1958. "Frankincense and Myrrh in Ancient South Arabia," *Journal of the American Oriental Society*, 78, 141-151.

______. 1960. "Frankincense and Myrrh," *The Biblical Archeologist*, 23, 69-95. (Reprinted 1964 in *The Biblical Archeologist Reader*, 2, 99-126, by Anchor Books, Garden City, New York.)

van den Berg, L. W. C. 1886. *Le Hadhramout et les colonies arabes dans l'archipel indien*. Batavia: Imprimerie du Gouvernement.

van den Branden, A. 1957. "La chronologie de Dedan et de Lihyan," *Bibliotheca Orientalis*, 14, 13-16.

Vilenčik, J. 1930. "Welchen Lautwert hatte ض im Ursemitischen?" *Orientalistische Literaturzeitung*, 33, 89-98.

Vollers, Karl. 1893. "The System of Arabic Sounds as based upon Sibaweih and Ibn Yaïsh," *Transactions of the Ninth International Congress of Orientalists*, 2, 130-154. London: Committee of the Congress.

______. 1894. "Arabisch und Semitisch," *Zeitschrift für Assyriologie*, 9, 165-217.

______. 1906. *Volkssprache und Schriftsprache im alten Arabien*. Strassburg: Truebner.

______. 1909. "Die arabischen Teile der Wiener Südarabischen Expedition," *Zeitschrift für Assyriologie*, 23, 97-106.

Wagner, Max. 1966. *Die lexicalischen und grammatikalischen Aramäismen im Alttestamentlichen Hebräisch*. Berlin: Alfred Töpelman.

Wald, Benji V. n.d. "Arabic Loanwords in a Generative Phonology of Swahili." Master's thesis, Columbia University.

Wallin, G. A. 1858. "Ueber die Laute des Arabischen und ihre Bezeichnung," *Zeitschrift der Deutschen Morgenländischen Gesellschaft*, 12, 599-665.

Walzer, R. 1965. "Al-Fārābī," *The Encyclopaedia of Islam*. new ed. Leiden: E. J. Brill.

Warburg, Otto. 1921. *Die Pflanzenwelt*. 3 vols. Leipzig: Bibliographisches Institut.

Wehr, Hans. 1966. *A Dictionary of Modern Written Arabic* (J. Milton Cowan, ed.). Ithaca, New York: Cornell University Press.

Wellhausen, Julius. 1961. *Reste arabische Heidentums*. 3. unveränderte Aufl. Berlin: W. Degruyter.

Wellsted, James R. 1840. *Travels to the City of the Caliphs*. 2 vols. London: Colburn.

Wevers, J. W. 1970. "Ḥeth in Classical Hebrew," *Essays on the Ancient Semitic World* (J. W. Wevers and D. B. Redford, eds.), 101-112.

Whorf, Benjamin Lee. 1946. "The Milpa Alta Dialect of Aztec," *Linguistic Structures of Native America*. (Cornelius Osgood, ed.), 367-397. New York: Viking Fund.

Winnett, F. V., and W. L. Reed. 1970. *Ancient Records from North Arabia*. Toronto: University of Toronto Press.

Winstedt, Richard O. 1927. *Malay Grammar*. 2nd ed. Oxford: Clarendon Press.

______. 1962. *An Unabridged Malay-English Dictionary*. 4th ed. Singapore: Marican.

Wissman, Hermann von. 1964. *Sammlung Eduard Glaser III (Sitzungsberichte der Osterreichischen Akademie der Wissenschaften, Philosophisch-historische Klasse,* 246). Vienna.

Wissman, Herman von,and Maria Höfner. 1952. "Beiträge zur historischen Geographie des vorislamischen Südarabien," *Abhandlungen der Geistes - und Sozialwissenschaftl. Klasse, Akademie der Wissenschaften und der Literatur in Mainz,* 219-385. Wiesbaden.

Wright, W. 1896. *A Grammar of the Arabic Language*. 3rd ed. Cambridge: University Press. (Reprinted 1967 by Cambridge University Press.)

Würthwein, Ernst. 1957. *The Text of the Old Testament*. Oxford: Basil Blackwell.

Yāqūt ibn ʕAbdullah. 1886. *Jacut's Geographisches Wörterbuch* (Ferdinand Wüstenfeld, ed.). Leipzig: Deutsche Morgenländische Gesellschaft.

Yushmanov, N. V. 1926. "La correspondance du Ḍâd arabe au ʕAyn araméen," *Comptes Rendus de l'Académie des Sciences de l'URSS*, part B, 41-4.

______. 1930. "Dannye Fresnel'ja o južno-arabskom narečii Eḫkili," *Akademiia nauk SSSR. Aziatskii muzei. Zapiski Kollegii. Vostokovedov...Moscow*,5, 379-391.

______. 1938. *Stroi arabskogo jazyka*. Leningrad. (Reprinted 1961 as *The Structure of the Arabic Language* (transl. by Moshe Perlmann) by the Center for Applied Linguistics, Washington, D.C.)

Zamaxšarī, Maḥmūd ibn ʕUmar al-. 1859. *Al-Mufaṣṣal fi al-Naḥw* (J. P. Broch , ed.). Oslo.

______. 1947. *Al-Kaššāf ʕan Ḥaqāʔiq (Ġawāmid) al-Tanzīl*. Beirut: Dār al-Kitāb al-ʕArabī.

Zeuss, I. 1871. *Grammatica Celtica*. 2nd ed. Berlin: Werdmann.

Zimmern, Heinrich. 1917. *Akkadische Fremdwörter als Beweis für babylonischen Kultureinfluss*. 2nd ed. Leipzig: J. C. Hinrich.

Index